Investing
in Children

Investing in Children

Work, Education, and Social Policy in Two Rich Countries

ARIEL KALIL
RON HASKINS
JENNY CHESTERS
editors

BROOKINGS INSTITUTION PRESS
Washington, D.C.

Library of Congress Cataloging-in-Publication data
Investing in children : work, education, and social policy in two rich countries / Ariel
Kalil, Ron Haskins, and Jenny Chesters, editors.
    p.   cm.
    Includes bibliographical references and index.
    Summary: "Presents new research by leading scholars in Australia and the United States
on economic factors that influence children's development and the respective social poli-
cies the two nations have designed to boost human capital development"—Provided by
publisher.
    ISBN 978-0-8157-2202-1 (pbk. : alk. paper)
    1. Children—Government policy—Australia. 2. Children—Government policy—
United States. 3. Children—Australia—Economic conditions. 4. Children—United
States—Economic conditions. 5. Australia—Social policy. 6. United States—Social
policy. 7. Child development—Australia. 8. Child development—United States. I.
Kalil, Ariel. II. Haskins, Ron. III. Chesters, Jenny.
    HQ792.A85I587 2012
    305.230973—dc23   2012006594

9 8 7 6 5 4 3 2

Printed on acid-free paper

Typeset in Adobe Garamond

Composition by R. Lynn Rivenbark
Macon, Georgia

Contents

Acknowledgments

E dited volumes based on conference proceedings require lots of work from an army of people. We first thank the organizations that sponsored the conference and this volume, primarily the Australian Department of Education, Employment and Workplace Relations; the Australian Institute of Family Studies; the Australian National University College of Business and Economics; the Center for Human Potential and Public Policy at the Harris School of Public Policy Studies at the University of Chicago; and the Annie E. Casey Foundation. We extend a special thanks to Andrew Leigh, currently a member of the Australian House of Representatives and formerly a professor at the Australian National University, for his help in generating enthusiasm in Australia for the conference, securing Australian sponsorship for the project, and for his inspiring dinner talk during the conference. We thank Peter Brandon from State University of New York–Albany and Bob Gregory from the Australian National University for help in planning the conference and activities associated with it. We are grateful to Peter McDonald, Peter Saunders, Bettina Cass, Janeen Baxter, Boyd Hunter, and Linda Harrison for their comments on the papers delivered at the conference. Laurel Spindel of the Harris School and Mary Jones of Brookings provided exceptionally competent help in coordinating the preparation of the chapters in this volume and in coordinating the work of all the authors with the Brookings Institution Press. Both played a vital role in bringing the chapters to their final form. We are, of course, grateful to all the authors as well. All mistakes in this volume are the responsibility of the editors.

1

Introduction

ARIEL KALIL, RON HASKINS, AND JENNY CHESTERS

A ustralia and the United States are two wealthy countries with similar levels of income per capita.[1] Although they are both democratic nations that share some historical links, both being former colonies of the United Kingdom, their political institutions differ markedly. Nevertheless, though the institutional settings for the development of public policy differ, the two countries are actively engaged in many similar policy discussions. Discussions include employment policy for the low-income population; poverty policy and strengthening the safety net for low-income families; early childhood education policy; and policies to increase postsecondary education.

The purpose of this volume is to present new research by leading scholars, using the most current high-quality data each country has to offer, to identify contemporary economic arenas in which government policy has a role to play by investing to promote children's potential. We focus on three different but interrelated economic arenas: parental employment; early childhood care and education; and children's educational attainment. These economic arenas are linked by virtue of being the fundamental elements of human capital development and economic success during adulthood in both the United States and Australia. In addition, they contribute greatly to the gross domestic product (GDP) of both nations. Consequently, each country has the potential to learn from the other about promising strategies to build up these important resources. The chapters in this volume also provide insights into the potential effectiveness of employment policies, education policies, and income redistribution policies as tools for encouraging human capital investment in children and reducing resource and achievement gaps. Authors of the chapters employ quantitative analysis of nationally representative data to identify how limited resources in each of these three arenas can compromise child development, and they discuss their findings

1

in terms of promising avenues for public policy. The volume includes several chapters making use for the first time of new Australian data that answer questions about contemporary policy problems that are common to both countries.

Policy Context Related to the Central Themes

There is a surprising degree of similarity in the domestic social issues faced by Australia and the United States. Here we review three important examples of that similarity, all of which are taken up in detail by the chapters that follow. The three issues are the emphasis in public policy on work by poor and low-income parents and the impacts of parental employment on children; policies that attempt to balance the need for child care while parents work with the goal of providing high-quality early childhood programs to boost the development and school readiness of children from poor families; and policies that promote postsecondary education among children from poor families.

Parental Employment

Beginning roughly in the 1980s and culminating with passage of welfare reform legislation in 1996, the United States gradually developed an effective strategy for increasing work and reducing poverty in families headed by poor mothers. Given the very high poverty rates of families headed by females and the large and increasing number of these families,[2] a successful antipoverty strategy in the United States must maintain a major focus on female-headed families. After the 1996 reforms, the major aim of which was to increase work rates of single mothers on welfare, there was a 40 percent increase over four years in employment by never-married mothers, a group that previously demonstrated very low work rates and exceptionally high rates of poverty and welfare use.[3] The rapid increase in employment by females heading families was accompanied by a rapid fall in poverty among children in these families and among black children (who live disproportionately in female-headed families). In fact, both poverty rates reached their lowest level ever at the turn of the century. Even today, after the most severe recession since the Great Depression of the 1930s and with continuing high levels of unemployment, the poverty rates among children in black families and female-headed families are lower than they were before the explosion of employment among low-income mothers.[4]

Three factors contributed to these notable increases in work and declines in poverty: the strong work requirements in welfare reform, the gradual construction of a system of work-related benefits for low-income workers with children, and a very strong economy that generated plentiful jobs. The 1996 welfare reforms dramatically altered the previous cash welfare program (Aid to Families with Dependent Children) by creating much stiffer work requirements backed by strong financial sanctions. The major thrust of the state programs that resulted from welfare reform was to require mothers to look for work and to help them find and apply for low-wage jobs. Most states provided mothers with a brief training program, usually lasting for only a few days, that helped them prepare a resume, search local newspapers and the Internet for job openings, contact prospective employers, and practice interviewing. If this type of job preparation training was the soft side of welfare reform, the harder side was that mothers who did not cooperate with the program and make a serious effort to prepare for and find work had their cash benefit cut. In a majority of states, mothers could lose their entire cash benefit if they did not meet the work requirements.[5] In addition, most mothers could not receive welfare benefits for more than five years, thereby signaling that in the end the mothers had almost no choice except to work.

Clearly, there was ongoing tension between the dual aims of U.S. social policy—to help the poor as well as to avoid welfare dependency—and following the 1996 reforms the pendulum swung in the direction of using stern measures to promote work and reduce dependency. In contrast with the demanding cash welfare reforms, the nation's work support system offered substantial financial rewards for low-income mothers who went to work in low-wage jobs. The development of the work support system over many years reflected the realization on the part of policymakers that if welfare inevitably provided people with incentives not to work, the solution was to provide incentives for people to work, even in low-wage jobs.[6] Nevertheless, despite many mothers' desire to work to support their families, long-term welfare reliance remained a problem. Sophisticated research published in the 1980s showed that of the families on cash welfare rolls at any given moment, about 65 percent had been on the rolls for eight years or more (counting repeat spells).[7]

Perhaps the most notorious example of the unfortunate disincentives to work in the old system was that if mothers went to work, they and their children often lost their Medicaid health care coverage. To reduce that disincentive, a series of reforms in the 1980s and 1990s resulted in medical coverage for all children below the poverty level and many children up to 133 percent of the poverty level, regardless of the mother's work status. Health coverage for low-income mothers also was expanded. Similarly, reforms at both the federal and state level increased the amount of money available for child care, and the food stamp program was reformed to make it easier for low-income working families to receive the benefit.

A study by the Congressional Budget Office published in 1998 showed that expansion of programs for child care, children's health insurance, and child tax credits based on earnings resulted in about a tenfold increase in federal and state support for low-income working families.[8] Thus, federal and state reforms of the work support system "made work pay," thereby increasing the incentive to work. If work requirements pushed mothers off welfare, work supports pulled them off.

The third element that accounted for the rise in employment and the decline in poverty during the 1990s was the strong U.S. economy. After the recession of 1990–91, GDP increased in real (inflation-adjusted) terms every year until the Great Recession began in 2007. The economy slowed after 2000, but between 1990 and 2000 GDP increased from $8.0 trillion to $11.2 trillion, a rise of 40 percent.[9] More to the point, between 1991 and 2000, the economy added over 18 million jobs.[10] The economy sputtered after 2000 and then plunged after 2007. Even so, as we have seen, employment of never-married mothers was still higher in 2009 than it had been in the early 1990s and poverty rates for black children and children in female-headed families were also lower than before welfare reform. A reasonable conclusion from this history is that the U.S. strategy of combining strong work requirements in welfare programs with attractive work supports is effective when the economy is expanding but less effective when the economy is stagnant.

Encouraging maternal employment is also of concern to policymakers in Australia, although in Australia there is a much weaker push to get low-income single mothers to work. In contrast to the U.S. low-wage, full-time workforce, the Australian workforce is relatively high wage but highly "casualised" (temporary), with 21 percent of employees working on a casual basis.[11] Casual employees are hired on a temporary basis with no security of tenure, and they are not entitled to any type of paid leave, including sick leave and recreation leave. To compensate for their lack of entitlements, they are paid up to an extra 15 to 25 percent of the hourly rate paid to permanent employees.[12] The percentage of employees engaged in part-time work in Australia, either on a casual or permanent basis, increased from 16 percent in August 1980 to 30 percent in August 2011.[13] However, being employed on a part-time basis allows mothers to combine paid work and domestic work without having to work excessively long hours. The Australian government also provides a 50 percent subsidy for child care to encourage mothers to take up paid work.

Although children growing up in single-parent families in Australia are more at risk of living in poverty than children in dual-parent families, generous welfare provisions lessen the impact. And the population of single-parent families is much smaller in Australia than in the United States. Between 1997 and 2009, the proportion of Australian families that were headed by single parents stayed around 20 percent. In 1997, 21.3 percent of children younger than fifteen years were living in single-parent families, but that percentage decreased to 17.9 percent in 2009 to 2010.[14]

In Australia, the federal government gives a single parent with a child under the age of eight up to $1,390 a month[15] (although the exchange rate between the U.S. dollar and the Australian dollar is set by the market, at the time of writing, one Australian dollar was approximately equal to one U.S. dollar), depending on the parent's income from other sources. Those earning more than $370 per month have their entitlement reduced by 40 cents for every extra dollar that they earn, but they can still receive a partial payment until their income from other sources exceeds $8,852 a month. Welfare payments are subject to an assets test, but the thresholds are quite generous and affect only those with assets valued at more than $186,750 if they own their own home or $321,750 if they do not own their own home.[16] Like other low-income Australians, single parents may also be eligible for a health care card, which entitles them to free or subsidized medical care for items not covered by the country's universal Medicare system. Although health care provided in public hospitals funded by the state and federal governments is free, in some cases waiting lists are long and many low-income people use their health care card to receive treatment for minor illnesses in the private system.

To encourage mothers to remain in the workforce, the federal government recently introduced universal paid parental leave. Parents who are primary caregivers are entitled to eighteen weeks of leave paid at the national minimum wage rate. Although the scheme is funded by the government, the payments are made by the caregiver's employer to maintain the link between the caregiver and the employer. To be eligible, the caregiver must have worked for ten of the thirteen months prior to the birth of the child and must have earned no more than $150,000 in the financial year (between July 1 and June 30) prior to the birth.[17]

The unemployment rate in Australia has declined significantly since the recession in 1993. At that time, 10.6 percent of the Australian workforce was unemployed. By contrast, around 5.1 percent of the workforce was unemployed in August 2011, despite an increase from 62.2 percent to 65.4 percent in the labor force participation rate of 15- to 64-year-olds.[18] The unemployment rate peaked at 6.1 percent in March 2009 during the global recession but steadily declined as the economy recovered. Of more concern in Australia is the proportion of unemployed people who have been out of work for more than fifty-two weeks—a concern that is shared in the United States. This proportion declined from 34 percent of the total number of unemployed people in 1994 to 13 percent in 2009 before increasing to 20 percent by June 2011. In other words, 120,000 of the 597,300 unemployed persons in Australia have been seeking employment for at least fifty-two weeks.[19]

Welfare payments to the unemployed are paid at a standard rate regardless of the person's skills or qualifications or the length of time that he or she has been unemployed. Designed to be a short-term measure, the Newstart Allowance of $1,055 a month consigns the long-term unemployed to living in poverty. Unemployed persons with dependent children are eligible for extra payments depending on the number of dependent children and their ages. Half of those classified as long-term unemployed have low skills and little education.[20]

In recognition of the financial difficulties that low-income earners have to contend with and the high effective marginal tax rates that people on welfare payments face, the Australian government increased the tax-free threshold on earned income. From July 1, 2012, the first $18,200 of earned income is tax free, meaning that 1 million workers will pay no tax and everyone earning less than $80,000 will receive a tax cut. This measure is designed to encourage those who are currently not in the workforce to participate and those receiving welfare payments to at least take on some paid work.

Although low-income mothers will benefit from paid parental leave and the increase in the tax-free threshold, their ability to remain in the workforce depends on the availability of child care. Rather than provide universal child care, the government provides subsidies to parents who then choose private child care providers. Parents with the highest incomes have more options than parents with low incomes, and that presents a barrier to many mothers seeking paid work. Australia and the United States share the problem of providing enough public support for child care to allow all low-income families to receive a child care subsidy, a topic to which we now turn our attention.

Early Care and Education

Policymakers in the United States can make the low-wage sector of the U.S. economy stronger and more effective by improving the work support system.[21] Perhaps the weakest link in the work support system is child care. Not only are the funds now available insufficient to provide a subsidy to all the low-income workers who qualify, but the quality of care is uneven.[22] As many observers have pointed out, the United States could achieve two policy goals if the federal and state governments spent more money to increase the number of low-income families receiving a child care subsidy while simultaneously improving the average quality of care to boost the development of children from low-income families and better prepare them for public schooling.[23]

The United States spends around $30 billion a year at the federal and state level on early education programs, state prekindergarten (pre-K) programs, and child care programs that are usually subject to some regulation but are of uneven quality.[24] About forty of the fifty states have their own preschool programs, some of which have been well evaluated and found to have positive impacts on the intellectual and social development of children, especially children from poor families.[25] Most reviewers of the programs agree that Head Start has modest but inconsistent impacts, whereas the child care programs supported by federal and state dollars, primarily through the Child Care and Development Fund (CCDF), are of exceptionally mixed quality, with the majority of programs being of mediocre quality.[26]

These CCDF programs are heavily criticized by scholars, advocates, and practitioners, who have launched two major lines of argument about the programs. First, too many working families do not receive subsidies. Despite the high level of expenditures and the numerous programs, there is still not enough money available to help every low-income family pay for child care, let alone enough for every working family regardless of income level. Research shows that low-income working families that do not receive subsidies pay an average of well over $2,000 or more a year on child care than similar families that have subsidies.[27] For low-income families without subsidies, help with child care would amount to a direct infusion of cash into their bank account.

A second criticism of American child care programs is that so many of them are of modest or worse quality. Even Head Start—which at $7 billion a year and an enrollment of well over 900,000 children is the biggest and most expensive preschool program designed explicitly to provide a quality preschool education—has been shown to produce modest results. A recent national, random-assignment evaluation showed only modest effects at the end of the program year (or, for some children, at the end of two years) and virtually no positive effects on test scores at the end of the first year of schooling.[28] In November 2011, the Obama administration implemented the biggest reform in the history of Head Start by subjecting programs to competition for their funding if they do not measure up in evaluations based in part on direct observations of teacher performance.[29] The conclusion of most scholars and preschool advocates is that high-quality programs can produce lasting positive impacts on child development and important outcomes even in adulthood, but that too few preschool programs are of high enough quality to produce such impacts.[30]

Tension between the quality and quantity of child care is a permanent feature of the U.S. child care system.[31] Quality child care would produce two important benefits: better development and school readiness for poor children and care for children while parents work. The problem is that high-quality care is expensive. The cost of Head Start for one child attending a full-day program is around $13,300 a year, and the average cost of the preschool programs offered by states, most of which are of high quality, is about $14,400 a year. By contrast, the average cost of the care now purchased by funds from the CCDF is about $9,100 a year, more than 30 percent less than Head Start and well over 35 percent less than the state preschool programs.[32]

The trade-off is obvious: pay a higher price and purchase better child development and school readiness at the cost of serving fewer families. But such a trade-off must also factor in the impact on working parents, especially single mothers. Mothers who do not get a child care subsidy might put their child in substandard care, which in turn could have a negative impact on the child's health and development. Alternatively, the mother might decide not to work, a decision that in most cases means that the mother and her children will live in poverty because U.S. welfare programs are not generous enough to lift a family above the poverty line unless the family has additional income.

The solution to the quality-versus-quantity dilemma is for government to spend more money on child care. Until recently, both the federal government and the states had been gradually increasing their expenditures on Head Start, state prekindergarten programs, and child care. But now, given the recession and the magnitude of the financial problems faced by both the states and the federal government, it will in all likelihood be many years before significant new funds are available to boost either the quantity or quality of preschool programs.

In Australia, evidence that children who attend an early childhood program perform better in school has encouraged the Australian government to develop initiatives designed to improve access to early childhood programs for all children, particularly those from low-income families. Currently, early childhood education is provided by a mix of state government–funded preschools, community and private preschools, and child care centers. The availability and cost of early childhood programs differ markedly across the states and territories. For example, in the Australian Capital Territory, the Northern Territory, South Australia, Tasmania, and Western Australia, all four-year-old children are eligible to attend a publicly funded preschool for between eleven and twelve hours a week at no cost to their parents. In Victoria, the state government partially funds preschool programs, but the parents must make some contribution to the payment. In New South Wales, some children attend government-funded preschools, but the majority attend community preschools or child care centers paid for by their parents. In Queensland, the state government ceased providing free preschools for all five-year-olds when universal full-time kindergarten was introduced in 2007, resulting in a dramatic decline in the proportion of Queensland children attending preschool.

According to the Australian Bureau of Statistics (ABS), in 2008 the median cost of preschool to Australian parents, after subsidies from governments, was $25 a week.[33] In 2009 to 2010, there were 213,446 children attending just over 4,800 preschools in Australia.[34] The total cost of providing preschool education to four-year-old children in Australia in 2006 was around $540,646,000, which equates to about $2,180 per child.[35] It should be noted, however, that preschool participation in Australia is not synonymous with child care, given how few hours Australian children attend preschool. Working parents must arrange for their children to be in child care before and after preschool; many working parents therefore elect instead to enroll their children in child care centers that have a preschool program. In 2008, fees ranged from around $50 to $70 a day, with average costs of around $287 a week per child (or $14,924 per year for full-time, year-round care).[36] The federal government subsidizes fees paid by parents to approved child care providers.

Although the federal government does not provide universal access to child care, it does provide generous subsidies so that parents can access private child care services. Parents who are working, looking for work, or engaged in training or study for at least fifteen hours a week can access up to fifty hours of subsidized child care a week. The subsidy, of just under $4 an hour, provides parents with up to $189 a week toward the cost of child care. Even parents who are not working or studying are eligible for up to twenty-four hours a week of subsidized care. Parents are also able to claim a tax rebate that provides up to $7,500 a year for out-of-pocket expenses—that is, the difference between the fees paid and the subsidy received from the government.[37]

In 2009, the Council of Australian Governments (COAG) endorsed a strategy to ensure that by 2013 all children would have access to fifteen hours a week of government-funded, play-based, early childhood education for forty weeks a year in a public, private, or community-based preschool or child care center in the year before they begin school.[38] The aim of the initiative is to ensure that all children, regardless of their family circumstances, have some exposure to early childhood education to better prepare them for school. The federal government is also working with the state and territory governments to improve the standard of care provided in child care centers by requiring staff to have formal qualifications relevant to their role. From 2014, all child care center staff either will have or will be working to acquire a Certificate III qualification (similar to a two-year community college degree in the United States) and at least 50 percent of the staff in each child care center or preschool will have or will be working to acquire a relevant diploma or higher-level qualification.[39] Child care centers will be staffed by early childhood educators and will provide a valuable link between informal education in the home and formal education in schools.

Total government expenditure on children's services was $4.7 billion in the 2009–10 financial year, with 80 percent of the funding being provided by the federal government. Of the $908 million provided by the state and territory governments, 84 percent was spent on the provision of preschool services.[40]

Educational Attainment

It is common knowledge that modern economies are fueled by education. The role of education is especially vital in the U.S. economy.[41] Every year over the past four decades, the family income of people with more education has been greater than that of people with less education.[42] At the bottom of the income distribution are high school dropouts; then, in ascending order, are people with a high school degree, people with some college, people with a two-year degree, people with a four-year degree, and people with a graduate or professional degree. Equally important, since the early 1990s only those with a four-year degree or higher have enjoyed rising family income. Even people with a two-year degree or some college have experienced stagnant incomes.[43]

Therefore, the key to economic reward in the United States is postsecondary education. Unfortunately, data from the U.S. Panel Study of Income Dynamics (PSID) show that there is a strong positive correlation between the income of parents and both the college enrollment and college graduation rates of their children. Only 34 percent of young adults from families with incomes in the bottom fifth (roughly below $20,000 in 2010)[44] enrolled in college, and only 11 percent—less than a third of those who entered—eventually obtained a four-year degree. By contrast, 79 percent of those whose parents came from the top income quintile (roughly $100,000 a year and above in 2010) entered college, and over half of them earned a four-year degree.[45]

The cost of postsecondary education is a barrier to obtaining a four-year degree for some young adults from poor and low-income families, although the United States has a variety of sources that provide nearly $155 billion in financial aid to undergraduate students and another $45 billion to graduate students.[46] The College Board reports that in 2010 the average annual cost of attendance at a public four-year institution for an in-state student was around $20,000, including tuition and fees, room and board, books and supplies, and transportation.[47] Students from poor families have a number of options for financing their education, including federal and state grant programs, federal and private loans, tax credits, and work-study programs. Over the decade beginning with the 1999–2000 academic year, student aid increased by around 5 percent a year, after figures were adjusted for inflation. However, the share of student aid that is means-tested has been declining, resulting in more student aid going to students from relatively well-to-do families.[48]

Even if a large amount of funding is available to help students from low-income families support postsecondary education, there are other serious barriers that make it difficult for them to get into college and complete a college degree. They include difficulty in learning about available aid, lack of knowledge about how to apply for college admission and for aid programs, and poor academic preparation for college. Students from low-income families are far more likely to suffer from all those problems than students from wealthier families.[49] As a result, even with the remarkable level of aid available to qualifying low-income students, they are still at a marked disadvantage in preparing for, getting into, and graduating from postsecondary institutions.

Not surprisingly, education is also positively related to labor force participation and income in Australia. Therefore the Australian government has developed a range of policies designed to encourage all Australians to complete secondary school and undertake further study or training. The labor force participation rate of university-educated men is 14 percentage points higher than for men with ten or fewer years of schooling. For women, there is a 20-percentage-point difference between the participation rates of those with a university degree and those with ten years or fewer of education.[50] In 2004, 91 percent of males and 84 percent of females between the ages of 15 and 64 years who had a university degree or higher were in the labor force. In contrast, just 76 percent of males and 56 percent of females between 15 and 64 years of age who had only eleven or fewer years of schooling were in the labor force.[51]

Apart from increased labor force participation rates, people having a higher education are less likely to be unemployed. Although the overall unemployment rate in Australia was 5.3 percent in 2010, the unemployment rate for people with a bachelor's degree was just 2.7 percent while the rate for those with ten or fewer years of schooling was 10 percent.[52] Despite the obvious advantages of pursuing higher levels of education, a sizable minority of Australian students do not complete secondary school, let alone undertake university study, thus restricting their employment options, constraining their lifetime earnings, and often imposing costs on government programs.

Year 12 completion rates vary according to socioeconomic status, with students from poorer families more likely to drop out. In 2006, 78 percent of students from high socioeconomic backgrounds (those living in areas where the wealthiest 25 percent of the population reside) completed Year 12, whereas just 59 percent of students from low socioeconomic backgrounds (those living in areas where the poorest 25 percent of the population reside) did so.[53] Of the students who completed Year 12, those from low socioeconomic backgrounds, having taken subjects that prepared them for vocational training, were less likely to qualify for university education. Those who do embark on vocational training can enjoy relatively high earnings and secure employment, especially if they successfully complete a trade certificate. However, employment opportunities in the skilled trades generally are not available in the numbers required to ensure that all non-academic students are successfully integrated into the labor force.

Students over the age of fifteen living in low-income families are eligible for the youth allowance, a welfare payment designed to keep young people in the education system longer. Students living at home receive $655 a month; those living away from home receive $842 a month. Students attending university often work part-time because the youth allowance does not provide an adequate income. Students can earn up to $611 a month before their youth allowance is affected. Income over that threshold reduces their youth allowance at the rate of 50 cents for every extra dollar. In 2010, just over 137,000 domestic undergraduate students received the youth allowance.[54]

University education in Australia is not free. Students have to make some contribution to the cost of their education, but they do not have to pay fees up front. All domestic university students are entitled to an interest-free loan from the government, which they repay once their taxable income reaches a particular threshold. This policy helps ensure that students from low socioeconomic backgrounds who are academically qualified are not deterred from undertaking university studies by financial considerations. Despite these measures, only 15 percent of low socioeconomic students attend university.[55]

Overview of the Chapters

Recalling that the major purpose of this volume is to review new social science research based on high-quality data about the three policy issues reviewed above, we provide here a brief overview of the volume's eight chapters on parental employment, early child care and education, and educational attainment of poor children.

Parental Employment

U.S. policy for low-income families has increasingly emphasized work as a requirement for the receipt of welfare benefits. Consequently, employment rates for mothers of very young children are at historically high levels, despite the adverse effects of the recent recession on the overall employment rate. Nevertheless, the United States struggles with the problem of long-term unemployment, a problem also shared by Australia. In each country, researchers and policymakers are concerned about the amount of time that parents can devote to work without harming children's development. The three chapters in this section draw on longitudinal data from both countries to illustrate linkages between employment stability, unemployment, and work hours and child development. These analyses can inform policymakers interested in the correlations between families' employment experiences and children's development and in provision of support to help families balance the demands of work and family.

Rebekah Coley and Caitlin McPherran Lombardi analyzed U.S. data from *Welfare, Children, and Families: A Three-City Study* for their chapter, "Dynamics of Early Maternal Employment in Low-Income Families." These data provide a detailed examination of the work experiences of low-income, mostly minority mothers of very young children over a six-year period in three large U.S. cities beginning in 1999. Not surprisingly, in the era immediately following welfare reform, the authors document high levels of maternal employment. The small share of low-income mothers who did not work in the two years following the birth of a child were less educated, had lower literacy skills, and were more reliant on disability payments from the Supplemental Security Income program than their peers who entered the labor market soon after the birth of a child. Nonetheless but also not surprisingly, job quality was low, as reflected by low wages and the lack of employer-provided health insurance, even though work intensity was quite high. Even after accounting for the greater education and better health of employed mothers, children of low-income mothers who were employed during their infancy showed significantly higher math skills as well as lower anxiety and fewer somatic, hyperactivity, oppositional, and conduct problems at age seven than their peers whose mothers remained unemployed during that period.

Yet among employed mothers, job instability and overly long weekly work hours were correlated with poorer developmental outcomes for children. These results thus suggest that policy efforts to promote low-income mothers' stable and consistent employment may prove beneficial for low-income children and families. The results also suggest the need for policies and programs to support work environments that allow women adequate time and flexibility to deal with the demands of caring for young children.

In examining the effects of long-term unemployment on children's development in "Family Joblessness and Child Well-Being in Australia," Matthew Gray and Jennifer Baxter produce findings that are compatible with those of Coley and Lombardi. Using the Longitudinal Study of Australian Children (LSAC), which collected data on children on three occasions between the ages four and nine, the authors measure joblessness by whether the lone parent or both parents were jobless at the time of each interview. Four results are especially important. First, nearly 60 percent of lone-parent families but only 10 percent of two-parent families were jobless at least once. Joblessness at all three waves was seen almost entirely among lone-parent families, nearly 18 percent of which were jobless on all three occasions; in contrast, only a little over 1 percent of the two-parent families were jobless on all three occasions. Second, on every outcome measure collected, longer exposure to joblessness was correlated with poorer outcomes. The most important correlate of joblessness was low education, reinforcing the importance of education in helping families avoid economic problems. Third, measures of parenting, especially consistency of parenting and hostility or anger in parenting, were found to be correlated with development outcomes. Finally, introducing control variables such as parenting style, parent education, and parent mental health reduced the strength of the relationship between joblessness and child outcomes, although the relationship nevertheless remained strong at all three waves.

The authors draw a number of interesting conclusions from their research, the most important of which are that persistent unemployment has negative effects on children's development and that the effects are more pronounced the longer the joblessness lasts and that parent education, mental health, and parenting style are important mediators of the impacts of joblessness. The authors also conclude that improving the employment rate of jobless lone parents should be a central role for public policy.

Lyndall Strazdins, Megan Shipley, Liana Leach, and Peter Butterworth also analyzed data from the Longitudinal Study of Australian Children for their contribution, entitled "The Way Families Work: Jobs, Hours, Income, and Children's Well-Being." In Australia, employment rates of parents differ markedly by gender. Although 92 percent of Australian fathers are employed and many are working at least fifty-two hours a week, just 66 percent of mothers in couple families and 59 percent of lone mothers are employed. The majority of mothers, both partnered and single, work on a part-time basis. With an aging population and a low birth rate, Australia will need to increase the labor force participation rate of the working-age population. The implementation of policies designed to encourage more mothers to enter the workforce, such as providing paid parental leave and child care subsidies, raises the issue of how an increase in mothers' paid work hours will affect families. As in the Coley and Lombardi chapter, Strazdins and colleagues' findings show that long work hours of parents have a negative impact on the well-being of young children. Therefore, a key goal of policy in this area is to design policies that minimize the time trade-offs faced by parents in order to encourage more mothers to undertake paid work.

Early Care and Education

A policy approach increasingly common to the United States and Australia is to target resources on improving the early learning experiences of economically disadvantaged children. Especially in the United States, child care is considered not only a work support for parents, which is critically important given large increases in mothers' employment, but also an early intervention strategy—one that is especially important for economically disadvantaged young children. As mentioned above, in the United States, low-income parents struggle to afford high-quality care, spending a greater proportion of their income on child care than their middle- and upper-income counterparts but obtaining lower-quality arrangements on average than their more affluent peers.

Anna Johnson and Rebecca Ryan analyze national longitudinal data from the U.S. Early Childhood Longitudinal Study–Birth Cohort (ECLS-B) in "The Impact of Child Care Subsidies on the Quality of Care That Two-Year-Old Children Experience." To help low-income families afford child care, the federal government provides child care subsidies through the state-administered CCDF, the federal government's largest child care program. The primary goal of the CCDF subsidy program, which was enacted as part of the 1996 welfare reform legislation, is to support the economic independence of low-income parents by reducing out-of-pocket child care costs, thereby facilitating parental employment and allowing low-income parents to keep more of their earnings.

Johnson and Ryan show that CCDF subsidies help low-income families with young children purchase higher-quality care than they would otherwise. Specifically, they find that subsidy receipt led to increased use of center care, which was higher in quality than home-based care, and to the use of higher-quality home-based care. However, according to this analysis, subsidy receipt does not increase quality of care among families of toddlers already using center-based care. It is possible that the supply of quality center-based care for very young, low-income children is too low for recipients to benefit from the increased purchasing power that subsidies afford. Improving the availability of high-quality center-based care is a key objective of policy targeting low-income families in the United States.

Frank Oberklaid, Sharon Goldfeld, and Tim Moore analyzed the 2009 Australian Early Development Index (AEDI) for their contribution, entitled "Early Childhood Development and School Readiness." Oberklaid and colleagues describe a wide variety of social services that have been made universally available to Australian children and families but point out that significant gaps in child development persist because these services have not been taken up by the families that need them most.

AEDI data, which reflect the cumulative environmental influences on children's development in the years from birth until school entry, demonstrate the negative impact of early disadvantage on children's development with regard to physical health and well-being; social competence; emotional maturity; language and cognitive skills; and communication skills and general knowledge. Although the majority of Australian children attend preschool and benefit from the opportunities to develop pre-literacy and numeracy skills, children living in disadvantaged communities, who are most at risk of developmental delays, are less likely to attend preschool. Children who do not fit well within the learning environment tend to do less well academically and socially, have lower educational levels on leaving school, are more likely to become teenage parents, and are more likely to have poor employment records and to become welfare recipients. Australian policymakers are in the process of implementing policies aimed at overcoming the long-term effects of disadvantage experienced in the early years. However, Oberklaid, Goldfeld, and Moore point out that providing universal access does not necessarily translate to universal participation.

Educational Attainment

The three chapters in this section, all drawn from U.S. data, illustrate how gaps in educational attainment are associated with family background and income inequality and how inequalities are passed along from early childhood through adolescence and across generations. Collectively, the results from these chapters point to the need for effective strategies to encourage lower-income students to enroll in postsecondary educational institutions. As the authors discuss and as we pointed out earlier in this introduction, states can intervene to make postsecondary education more affordable for low-income students by establishing sliding-scale tuition schedules while the federal government could allocate increased support to new and existing financial aid programs for low-income youth. Also needed for this population are new approaches that address information barriers to entering and, especially, to graduating from college.

In "Economic Inequality and Children's Educational Attainment," Mary Campbell, Robert Haveman, and Barbara Wolfe investigate whether a persistent increase in economic inequality among families and geographic areas has implications for the educational attainment of children who have experienced increasing inequality. To do so, they draw on longitudinal data on about 1,200 children who were observed over a period of thirty years in the U.S. Panel Study of Income Dynamics. They first relate the family and geographic factors that exist while children are growing up to their educational attainments as young adults (completed years of schooling and graduation from high school). They then simulate the effects of increases in inequality in three family economic variables—family income (relative to needs), family wealth, and the increase in the Gini index for the state of residence on schooling attainment. Their simulation of the effects of increased inequality on the distribution of children's educational attainments uses the coefficients estimated in a model of educational attainment adjusted to reflect increased inequality. They find a small negative effect of increased inequality on the average level of schooling of these youths, along with significant increases in the inequality of their schooling attainments.

The chapter by Kathleen Mullan Harris and Hedwig Lee, "Pathways of Social Disadvantage from Adolescence into Adulthood," is an original report from an important longitudinal study of the transition from adolescence to adulthood. The National Longitudinal Study of Adolescent Health (Add Health) has now collected four waves of data from a large sample of young people who were in grades 7 to 12 when the study began in 1994 and were between the ages of 24 and 32 years at the time that the fourth wave of data was collected.[56] The longitudinal design of the study and the extensive information collected on the adolescents' families, peers, neighborhoods, and schools as they made the crucial transition from adolescence to adulthood permit careful study of the associations between the youth's social environment and outcomes in young adulthood, including educational attainment, poverty or welfare status, and subjective social status. Harris and Lee emphasize that their analysis shows that the disadvantages experienced by many adolescents, especially minorities, occur in a variety of social settings, including their family, their peer group, their school, and their neighborhood and that those disadvantages are cumulative.

Nonetheless, adolescents can increase their upward mobility in early adulthood if they make good choices, such as by finishing high school (at a minimum), avoiding teen pregnancy, and getting a job and avoiding idleness when they complete their education. The study also shows that engagement in civic activities promotes upward mobility, especially for females. From these and similar results, the authors conclude that intervention programs should target several of the social contexts in the lives of disadvantaged students, especially by encouraging civic participation and promoting mentor relationships. The goal of the mentors and programs that facilitate civic participation should be to help disadvantaged adolescents to avoid dropping out of school, teen pregnancy, and idleness.

Complementing the Harris and Lee chapter, the chapter by Patrick Wightman and Sheldon Danziger, entitled "Poverty, Intergenerational Mobility, and Young Adult Educational Attainment," uses data from the PSID to examine the intergenerational transmission of poverty and inequality. They investigate the relationship between family background and young adult outcomes and the extent to which inequalities in parental socioeconomic status (SES, as measured either by income or by educational attainment) may have affected young adult educational attainment over the past thirty years. Despite several decades of spending on compensatory education programs, from preschool through college, over the period of study, the authors find no evidence that the gaps in college completion (earning a four-year degree by the age of 25 years) between young adults from low-income and those from high-income families narrowed among cohorts from the mid-1950s through the early 1980s. Nor do they find any such evidence for gaps between young adults from low-education and those from high-education families. The authors also examine educational attainment differences by SES in a three-generation context, focusing on the outcomes of young adults around the age of 19 years raised by low-income parents who were themselves raised in low-income households. The results show that educational attainment is lower both for those whose own childhood SES was low and for those whose parents' childhood SES was low. The authors conclude that equality of educational opportunity in the United States has not improved since the beginning of the War on Poverty in the mid-1960s.

Summary and Implications

This volume examines perennial issues of social policy that Australia and the United States have in common and that both nations spend billions of dollars and at least as much political capital trying to solve or minimize. Three specific issues that receive extensive treatment in the eight chapters included in the volume are employment of the poor and the attendant problem of child care; the trade-offs between inexpensive means of caring for children while parents work and more expensive, high-quality early childhood education programs that can boost development and promote school readiness; and the role of postsecondary education in equalizing opportunity.

An important feature of the chapters—and indeed the major reason that we organized the conference and this volume—is that they all explore these vital policy issues by using original empirical research based on high-quality longitudinal datasets from their respective countries. The policymakers and to a lesser extent foundations of both nations have made extensive investments in creating longitudinal datasets that allow researchers to accurately describe the course of social problems over time and to study the underlying social and demographic conditions related to these problems. The authors capitalize on two Australian datasets (the Longitudinal Study of Australian Children and the Australian Early Development Index) and four U.S. datasets (the Panel Study of Income Dynamics, the Early Childhood Longitudinal Survey–Birth Cohort, the Three-City study, and the National Longitudinal Study of Adolescent Health) to present original analyses of parental employment, early childhood care and education, and educational attainment. All of the authors draw implications for social policy from their empirical analyses.

The chapters on parental employment are timely because many nations with advanced economies have now embarked on policies intended to boost the employment of their adult population, including parents, because of the crisis in funding the welfare state.[57] But parental employment—especially in single-parent families—raises serious questions about child development. The chapters in this section show that children demonstrate better development if their parents work and have higher income but that working long hours at low-wage work by either both parents or by lone parents is associated with problems in the academic and socioemotional development of children. On the other hand, long-term joblessness is also inimical to children's development. The policy implications of these findings are that the current emphasis on high employment rates of both parents in two-parent families and of lone parents can boost family income and have either a neutral or positive impact on children's development. However, given the potential negative impacts of long hours and low wages on child development, governments would be wise to provide supports such as child care, wage supplements, parental leave, and employment and training, which subsidize the income of low-income parents, help parents to maintain job stability, and promote advancement to better jobs with higher pay and better benefits and working conditions.

The chapters in the section on early care and education assume that high-quality early education is a key to the development of disadvantaged children and explore the conditions that support it. Without government subsidies, poor parents are not able to afford high-quality care and therefore miss an opportunity to boost the development of their children; in some circumstances, their children are harmed by being exposed to inadequate care. Even with government subsidies, families do not always select higher-quality center-based care. Equally problematic, representative national data from Australia indicate that communities that have a large share of disadvantaged families do not have adequate programs to promote the development of poor children, who then arrive at the school door already far behind children from more advantaged families. The implication of these chapters is that higher child care subsidies would promote selection of somewhat higher-quality care by parents. Ensuring that more children receive high-quality care also requires raising the overall quality of care available in local communities. Oberklaid and his coauthors conclude, however, that even greater subsidies and higher-quality care will be inadequate to achieve meaningful progress toward equal opportunity. Rather, a much more aggressive preschool strategy is required in which children with bigger problems receive both high-quality care and individual supports as well as treatment for themselves and their parents.

The three chapters on educational attainment produce a rather stark picture of educational disadvantage in the United States. The chapters show the wide range of disadvantages faced by children from low-income families, including disadvantages in their families, peer group, school, and neighborhood during the crucial transition to adulthood and the impact of rising inequality in widening the already considerable gap in educational achievement, especially between black and white children. The Wightman and Danziger chapter shows that the gap in college achievement between children of upper-income and low-income parents has widened by as much as 50 percent across three generations. Thus, the impact of low income reaches across generations. As Wightman and Danziger conclude and the other authors in this section imply, the long history in the United States of focusing policies on reducing the gap in educational opportunity have largely failed. The authors conclude that the country must intensify its efforts to boost the development of poor children during the pre-school years, do a much better job of preparing them for college, and find more effective ways of helping them finance the ever-increasing costs of a college education. The chapter by Harris and Lee also emphasizes the importance of civic participation and mentoring in helping poor children make more responsible personal decisions, such as to stay in school and avoid teen pregnancy.

Taken together, these studies show that Australia and the United States share similar social problems associated with the tangled relationship between poverty, poor education, low-wage work, and low family income. Researchers and policymakers from both sides of the Pacific have much to learn from each other's social problems and policy responses. We believe that this volume moves us closer to that goal.

Notes

1. In 2010, per capita income in the United States was about $47,000 while per capita income in Australia was $40,000. See International Monetary Fund, "Gross Domestic Product Based on Purchasing-Power-Parity (PPP) Per Capita GDP," World Economic Outlook database, September 2011 (www.imf.org/external/pubs/ft/weo/2011/02/weodata/index.aspx).

2. The poverty rate for female-headed families is about four to five times the rate for married-couple families. In 2010, for example, there was an approximately fivefold difference: 31.6 percent of families with a single female household head were in poverty but only 6.2 percent of married-couple families. Carmen DeNavas-Walt, Bernadette D. Proctor, and Jessica C. Smith, *Income, Poverty, and Health Insurance Coverage in the United States: 2010* (U.S. Census Bureau, 2011), table B-3. At any given moment, about 25 percent of American children are living in a female-headed family; see U.S. Census Bureau, "America's Families and Living Arrangements: 2011," table C-3 (www.census.gov/population/www/socdemo/hh-fam/cps2011.html).

3. Calculations based on Brookings tabulations of data from the Current Population Survey, "Annual Social and Economic Supplement,"1980–2010. The specific employment-to-population ratios were 46.5 for 1995 and 66.0 for 1999, yielding an increase of 41.9 percent. See also Ron Haskins, "Balancing Work and Solidarity in the Western Democracies," Discussion Paper (Berlin: Social Science Research Center Berlin [WZB], October 2010).

4. The poverty rate for families with a female householder (no husband present) with children was 41.5 percent in 1995, 33.0 percent in 2000, 38.5 percent in 2009, and 40.7 percent in 2010. See DeNavas-Walt, Proctor, and Smith, *Income, Poverty, and Health Insurance Coverage*, table B-3.

5. Gretchen Rowe and Tracy Roberts, *The Welfare Rules Databook: State Policies as of July 2000* (Washington: Urban Institute, 2004).

6. Sheldon Danziger and others, "Does It Pay to Move from Welfare to Work?" *Journal of Policy Analysis and Management*, vol. 21, no. 4 (2002), pp. 671–92; James J. Heckman, Robert J. LaLonde, and Jeffrey A. Smith, "The Economics and Econometrics of Active Labor Market Programs," in *Handbook of Labor Economics*, vol. 3, edited by Orley Ashenfelter and David Card (Amsterdam: North Holland, 1999).

7. Mary Jo Bane and David Ellwood, *Welfare Realities: From Rhetoric to Reform* (Harvard University Press, 1994), table 2.3, p. 39.

8. Congressional Budget Office, "Policy Changes Affecting Mandatory Spending for Low-Income Families Not Receiving Welfare" (Washington, 1998).

9. Office of the President, *Economic Report of the President* (U.S. Government Printing Office, 2011), p. 190.

10. Ibid., p. 234.

11. Australian Bureau of Statistics, *Employee Earnings and Hours, Australia: May 2010*, No. 6306.0, "Summary of Findings" (http://www.abs.gov.au/ausstats/abs@.nsf/mf/6306.0).

12. Australian Council of Trade Unions, "Casual Workers Factsheet" (www.actu.org.au/HelpDesk/YourRightsfactsheets/CasualWorkers.aspx [November 23, 2011]).

13. Australian Bureau of Statistics, *Labour Force: September 2011*, No. 6202.0, table 01 (2011) (www.abs.gov.au).

14. Australian Bureau of Statistics, *Family Characteristics: 2009–10*, No. 4442.0, "All Children, Family Type by Age of Child, 1997, 2003, 2006–07, 2009–10" (2011) (www.abs.gov.au).

15. Centrelink, *Payments* (Australian Government Department of Human Services, 2011) (www.centrelink.gov.au/internet/internet.nsf/payments/parenting_rates.htm).

16. Centrelink, *Payments: Assets Test* (Australian Government Department of Human Services, 2011) (www.centrelink.gov.au/internet/internet.nsf/payments/chartab.htm#a).

17. Centrelink, *Individuals: Paid Parental Leave Scheme Eligibility* (Australian Government Department of Human Services, 2011) (www.centrelink.gov.au/internet/internet.nsf/individuals/ppl_working_parents_eligibility.htm).

18. Australian Bureau of Statistics, *Labour Force*, table 01.

19. Australian Bureau of Statistics, *Australian Social Trends September 2011: Long-Term Unemployment*, No. 4102.0 (2011) (www.abs.gov.au).

20. Ibid.

21. In a study of men's wages, Gary Burtless and Ron Haskins showed that wages at the 10th percentile have not increased in nearly four decades. See Gary Burtless and Ron Haskins, "Inequality, Economic Mobility, and Social Policy," in *Understanding America: The Anatomy of an Exceptional Nation*, edited by Peter H. Schuck and James Q. Wilson (New York: Public Affairs, 2008), pp. 495–538.

22. Deborah L. Vandell and Barbara Wolfe, "Child Care Quality: Does It Matter and Does It Need To Be Improved?" (Washington: U.S. Department of Health and Human Services, 2000) (http://aspe.hhs.gov/hsp/ccquality00/ccqual.htm).

23. Teresa Eckrich Sommer and P. Lindsay Chase-Lansdale, "Early Childhood Education Centers and Mothers' Postsecondary Attainment: A New Conceptual Framework for a Dual-Generation Education Intervention," *Teachers College Record*, forthcoming.

24. Ron Haskins and W. Steven Barnett, *Investing in Young Children: New Directions in Federal Preschool and Early Childhood Policy* (Brookings, 2010).

25. W. Steven Barnett and others, *Effects of Five State Prekindergarten Programs on Early Learning* (New Brunswick, N.J.: National Institute of Early Education Research, 2007).

26. Robert C. Pianta and others, "The Effects of Preschool Education: What We Know, How Public Policy Is Not Aligned with the Evidence Base, and What We Need to Know," *Psychological Science in the Public Interest,* vol. 10, no. 2 (2009), pp. 49–88, and W. Steven Barnett, "Effectiveness of Early Educational Intervention," *Science,* vol. 333, no. 6045 (2011), pp. 975–78, but see David Deming, "Early Childhood Intervention and Life-Cycle Skill Development: Evidence from Head Start," *American Economic Journal: Applied Economics,* vol. 1, no. 3 (2009), pp. 111–34.

27. Nicole D. Forry, "The Impact of Child Care Subsidies on Low-Income Single Parents: An Examination of Child Care Expenditures and Family Finances," *Journal of Family Economic Issues,* vol. 30, no. 1 (2009), pp. 43–54, see tables 2 and 4.

28. Administration for Children and Families, "Head Start Impact Study: Final Report," January 2010 (www.acf.hhs.gov/programs/opre/hs/impact_study/reports/impact_study/hs_impact_study_final.pdf). But for an evidence-based argument that Head Start does produce some long-term impacts, see Deming, "Early Childhood Intervention and Life-Cycle Skill Development."

29. Ron Haskins and W. Steven Barnett, "Finally, Obama Administration Is Putting Head Start to the Test," *Washington Post,* October 11, 2011; Federal Register, "Designation Renewal of Head Start Grantees," Proposed Rule by the Children and Families Administration, September 22, 2011.

30. Pianta and others, "The Effects of Preschool Education"; Barnett, "Effectiveness of Early Educational Intervention."

31. Ron Haskins, "Is Anything More Important than Day-Care Quality?" in *Child Care in the 1990s: Trends and Consequences,* edited by Alan Booth (Hillsdale, N.J.: Erlbaum, 1992), pp. 101–15.

32. These figures are based on cost-of-care estimates by Doug Besharov and colleagues. The Besharov figures are for 2005; we inflated his 2005 estimates by the GDP deflator to estimate costs in 2010 dollars; see Douglas J. Besharov, Justus A. Myers, and Jeffrey S. Morrow, "Costs per Child for Early Childhood Education and Care" (University of Maryland, Welfare Reform Academy, August 2007).

33. Steering Committee for the Review of Government Service Provision, *Productivity Commission Report on Government Services 2011* (Australian Government Productivity Commission, 2011) (www.pc.gov.au/gsp/reports/rogs/2011).

34. Early Childhood Development Workforce, *Overview* (Australian Government Productivity Commission, 2011) (www.pc.gov.au/__data/assets/pdf_file/0011/110504/03-early-childhood-overview.pdf).

35. Marilyn Harrington, *Preschool Education in Australia* (Parliament of Australia, 2008) (www.aph.gov.au/library/pubs/bn/2007-08/PreschoolEdAustralia.htm#_Toc198010805).

36. Office of Early Childhood Education and Child Care, *State of Child Care in Australia* (Australian Government Department of Education, Employment, and Workplace Relations, 2010) (www.mychild.gov.au/documents/docs/StateChildCareAus.pdf).

37. Centrelink, "2011 Payments" (www.centrelink.gov.au/internet/internet.nsf/payments/ccr_rates.htm).

38. Harrington, *Preschool Education in Australia.*

39. Early Childhood Development Workforce, *Overview.*

40. Steering Committee for the Review of Government Service Provision, *Productivity Commission Report*.

41. Claudia Goldin and Lawrence F. Katz, *The Race between Education and Technology* (Cambridge, Mass: Belknap, 2008).

42. Ron Haskins, "Education and Economic Mobility," in *Getting Ahead or Losing Ground: Economic Mobility in America*, edited by Julia B. Isaacs, Isabel V. Sawhill, and Ron Haskins (Washington: Brookings and the Pew Charitable Trusts, 2009), pp. 81–104.

43. Ron Haskins and Isabel Sawhill, *Creating an Opportunity Society* (Brookings, 2009), p. 127.

44. DeNavas-Walt, Proctor, and Smith, *Income, Poverty, and Health Insurance Coverage in the United States: 2010*, p. 10.

45. Ron Haskins, Harry Holzer, and Robert Lerman, *Promoting Economic Mobility by Increasing Postsecondary Education* (Washington: Economic Mobility Project, Pew Charitable Trusts, 2009), p. 12.

46. College Board, "Trends in Student Aid: 2010" (New York: 2011).

47. College Board, "Trends in Student Pricing: 2010" (New York: 2011).

48. College Board, "Trends in Student Aid: 2010."

49. Haskins, Holzer, and Lerman, *Promoting Economic Mobility*.

50. Patrick Laplange, Maurice Glover, and Anthony Shomos, "Effects of Health and Education on Labour Force Participation," Staff Working Paper (Melbourne, Australia: Australian Government Productivity Commission, 2007) (www.pc.gov.au/__data/assets/pdf_file/0019/63190/healthandeducation.pdf).

51. Ibid.

52. Authors calculations from Australian Bureau of Statistics, *Education and Work*, No. 6227.0, table 10 (2011) (www.abs.gov.au).

53. Centre for the Study of Higher Education, *Participation and Equity: A Review of the Participation in Higher Education of People from Low Socioeconomic Backgrounds and Indigenous People*, report prepared for Universities Australia (University of Melbourne, 2008).

54. Department of Families, Housing, Community Service, and Indigenous Affairs, "Income Support Customers: A Statistical Overview 2010" (2011) (www.fahcsia.gov.au/about/publicationsarticles/research/statistical/Pages/stp_9.aspx).

55. Department of Education, Employment, and Workplace Relations, "Transforming Australia's Higher Education System" (2009) (www.deewr.gov.au/HigherEducation/Documents/TransformingAusHigherED.pdf).

56. For background on the Add Health study, see "Add Health" (www.cpc.unc.edu/projects/addhealth).

57. Ivar Lodemel and Heather Trickey, "'An Offer You Can't Refuse': Workfare in International Perspective" (Bristol, U.K.: Policy Press, 2001).

2

Dynamics of Early Maternal Employment in Low-Income Families

REBEKAH LEVINE COLEY AND

CAITLIN MCPHERRAN LOMBARDI

Recent social policy shifts in the United States have sought to promote maternal employment in order to improve poor families' economic resources and self-sufficiency, support healthy family functioning, and promote child development. One concern raised in policy debates highlights employment among new parents. Contrasting arguments have been made concerning whether public resources should be used to provide economic support to new mothers to remain out of the labor force or whether a quick entry or return to work after childbirth will best promote economic and family stability. These debates are heightened when the target is low-income families, who often lack a second potential wage earner and hence must rely on mothers' wages or public support.[1]

The United States is an outlier on the world stage with respect to the social policy issues surrounding early maternal employment. The United States is currently the only wealthy industrialized country that does not provide federal paid leave for mothers following childbirth.[2] Although the Family Medical Leave Act (FMLA) provides job-protected unpaid leave for twelve weeks for the birth or adoption of a new child or other family health issues, less than half of working mothers meet the eligibility requirements, with poor, single, and African American women having lower eligibility than their more advantaged counterparts.[3] Even among eligible mothers, many cannot afford to lose all employment income for three months and hence do not take the leave to which they are entitled.[4] The private sector does not adequately fill this unmet need as only an estimated 8 percent of private employers offer paid parental leave.[5] Moreover, poor women are propelled into the labor market in the months immediately following childbirth by policy levers besides the lack of federal financial support for women remaining at home with their children. U.S. federal welfare policy has become more stringent over the past two decades, implementing strict work requirements as well as additional work supports for working parents. Currently some states' welfare policies provide no employment exemption for childbirth, and forty-six states require welfare recipients to work by the time their child is 12 months old.[6]

In light of these policies and their potential implications for families and children, a central question for researchers concerns the repercussions of employment among mothers of newborn children. Research on the effects of maternal employment has focused primarily on middle-income, European American children in the United States. The literature generally shows few associations between mothers' work status and children's development.[7] An exception to this pattern is a fairly consistent negative link between maternal employment begun in a child's first year of life and later child cognitive and socioemotional development found in middle-income, European American samples.[8] Full-time early maternal employment has been found to be especially detrimental to children's later functioning.[9]

Maternal employment during infancy may pose harm because it hampers child-parent attachment, places additional demands on mothers at a time when their child requires the most care, and requires mothers to secure quality child care for their infants, which is often of limited availability and expensive. Attachment theory suggests that time spent working may reduce the amount of time and opportunities that a mother has to build the sensitive, responsive parenting skills that are essential to the development of her child's secure attachment.[10] Furthermore, the high care demands of infants combined with balancing employment and parenting at this developmental stage may be especially stressful for mothers, negatively influencing maternal well-being and family functioning and ultimately affecting child outcomes.[11] On a practical level, most employed mothers must find child care outside of their home, which research has shown to be challenging due to a lack of affordable, quality infant care options.[12]

These arguments suggest that early entry into employment may be harmful for young children. However, there has been a notable gap in determining the impact for low-income families. This is an especially relevant distinction to make because the most rapid increase in maternal employment in the United States in recent years has occurred among single, low-income mothers. That increase is widely assumed to be the result of policies aimed at increasing employment among economically disadvantaged mothers, such as the work requirements instituted as part of welfare reform and expansion of the earned income tax credit. At the time of the federal welfare changes in 1996, in which a cash assistance entitlement program was replaced with a time-limited cash benefit requiring work, proponents argued that reducing the safety net for low-income women would propel them into the labor market and put them in a position to better support their families over the long term and hence encourage healthy child development.[13] And indeed the proportion of working single mothers grew dramatically between 1993 and 2000.[14]

For low-income families, the benefits of maternal employment may outweigh negative factors, with mothers' work bringing needed economic resources to families and a psychological boost to mothers.[15] Research on the influence of employment on maternal functioning and parenting in low-income families with older children has found that, in general, maternal employment is positively linked with mothers' mental health as well as with mother-child relationships, parenting, and the quality of home environments.[16] Psychological models argue that the economic and social resources derived from employment may, in turn, support children's development, promoting core cognitive skill development through access to cognitively enriching resources as well as supporting emotional and behavioral functioning through stable, responsive, and high-quality relationships and environments.[17]

Few studies have addressed the hypothesis that early maternal employment may not pose a threat to the development of infants from low-income families. Among the existing studies drawing from rich, longitudinal datasets, results are somewhat mixed. One recent study of children in low-income families found early maternal employment to predict enhanced emotional and behavioral functioning among children at the age of seven years, with no significant links for children's cognitive skills.[18] Other studies have replicated the pattern of no significant links between early maternal employment and children's later cognitive skills among African American and Hispanic children (not all of whom were low-income) but have found mixed results for behavioral functioning.[19]

In short, existing research is somewhat equivocal concerning whether early maternal employment is harmful for young children in low-income families. One explanation for the lack of consistency may be related to the labor market experiences of low-income mothers and the policies that encouraged their employment. Some critics of U.S. employment policies targeting low-income families argue that many poor parents lack the education and job training support required to obtain a quality job with opportunities for advancement. A host of barriers to employment have been noted among poor parents, including limited education and skills, fragile mental health, and substance abuse problems.[20] Low-income women's employment therefore may be of poor or variable quality, with some women having stable jobs with decent pay and benefits but others obtaining low pay and minimal benefits or experiencing work instability and frequent transitions in and out of employment. The quality and stability of work may in turn have important implications for child functioning.

Research that goes beyond assessing mothers' employment status to considering the dynamics and quality of their employment experiences is sparse. Although studies have shown that employment rates of disadvantaged women increased following welfare reform in the late 1990s, such research also notes that many former welfare recipients obtained jobs with low pay, high turnover, and limited benefits and others remained unemployed or underemployed (that is, they worked part-time but wanted more hours).[21]

Researchers know little about how job characteristics such as pay and benefits, work hours and consistency, and work stability may influence the well-being of low-income children.

Experimental assessments of antipoverty employment programs have found that programs that increased mothers' employment hours and family incomes had positive effects on school-age children's later achievement and social behaviors but found no significant effects on the functioning of younger children.[22] Correlational research has similarly failed to find a significant link between greater employment hours among low-income mothers of infants and later child functioning.[23] It is notable that little research has assessed the quality of disadvantaged mothers' employment more carefully, considering factors such as wages, access to health insurance and other benefits, or flexibility. Finally, some researchers have drawn attention to instability in women's employment trajectories. Each transition in employment among parents of young children requires adjustments in family processes and child care practices and hence may impede healthy child development. Results linking job instability with child outcomes suggest that unstable employment may pose risks to children that are not evident with continuous employment or continuous unemployment.[24]

Taken together, this limited research suggests that maternal employment in low-income families could be positively, neutrally, or negatively linked with children's outcomes, depending on employment dynamics. Unemployment, low-quality employment, and employment patterns characterized by instability appear harmful compared with continuous employment in a good-quality job. The literature has focused primarily on older children and adolescents, giving less attention to very young children, who are at a centrally important stage of development. We know little about the employment experiences of low-income mothers of infants and how their experiences are associated with children's healthy development as they reach school age. Understanding the dynamics of employment among mothers of young children is paramount to resolving further policy debates and developing initiatives concerning parental leave, work promotion, and family support.

We used a rich longitudinal dataset on low-income families in the United States from *Welfare, Children, and Families: A Three-City Study* (the Three-City Study) to assess the employment experiences of low-income mothers over the two-year period following the birth of a child. We first sought to provide a rich descriptive view of women's labor market experiences in the years after childbirth, considering the status, timing, extent, consistency, and quality of women's employment. Our second goal was to assess the repercussions of early maternal employment for children, considering links between maternal employment characteristics and children's cognitive, behavioral, and emotional functioning as they entered middle childhood.

Method

The data for our empirical analyses were drawn from the main survey component of the Three-City Study, a longitudinal, multi-method study of the well-being of low-income children and families in the United States. This study was initiated following the passage of a new set of policies in the United States that sought to increase low-income mothers' economic independence and engagement in the labor force and decrease their reliance on government cash benefits by imposing restrictions on welfare eligibility; establishing work requirements for welfare recipients, including mothers of infants and toddlers; and increasing work supports, such as wage supplements and child care subsidies, for all low-wage parents. These changes, initiated in the mid- to late 1990s, occurred during a notable economic expansion characterized by a very low unemployment rate of 5.3 percent and rising median household incomes.[25] In sum, the Three-City Study was designed to assess a sample of families headed primarily by unmarried mothers who were under substantial pressure to obtain paid employment, with variable public support for balancing employment and parenthood.

Sampling and Data Collection

The Three-City Study followed a stratified, random sample of over 2,400 low-income children and mothers, drawn from high- and moderate-poverty neighborhoods in three large U.S. cities: Boston, Massachusetts; Chicago, Illinois; and San Antonio, Texas. Within each family in the study, one focal child was selected. Due to our primary interest in mothers of young children, we restricted our analysis to the Three-City Study families with focal children from birth to the age of 23 months in wave 1 ($N = 444$); these children were followed for six years, until the average age of seven years. The mothers in this sample were primarily unmarried (74 percent); most were from ethnic and racial minority groups, primarily African American (42 percent) and Hispanic (55 percent); and all were low income, with 73 percent reporting household incomes below the U.S. federal poverty level at the beginning of the study.

Data were collected through a series of individual, in-person interviews and assessments with mothers and focal children over a six-year period. The first wave of interviews was completed in 1999 (90 percent screening rate; 83 percent interview response rate); the second wave in 2000–01 (88 percent retention rate); and the third wave in 2005 (80 percent retention rate of wave 1 respondents). Interviews were conducted in English or Spanish by professional, trained interviewers, and all respondents were paid for their participation in the study.[26] All of our analyses incorporated sampling weights that adjust for selection criteria and differential response and make the sample representative of infants and mothers in low-income families in low-income neighborhoods in the three cities. A relatively small amount of missing data was apparent, ranging from 0 to 16 percent across study variables. Missing data were imputed using an expectation maximization technique employing a maximum likelihood approach, leading to a stable sample across all analyses.

Measures

Measures for this research were drawn from numerous sources. Mothers reported on their work experiences as well as on child and family characteristics. Both mothers' reports and direct assessments were used to assess focal child functioning.

Maternal Employment Variables

Numerous aspects of mothers' employment dynamics were assessed through an extensive series of questions to mothers concerning their job experiences for each job that lasted at least two months over the two-year period prior to the first interview and the period from the first to the second interview. From these data, we created a set of measures on mothers' employment experiences from the time of the focal child's birth until his or her second birthday. Employment effort was measured with a continuous variable of the number of hours per week employed. Employment quality was assessed through a continuous variable assessing average hourly wage rates and a variable denoting whether the mother had received health insurance from her employer during the two-year period. Employment stability also was assessed with two variables: a count variable of the number of months worked over the two-year period and a count of the number of different jobs held over the two-year period.

Child Functioning

Two aspects of child functioning were measured at wave 3, when children averaged seven years of age: cognitive skills and behavioral-emotional functioning, assessed with full-scale, well-validated developmental assessment measures. Children's cognitive skills were directly assessed by field interviewers using the Woodcock-Johnson Psycho-Educational Battery Revised (WJ-R) Letter-Word Identification and Applied Problems subtests to assess children's reading and math skills.[27] Scores were standardized according to national norms. Children's emotional and behavioral functioning was measured using mothers' reports on the full Child Behavior Checklist (CBCL/6-18).[28] This extensively used, validated scale measures numerous aspects of children's emotional and behavioral functioning with new subscales based on the *Diagnostic and Statistical Manual of Mental Disorders* assessing symptoms of affective problems, anxiety problems, somatic problems, attention deficit hyperactivity (ADHD) problems, oppositional defiant problems, and conduct problems.[29] Internal consistency estimates for the six subscales ranged from α = .64 to .83 in the Three-City Study, and scores were standardized according to national norms.

Child and Mother Covariates

In addition to the primary variables of interest, a number of child and family characteristics were assessed that are important to consider because they might select mothers into employment and also might affect child functioning. All covariates were measured at wave 1 unless otherwise noted. Covariates included child race/ethnicity, coded as African American, Hispanic (of any race), or white/other; child gender; and child age in months. Additional child variables included an indicator for low birth weight (< 2,500 grams) and a second indicator of whether the child showed a likelihood of developmental delays in communication, fine motor skills, gross motor skills, problem solving, or personal-social realms, assessed with the Ages and Stages Questionnaire (ASQ).[30]

Covariates for mothers, which also were measured at wave 1 unless otherwise noted, included demographic and human capital characteristics. Mother's age was measured in years. Education was coded categorically as less than a high school diploma, a high school diploma or GED, or more than a high school diploma. Mothers' literacy skills were assessed at wave 2 with the WJ-R Letter-Word Identification subscale, using standard scores.[31] Mothers' marital status was designated as married or single, and an additional dummy variable indicated whether the mother had an employed spouse in the household. The number of children in the household was assessed linearly. An indicator of whether the mother was employed in the year prior to the focal child's birth was included, as was a measure of the mother's employment at wave 3 (an indicator of whether the mother had been employed for the majority of the prior eleven months), when child functioning was assessed, to adjust for the concurrent link between mothers' employment and child functioning at wave 3. We also controlled for whether the mother or child received welfare in the two-year period prior to the wave 1 interview and for total family income, assessed through an income-to-needs ratio comparing the total household income to the federal poverty line.

Sample Description

Table 2-1 (first column) presents descriptive statistics for the sample. As noted above, the sample was economically and socially disadvantaged. Most mothers were young, of an average age of 25 years, and only 37 percent had pursued education beyond a high school diploma. More than four of five mothers had received welfare at some point in the two years prior to the first interview, although nearly half also had been employed in the year prior to the focal child's birth. Just over one-fourth of mothers were married, and only 18 percent had an employed spouse. The average household income was below the federal poverty line at the beginning of the study (income-to-needs ratio of 0.88), rising to just over the poverty line in the second and third waves.

Results

This section presents a descriptive assessment of mothers' work experiences in the two years following childbirth and a comparison of child and maternal characteristics of employed and unemployed mothers during that period, followed by a discussion of the repercussions of maternal work on children's well-being.

Mothers' Employment Experiences Following Childbirth

The first goal of this analysis was to assess patterns of employment among low-income mothers following the birth of a new child. The top panel of table 2-1 presents descriptive data on mothers' employment experiences over the twenty-four months following the focal child's birth, with the first column showing data for all mothers in our analytic sample and the second column showing data for the subsample with some employment experience. These data show a high level of labor market participation, with nearly three-quarters (73 percent) of mothers employed within the two years following childbirth and 27 percent of mothers remaining out of the paid labor market that entire time. Data on the timing of employment (not shown) indicated that 41 percent of mothers

Table 2-1. *Descriptives of Study Variables*[a]

Variable	Total sample (N = 444)	Total employed (n = 324)	Total unemployed (n = 120)
Mother's employment characteristics at 0–24 months			
Hours worked/week (number)	26.25 (16.00)	32.92 (10.16)	-
Part-time, < 30 hours/week (%)	19.14	26.15	-
Full-time, 30–40 hours/week (%)	46.49	63.66	-
Overtime, > 40 hours/week (%)	7.21	9.85	-
Hourly wage (dollars)	6.32 (3.95)	7.91 (2.64)	-
Health insurance (%)	20.61	25.94	-
Months worked (number)	10.83 (8.85)	13.62 (7.84)	-
Jobs (number)	1.16 (0.90)	1.46 (0.77)	-
One job (%)	44.59	60.92	-
Two or more jobs (%)	28.60	39.08	-
Child characteristics at wave 1			
Age (months)	12.64 (6.78)	12.48 (6.72)	13.22 (7.00)
Boy (%)	48.14	48.62	43.89
Girl (%)	51.86	51.38	56.11
Hispanic (%)	54.98	53.56	62.43
Black (%)	42.08	43.69	33.79
White (%)	2.94	2.75	3.78
Developmental delay (%)	28.68	27.46	35.09
Low birth weight (%)	5.26	5.26	8.95

(continued)

entered the labor market prior to six months after childbirth and that 54 percent did so by twelve months. Mothers worked an average of 26 hours per week; mothers who were employed worked an average of 33 hours, indicating that full-time work was common even among mothers of infants. Indeed, among working mothers, only 26 percent worked part-time (< 30 hours per week), 64 percent worked full-time (thirty to forty hours), and 10 percent worked more than forty hours per week, which we term overtime.

Although work intensity was quite high, job quality was low. Employed mothers' wages averaged less than $8 an hour, and only a quarter of employed mothers received employer-sponsored health insurance at any point during the two-year period. In 1999, the federal minimum wage in the United States was $5.15 per hour (it stayed at this level for a decade, over the entire period covered by this study). Closer examination of our data indicated that 7 percent of employed mothers earned less than the minimum wage, taking primarily informal jobs such as babysitting. Finally, the data reveal a moderate level of work

Table 2-1. *Descriptives of Study Variables*[a] *(Continued)*

Variable	Total sample (N = 444)	Total employed (n = 324)	Total unemployed (n = 120)
Mother characteristics at wave 1			
Mother cognitive skills	89.66 (16.59)	91.26 (14.68)**	83.14 (21.65)**
Less than high school (%)	35.11	30.86 ***	52.27 ***
High school or GED (%)	27.62	27.72	25.58
More than high school (%)	37.27	41.42 ***	22.15 ***
Employed before birth (%)	46.51	55.57 ***	12.1 ***
Welfare receipt in last 2 years (%)	81.04	80.15	84.08
Mother is married (%)	26.33	26.00	28.17
Working spouse (%)	18.36	16.35	26.47
Children (number)	2.62 (1.57)	2.58 (1.61)	2.85 (1.33)
Age of mother (years)	25.38 (6.94)	24.84 (5.94)	27.65 (9.60)
Income-to-needs ratio	0.89 (0.63)	0.96 (0.67)**	0.69 (0.44)**
Child characteristics at wave 3			
Age (months)	82.72 (7.57)	82.52 (7.52)	83.27 (7.70)
Reading skills	102.10 (16.90)	102.16 (16.53)	101.89 (18.27)
Math skills	95.96 (18.11)	96.49 (18.54)	93.93 (16.28)
Affective problems	54.34 (5.47)	54.06 (5.47)	55.39 (5.36)
Anxiety problems	54.51 (5.36)	53.97 (5.00)***	56.54 (6.14)***
Somatic problems	54.75 (5.61)	54.32 (5.36)**	56.37 (6.21)**
Hyperactivity problems	54.93 (6.02)	54.58 (5.92)*	56.24 (6.24)*
Oppositional problems	54.85 (5.92)	54.58 (5.82)	55.86 (6.23)
Conduct problems	55.04 (6.33)	54.18 (5.54)***	58.29 (7.93)***

a. Table presents percents or means; standard deviations are in parentheses. Significant differences between the unemployed and employed sample groups are denoted as follows: *$p < .10$, **$p < .05$, ***$p < .01$.

stability. On average, women were working in about half of the twenty-four months under consideration. That average masked quite a bit of variability, however, with one-quarter working six months or less and one-third working twenty months or more. Nearly one-fifth of the employed mothers reported working all twenty-four months. Work instability was moderate, with 39 percent of employed mothers having two jobs or more during the two-year period.

Comparing Employed and Unemployed Mothers

As a second descriptive question, we considered differences between mothers who were employed in the two-year period following the focal child's birth and those who remained out of the labor market during that time. The second and third columns of table 2-1 present data on the two groups that show notable similarities in child characteristics, with no significant differences between the groups in child gender, age, race/ethnicity, or early health problems. On the other hand, differences were apparent in maternal characteristics. Replicating prior research, these data indicate that employed mothers had greater literacy skills and more education than unemployed mothers. Employed mothers also had a stronger work history, being more likely to have been employed during the year prior to childbirth. Interestingly, however, employed mothers were no less likely to have been on welfare than unemployed mothers, with over four of five mothers having received welfare in the prior two years. In addition, there were no significant differences between employed and unemployed mothers in mothers' marital status, presence of an employed spouse, number of children, or mothers' age.

The lack of differences in welfare receipt and having an employed spouse raises the question of how economically disadvantaged women without paid employment were surviving financially. Our data contained extensive information on households' income sources from numerous public programs. Additional descriptive analyses indicated that unemployed mothers were significantly more likely than employed mothers to have received Supplemental Security Income (SSI) (28 percent of unemployed mothers and 6 percent of employed mothers) in the two-year period prior to the first interview and were slightly more likely to live in public housing (54 percent and 41 percent, respectively). However, there were no significant differences in recent receipt of Medicaid (94 percent versus 81 percent), Women, Infants, and Children (WIC) food support (89 percent versus 83 percent), or other housing subsidies (10 percent versus 16 percent). Considering the income of other family members, employed mothers lived in households with more adults (2.02 adults versus 1.73), but there was no difference in monthly earned income from other adults in the household ($565 a month for employed mothers and $660 a month for unemployed mothers). All told, considering all sources of cash income and food stamps, unemployed mothers were notably more likely to be poor, with an average income-to-needs ratio of 0.69 for unemployed- and of 0.96 for employed-mother families. Although this difference indicates the importance of mothers' earned income in supporting their families, it is notable that the household income of employed mothers remained, on average, below the poverty line.

Links between Maternal Employment and Children's Functioning

EMPLOYMENT STATUS AND CHILD FUNCTIONING. After considering mothers' employment experiences in the two-year period following childbirth, we next sought to assess whether patterns of maternal employment during a child's infancy had repercussions for later child well-being. We first considered the bivariate descriptive results for children of employed and unemployed mothers, presented in the bottom panel of table 2-1. There were no significant differences in children's reading or math skills at age seven between families in which mothers were in the paid labor force in the two years following childbirth and families in which mothers remained unemployed. However, numerous differences emerged in emotional and behavioral functioning. Children of employed mothers had significantly lower levels of anxiety problems, somatic problems, and conduct problems and marginally lower hyperactivity problems.

Multivariate analyses that compared child functioning in these two groups while adjusting for differences in child, mother, and family characteristics replicated these patterns, as shown in table 2-2. Two analytic techniques were employed: ordinary least squares (OLS) regression analyses, adjusting for the child, mother, and family characteristics in table 2-1, and propensity score matching techniques, in which correlational data are restructured to mimic randomized experimental data that match characteristics of an experimental group and a control group, leading to a less biased estimate of the treatment effect.[32] Results of the OLS models indicated that children of mothers who were employed during their infancy showed significantly higher math skills as well as lower anxiety and somatic, hyperactivity, oppositional, and conduct problems at age seven than their peers whose mothers remained unemployed during that period. The propensity score matching models largely replicated these findings, showing that early maternal employment was linked with enhanced functioning in middle childhood for children from economically disadvantaged families.

EMPLOYMENT INTENSITY, QUALITY, AND STABILITY AND CHILDREN'S FUNCTIONING. Having shown that mothers' employment status predicted enhanced functioning of children, we next sought to explore the implications of maternal employment experiences in richer detail by considering the dynamics of mothers' work in terms of intensity, quality, and stability. For these analyses we focused only on the employed mothers, assessing how the five maternal work characteristics (weekly work hours, wages, insurance coverage, months employed, and job stability) were related to children's functioning at the age of seven years. In initial models we considered whether these variables functioned linearly or nonlinearly. Insurance receipt was a dichotomous variable, and job instability was also coded dichotomously, distinguishing women with one job (61 percent) from those who had two or more jobs (39 percent) during the two-year period following childbirth. Both hourly wages and months employed functioned linearly. However, we found that work hours were related to children's functioning in a nonlinear fashion, and thus we distinguished part-time hours (less than thirty hours per week), full-time hours (thirty to forty hours per

Table 2-2. *Main Effect of Employment between Birth and Age of Two Years on the Development of Cognitive Skills and Behavior[a] Problems at Age Seven*

Independent variable	WJ letter-word	WJ applied problems	Affective problems	Anxiety problems	Somatic problems	Attention deficit/hyperactivity	Oppositional defiant problems	Conduct problems
OLS model								
Employed	−0.33	6.05	−1.11	−2.22	−4.00	−2.46	−2.58	−5.21
	(3.13)	(3.04)**	(1.04)	(1.12)**	(1.20)***	(1.10)**	(1.26)**	(1.40)***
F statistic	3.57	2.54	2.91	1.55	3.07	2.03	2.08	1.61
R^2	0.21	0.16	0.15	0.09	0.19	0.12	0.12	0.12
Propensity score model								
Employed	−1.65	4.83	−1.73	−2.24	−4.17	−2.34	−2.66	−5.28
	(4.33)	(4.14)	(1.27)	(1.16)*	(1.51)***	(1.31)*	(1.33)**	(1.57)***
F statistic	2.79	4.45	5.31	2.54	3.75	2.53	2.10	1.69
R^2	0.27	0.37	0.32	0.21	0.30	0.28	0.28	0.27

a. Employed group is compared with the omitted category "no employment." All analyses controlled for the wave 1 value of mother age, mother education, mother marital status, number of minors in the household, working spouse, mother employed in year prior to birth, mother receipt of welfare in last two years, child gender, child age, child race/ethnicity, child low birth weight, child developmental delay at birth, child in formal child care, child in informal child care, household income-to-needs ratio, mother cognitive skills at wave 2, and mother recently employed at wave 3. * $p < .10$, ** $p < .05$, *** $p < .01$.

week), and overtime hours (more than forty hours per week). OLS regression models assessed prospective links between the five work characteristics and children's functioning at age seven, again adjusting for the set of child, mother, and family characteristics shown in table 2-1.

Results, presented in table 2-3, highlight the importance of mothers' work intensity and work stability during their children's infancy. Specifically, results suggest that working extensive hours was associated with lower child well-being. Working overtime, more than forty hours per week, was associated with lower reading and math skills for children at age seven than were working part-time or full-time. Similarly, working overtime was associated with greater levels of behavior problems in children—including higher hyperactivity, oppositional, and conduct problems—than were working part-time or full-time.

Job stability also was important for children. In particular, greater months of employment were associated with lower affective, hyperactivity, oppositional, and conduct problems and marginally lower anxiety problems. Greater months of employment also predicted higher math skills among children. Having more than one job, on the other hand, predicted heightened oppositional and marginally higher conduct problems. In contrast to the importance of work intensity and stability for children's well-being, results suggest that job quality was not significantly linked with children's functioning. Receiving health insurance through one's employer was not associated with children's cognitive, behavioral, or emotional functioning. And paradoxically, one significant result indicated that higher maternal wages were associated with lower math skills among children.

Discussion

As both maternal employment and single-mother families have become more prevalent among wealthy countries, particularly the United States, concerns have arisen over the repercussions of mothers' efforts to combine parenting and labor force participation. These concerns are heightened for low-income mothers, who often lack the human capital resources to obtain high-quality employment with supportive benefits and the financial capital to purchase child and family care supports in the private market; they may also lack the social capital to help them balance the demands of work and parenting to optimally support their children's healthy development.

To address these concerns, nearly all wealthy countries have implemented a series of supportive family policies, including paid, job-protected leave for parents of newborn children. Indeed, other wealthy countries provide fully paid parental leave averaging about twenty-five weeks to allow new parents to focus

Table 2-3. *OLS Regression Models: Employment Characteristics Predicting Child Outcomes at Age Seven*[a]

Characteristic	Reading skills	Math skills	Affective problems	Anxiety problems	Somatic problems	Hyperactivity problems	Oppositional problems	Conduct problems
Part-time work	-0.55 (2.69)[a]	2.84 (3.38)[a]	-0.72 (0.91)	-0.33 (0.82)	-1.2 (0.9)	0.23 (0.91)	0.68 (0.95)	0.84 (0.79)[a]
Overtime work	-12.12 (3.87)***[a]	-11.13 (4.12)***[a]	0.92 (1.28)	0.17 (1.68)	-1.31 (1.6)	3.16 (1.4)**	3.59 (1.39)**	3.82 (1.45)***[a]
Hourly wage	-0.62 (0.47)	-1.09 (0.55)**	-0.17 (0.19)	-0.06 (0.17)	0.15 (0.19)	0.11 (0.22)	0.04 (0.18)	-0.16 (0.15)
Insurance	-3.45 (2.57)	-1.09 (3.38)	1.13 (1.2)	0.69 (1.03)	0.03 (1.11)	1.53 (1.34)	-1.31 (0.89)	0.59 (1.04)
Months employed	0.30 (0.19)	0.76 (0.26)***	-0.14 (0.07)***	-0.10 (0.06)*	-0.01 (0.07)	-0.18 (0.07)**	-0.15 (0.07)**	-0.18 (0.07)**
Multiple jobs	-1.56 (2.37)	-2.4 (3.28)	0.6 (0.83)	0.83 (0.79)	0.14 (0.91)	0.82 (0.84)	1.86 (0.84)**	1.62 (0.84)*
Constant	85.51 (15.81)***	86.29 (20.24)***	51.05 (5.96)***	46.26 (5.98)***	46.71 (6.29)***	49.41 (5.97)***	39.52 (5.84)***	49.65 (5.29)***
F statistic	3.43***	2.34***	2.03***	1.23	1.69**	3.54***	4.48***	2.49***
R^2	0.30	0.24	0.19	4.88	0.14	0.18	0.26	0.18

a. Employed groups are compared with the omitted category "no employment." Within each column, groups with shared superscript letters are different from each other at the $p < .05$ level. All analyses controlled for the wave 1 value of mother age, mother education, mother marital status, working spouse, number of minors in the household, mother employment in year before birth, mother receipt of welfare in last two years, income-to-needs ratio, child gender, and child race/ethnicity as well as mother cognitive skills at wave 2 and child age at wave 3. $*p < .10$, $**p < .05$, $***p < .01$.

full-time on parenting without notable economic repercussions.[33] Other common family supports include government-funded child care to provide alternative care arrangements for young children of working parents and additional cash and noncash benefits, such as child payments, government-funded health insurance, and special protections for poor families.[34] The United States is an outlier, lacking paid parental leave for parents of newborns, having limited government-funded health insurance, and employing more targeted cash and noncash aid to parents and children than most other countries.[35] Moreover, welfare policy in the United States now requires nearly all recipients to work, even mothers with new infants. In this policy context many new mothers in the United States are economically required to enter or return to work very soon after childbearing. It is perhaps not surprising, then, that the United States has especially high rates of maternal employment, with 63 percent of new mothers returning to the labor force within one year of childbirth and 64 percent of mothers of children under the age of six being employed.[36]

Maternal Employment Dynamics

In response to these demographic and policy trends, this chapter seeks to provide a rich and detailed view of the labor force experiences of low-income mothers following the birth of a new child and to explore the repercussions of mothers' early employment dynamics for child well-being. Assessing data on a representative sample of low-income families with young children from three major U.S. cities, we highlight the substantial work effort among low-income mothers with infants as well as the predominance of jobs with limited pay and benefits. Nearly three-fourths of the sample reported working within the two-year period after childbirth, most prior to their child's first birthday. Work intensity was high, with the majority of employed mothers (73 percent) working full-time or overtime (thirty hours per week or more). And yet the payoffs to employment were relatively limited, with wages averaging less than $8 an hour and only a quarter of mothers receiving employer-sponsored health insurance. At the mean wage rate and weekly hours for our sample, that leads to an annual work income of just over $13,500 for full-year employment, just about equal to the federal poverty rate for a mother with two children in 1999. Yet the data also indicate that few mothers worked in all months of the study period, highlighting that incomes from employment did not raise most families above the poverty line.

Together, these descriptive data suggest that although many mothers in this representative low-income urban sample were engaged in the labor market to a relatively high degree, they remained economically insecure. To be sure, many women had additional sources of income, drawn from a variety of public sources such as welfare, food stamps, and WIC and from family sources includ-ing employed spouses. Yet average family income remained below the poverty line, suggesting the economic fragility of disadvantaged families with young children. Growing empirical research from a variety of fields has uncovered the importance of the initial years of life in providing the basis for healthy function-ing throughout the lifespan and has argued for the heightened consequences of economic and social resources during this stage.[37] Together, these results suggest the need for greater policy attention to supporting families with young children.

COMPARING EMPLOYED AND UNEMPLOYED MOTHERS. Although the major-ity of mothers in this study were employed to some extent during the two years after childbearing, about a quarter remained out of the labor force. Results indi-cate that skills and experience may have played a role in selecting mothers into or out of employment. Women with lower education, more limited literacy skills, and lack of work experience in the year prior to childbirth were signifi-cantly less likely to work after having a new child. On the other hand, a variety of child and mother characteristics and family structure characteristics did not distinguish employed and unemployed mothers. Nor did welfare, food stamp, Medicaid, or WIC receipt or having an employed spouse in the household, although receiving SSI and public housing assistance was associated with a lower likelihood of employment. In short, these patterns indicate that employed and unemployed mothers differed on some important characteristics, most notably human capital characteristics, although they also shared many similarities in their family environments and receipt of public services and programs.

MATERNAL EMPLOYMENT DYNAMICS AND CHILDREN'S FUNCTIONING. The descriptive results from this work highlight the variability in employment expe-riences among low-income women with young children. The second goal of this research was to assess whether mothers' early employment experiences had repercussions for their children's healthy development. Controlling for differ-ences in child, mother, and family characteristics, we found that children whose mothers were employed during their infancy exhibited greater math skills and lower levels of emotional and behavioral problems across numerous realms than their peers with unemployed mothers. These results are in contrast to research with middle-class and European American samples, which has suggested that early maternal employment may be detrimental to children's later functioning.[38] There are numerous potential reasons for the discrepancy. Within low-income families, the economic and social resources gained through employment may be more influential with respect to family functioning and child well-being, increasing total family income, improving mothers' self esteem and mental health, and supporting more enriching and stable home and alternative care environments.[39] On the other hand, given the significant barriers to finding high-quality, stable employment faced by disadvantaged mothers with children, many have hypothesized that low-quality or unstable work experiences may predominate, potentially with deleterious consequences for children.[40]

In order to further explore the complexities of links between maternal employment and children's functioning, analyses further considered the five characteristics of employment dynamics, including work intensity (hours), quality (wages and health insurance), and stability (consistency and instability). These results highlighted three main patterns, with consistent findings for job intensity and consistency but not for job quality.

One primary pattern indicated the importance of work consistency, with a greater number of months worked by mothers associated with improved cognitive skills as well as emotional and behavioral functioning in children as they entered middle childhood. This result suggests that even very quick entry into employment following childbearing is not detrimental for low-income children, replicating prior research, and also indicates potential benefits of remaining stably employed.[41] The importance of stability was further highlighted by the negative effects of having multiple jobs on children's behavior problems. It is important to note that our data may have undercounted job cycling and instability because they covered only jobs that lasted two months or more. Job consistency and stability might enhance the stability of family processes and care arrangements for children, providing the regularity and predictability that is important for healthy early development.

The benefits of employment consistency (the number of months worked) suggest that more work is better. However, consideration of employment intensity, assessed as hours worked per week, tempers this interpretation. Results found that although both part-time and full-time employment were linked with enhanced child functioning, overtime work, defined as more than forty hours per week, predicted both lower cognitive skills and heightened behavior problems among children. These results were notable in size, with detriments of 12 points, about two-thirds of a standard deviation, on the cognitive scores and increases of more than one-half of a standard deviation on the measures of behavior problems. Given the high time and energy demands of parenting infants and infants' needs for consistent and responsive caregiving, it is perhaps not surprising that working overtime appears detrimental.

In contrast to results for mothers' employment consistency and intensity and children's later functioning, results for employment quality and children's later functioning found essentially no significant links between the two. Neither wages nor receipt of employer-provided health insurance was related to children's cognitive and behavioral skills in a consistent fashion. Given the exclusive focus on low-income families in this sample, employment wages were uniformly low and relatively few women received health insurance. Other research reiterates the poor quality of employment among women with limited education and skills in the United States, with few receiving paid vacations and sick time, regular wage increases, flexible work schedules, or autonomy in performing work tasks.[42] These patterns reflect larger economic and business shifts that have occurred in the United States in recent decades as decent paying and stable manufacturing jobs have left the country, less stable and poorly remunerated service jobs have increased, and wages have stagnated for less skilled workers.[43] Hence, one hypothesis for the lack of links between work quality and child functioning in the current study is a lack of variability in work quality.

Conclusions

Results from our research suggest that policy efforts to enhance mothers' labor market success, particularly the stability and consistency of mothers' employment, may prove beneficial for low-income children and families. As proponents of welfare reform argued in the 1990s, in the social context of the U.S. market economy, with the growing normativeness of maternal employment and limited public supports for families, moving onto and up the employment ladder may provide the surest route to economic stability, healthy family functioning, and hence enhanced child development. However, the results also reiterate the broader trends in the U.S. labor market, in which the combination of workers with limited education and skills and an economy with a restricted need for lower-skilled workers creates a market that does not provide jobs with adequate pay, benefits, and supports for workers at the bottom of the economic ladder. Poor women in particular tend to have limited access to support and accommodation from their employers, indicating the need for broader policy levers in these areas.

For mothers of infants and young children, in particular, achieving stable employment also requires making notable accommodations and sacrifices. In addition to gaining adequate economic resources, mothers must balance the significant time and energy demands of parenting and holding a job simultaneously and must secure safe and reliable care for their children. Indeed, our results indicate that when mothers focused too much of their time on employment, their children's healthy development suffered. These results suggest the need for social policies and programs to support work environments that allow women adequate time and flexibility to deal with the demands of caring for young children.

Potential policy levers include paid parental leave policies providing adequate economic resources and employment security to new mothers, which are virtually nonexistent for low-income mothers in the United States though they are common in other wealthy countries.[44] Additional policy mechanisms could target individual parents, seeking to improve the education and work skills of disadvantaged parents, or target workers with minimum wage laws, wage supplements, and access to health insurance and other benefits such as paid sick and vacation leave. Finally, policies can more directly target children, through increased supports for high-quality, accessible, and reliable child care for infants and preschoolers. Policies of other wealthy countries provide numerous models that the United States can employ to support maternal employment, promote family-work balance, and help to secure the healthy functioning of children and families.

Notes

1. Ron Haskins, *Work over Welfare: The Inside Story of the 1996 Welfare Reform Law* (Brookings, 2006).

2. Jane Waldfogel, "The Role of Family Policies in Anti-Poverty Policy," Discussion Paper 1351-08 (Madison, Wis.: Institute for Research on Poverty, 2009).

3. Commission on Family and Medical Leave, "A Workable Balance: Report to Congress on Family and Medical Leave Policies" (U.S. Department of Labor, 1996); Sandra Hofferth, "Effects of Public and Private Policies on Working after Childbirth," *Work and Occupations*, vol. 23, no. 4 (1996), pp. 378–404; Katherin Ross Phillips, "Parent Work and Child Well-Being in Low-Income Families," Occasional Paper 56 (Washington: Urban Institute, 2002).

4. Commission on Family and Medical Leave, "A Workable Balance"; Jane Waldfogel, "International Policies toward Parental Leave and Child Care," *Future of Children*, vol. 11 (2001), pp. 99–111.

5. Commission on Family and Medical Leave, "A Workable Balance."

6. Jane Waldfogel, *What Children Need* (Harvard University Press, 2006).

7. Nazli Baydar and Jeanne Brooks-Gunn, "Effects of Maternal Employment and Child-Care Arrangements on Preschoolers' Cognitive and Behavioral Outcomes: Evidence from the Children of the National Longitudinal Survey of Youth," *Developmental Psychology*, vol. 27, no. 6 (1991), pp. 932–45; Wendy A. Goldberg and others, "Maternal Employment and Children's Achievement in Context: A Meta-Analysis of Four Decades of Research," *Psychological Bulletin*, vol. 134, no. 1 (2008), pp. 77–108; Christopher J. Ruhm, "Parental Employment and Child Cognitive Development," Working Paper 7666 (Cambridge, Mass.: National Bureau for Economic Research, April 2000).

8. Baydar and Brooks-Gunn, "Effects of Maternal Employment and Child-Care Arrangements"; Francine D. Blau and Adam J. Grossberg, "Maternal Labor Supply and Children's Cognitive Development," *Review of Economics and Statistics*, vol. 74 (1992), pp. 474–81; Sonalde Desai, Lindsay Chase-Lansdale, and Robert T. Michael, "Mother or Market? Effects of Maternal Employment on the Intellectual Ability of a 4-Year-Old," *Demography*, vol. 26,

no. 4 (1989), pp. 545–61; Wen-Jui Han, Jane Waldfogel, and Jeanne Brooks-Gunn, "The Effects of Early Maternal Employment on Later Cognitive and Behavioral Outcomes," *Journal of Marriage and the Family*, vol. 63, no. 2 (2001), pp. 336–54; Jennifer L. Hill and others, "Maternal Employment and Child Development: A Fresh Look Using Newer Methods," *Developmental Psychology*, vol. 41, no. 6 (2005), pp. 833–50.

9. Jeanne Brooks-Gunn, Wen-Jui Han, and Jane Waldfogel, "First-Year Maternal Employment and Child Development in the First 7 Years," *Monographs of the Society for Research in Child Development*, vol. 75, no. 2 (2010); Jeanne Brooks-Gunn, Wen-Jui Han, and Jane Waldfogel, "Maternal Employment and Child Cognitive Outcomes in the First Three Years of Life: The NICHD Study of Early Child Care," *Child Development*, vol. 73, no. 4 (2002), pp. 1052–72.

10. John Bowlby, *Maternal Care and Mental Health* (Geneva, Switzerland: World Health Organization, 1951); P. Lindsay Chase-Lansdale and Margaret Tresch Owen, "Maternal Employment in a Family Context: Effects on Infant-Mother and Infant-Father Attachment," *Child Development*, vol. 58 (1987), pp. 1505–12.

11. Glen Elder, "The Life Course and Human Development," in *Handbook of Child Psychology*, vol. 1, *Theoretical Models of Human Development*, edited by William Damon and Richard Lerner (New York: Wiley, 1997), pp. 939–91; Toby L. Parcel and Elizabeth G. Menaghan, "Early Parental Work, Family Social Capital, and Early Childhood Outcomes," *American Journal of Sociology*, vol. 99 (1994), pp. 972–1009.

12. NICHD Early Child Care and Youth Development Study, "Child Care in the First Year of Life," *Merrill-Palmer Quarterly*, vol. 43 (1997), p. 340–60; Diane Paulsell and others, *Partnerships for Quality: Improving Infant-Toddler Child Care for Low-Income Families* (Princeton: Mathematica Policy Research, 2002).

13. Haskins, *Work over Welfare*.

14. Kristen Shook Slack and others, "Family Economic Well-Being Following the 1996 Welfare Reform: Trend Data from Five Non-Experimental Panel Studies," *Children and Youth Services Review*, vol. 29, no. 6 (2007), pp. 698–720.

15. Gary S. Becker and Nigel Tomes, "Human Capital and the Rise and Fall of Families," *Journal of Labor Economics*, vol. 4, no. 3, part 2 (1986), pp. S1–S39; Greg J. Duncan and Jeanne Brooks-Gunn, *Consequences of Growing Up Poor* (New York: Russell Sage Foundation, 1997); Elizabeth Harvey, "Short-Term and Long-Term Effects of Early Parental Employment on Children of the National Longitudinal Survey of Youth," *Developmental Psychology*, vol. 35, no. 2 (1999), pp. 445–59; C. Cybele Raver, "Does Work Pay Psychologically As Well As Economically? The Role of Employment in Predicting Depressive Symptoms and Parenting among Low-Income Families," *Child Development*, vol. 74, no. 6 (2003), pp. 1720–36.

16. Sylvia Beyer, "Maternal Employment and Children's Academic Achievement: Parenting Styles as Mediating Variable," *Developmental Review*, vol. 15 (1995), pp. 212–53; Aurora P. Jackson and Chien-Chung Huang, "Parenting Stress and Behavior among Single Mothers of Preschoolers: The Mediating Role of Self-Efficacy," *Journal of Social Service Research*, vol. 26, no. 4 (2000), pp. 29–42; Aurora P. Jackson, Peter M. Bentler, and Todd M. Franke, "Low-Wage Maternal Employment and Parenting Style," *Social Work*, vol. 53 (2008), pp. 267–78; JoAnne M. Youngblut and others, "Maternal Employment and Parent-Child Relationships in Single-Parent Families of Low-Birth-Weight Preschoolers," *Nursing Research*, vol. 47, no. 2 (1998), pp. 114–21.

17. Rand D. Conger and others, "A Family Process Model of Economic Hardship and Adjustment of Early Adolescent Boys," *Child Development*, vol. 63 (1992), pp. 526–41.

18. Rebekah Levine Coley and Caitlin McPherran Lombardi, "Long-Term Effects of Early Maternal Employment on Low-Income Children's Functioning," forthcoming.

19. Lawrence Berger and others, "First-Year Maternal Employment and Child Outcomes: Differences across Racial and Ethnic Groups," *Children and Youth Services Review*, vol. 30, no. 4 (2008), pp. 365–87; Jane Waldfogel, Wen-Jui Han, and Jeanne Brooks-Gunn, "The Effects of Early Maternal Employment on Child Cognitive Development," *Demography*, vol. 39, no. 2 (2002), pp. 369–92.

20. Sheldon Danziger and others, "Barriers to the Employment of Welfare Recipients," in *Prosperity for All*, edited by Robert Cherry and William M. Rodgers (New York: Russell Sage Foundation, 2000), pp. 245–78.

21. Rucker C. Johnson and Mary E. Corcoran, "The Road to Economic Self-Sufficiency: Job Quality and Job Transition Patterns after Welfare Reform," *Journal of Policy Analysis and Management*, vol. 22, no. 4 (2003), pp. 615–39; Raver, "Does Work Pay Psychologically As Well As Economically?" pp. 1720–36.

22. Aletha C. Huston and others, "Impacts on Children of a Policy to Promote Employment and Reduce Poverty for Low-Income Parents: New Hope after 5 Years," *Developmental Psychology*, vol. 41 (2005), pp. 902–18; Pamela A. Morris and Lisa A. Gennetian, "Identifying the Effects of Income on Children's Development Using Experimental Data," *Journal of Marriage and Family*, vol. 65 (2003), pp. 716–29; Pamela A. Morris and Charles Michalopoulos, "Findings from the Self-Sufficiency Project: Effects on Children and Adolescents of a Program That Increased Employment and Income," *Applied Developmental Psychology*, vol. 24 (2003), pp. 201–39.

23. Coley and Lombardi, "Long-Term Effects of Early Maternal Employment."

24. Rucker C. Johnson, Ariel Kalil, and Rachel E. Dunifon, *Mothers' Work and Children's Lives* (Kalamazoo, Mich: W.E. Upjohn Institute for Employment Research, 2010); Ariel Kalil, Rachel E. Dunifon, and Sheldon K. Danziger, "Does Maternal Employment Mandated by Welfare Reform Affect Parenting Behavior?" in *For Better or Worse: Welfare Reform and the Well-Being of Children and Families*, edited by Greg J. Duncan and P. Lindsay Chase-Lansdale (New York: Russell Sage Foundation, 2001), pp. 154–78; Ariel Kalil and Kathleen M. Ziol-Guest, "Single Mothers' Employment Dynamics and Adolescent Well-Being," *Child Development*, vol. 76, no. 1 (2005), pp. 196–211; Mary Secret and Claudia Peck-Heath, "Maternal Labor Force Participation and Child Well-Being in Public Assistance Families," *Journal of Family Issues*, vol. 25, no. 4 (2004), pp. 520–41.

25. William C. Goodman and Randy E. Ilg, "Employment in 1996," *Monthly Labor Review* (February 1997), p. 3.

26. For further details about the sample and study components, see Pamela Winston and others, "Welfare, Children, and Families: A Three-City Study, Overview, and Design Report," 1999 (www.jhu.edu/~welfare).

27. Richard W. Woodcock and Mary B. Johnson, *Woodcock-Johnson Psycho-Educational Battery Revised* (Itasca, Ill.: Riverside, 1990); Richard W. Woodcock and Ana F. Munoz-Sandoval, *Bateria Woodcock-Munoz: Pruebas de Aprovechamiento Revisada* (Itasca, Ill.: Riverside, 1996).

28. Thomas M. Achenbach and Leslie A. Rescorla, *Manual for the ASEBA School-Age Forms and Profiles* (University of Vermont, Research Center for Children, Youth, and Families, 2001).

29. Thomas M. Achenbach, Levant Dumenci, and Leslie A. Rescorla, "DSM-Orientated and Empirically Based Approaches to Constructing Scales from the Same Item Pools," *Journal of Clinical Child and Adolescent Psychology*, vol. 32, no. 3 (2003), pp. 328–40.

30. Jane K. Squires, LaWanda Potter, and Diane D. Bricker, *The ASQ User's Guide* (Baltimore, Md.: Paul H. Brookes, 1999).

31. Woodcock and Johnson, *Woodcock-Johnson Psycho-Educational Battery Revised*; Woodcock and Munoz-Sandoval, *Bateria Woodcock-Munoz: Pruebas de Aprovechamiento Revisada*.

32. Rajeev H. Dehejia and Sadek Wahba, "Propensity Score Matching Methods for Non-experimental Causal Studies," *Review of Econometrics and Statistics*, vol. 84 (2002), pp. 151–61; Donald B. Rubin, "Estimating Causal Effects from Large Data Sets Using Propensity Scores," *Annals of Internal Medicine*, vol. 127 (1997), pp. 757–63.

33. Waldfogel, "The Role of Family Policies in Anti-Poverty Policy."

34. Ibid.

35. Bruce Bradbury and others, "Inequality During the Early Years: Child Outcomes and Readiness to Learn in Australia, Canada, United Kingdom, and United States," prepared for 31st General Conference of the International Association for Research in Income and Wealth, August 22–28, 2010; Jane Waldfogel, "What Other Nations Do: International Policies toward Parental Leave and Child Care," *Future of Children,* vol. 11 (2001), pp. 99–111.

36. Bureau of Labor Statistics, "Women in the Labor Force: A Databook," September 2009 (www.bls.gov/cps/wlf-databook2009).

37. Duncan and Brooks-Gunn, *Consequences of Growing Up Poor*; James J. Heckman, "Skill Formation and the Economics of Investing in Disadvantaged Children," *Science*, vol. 312, no. 5782 (2006), pp. 1900–02; Jack P. Shonkoff and Deborah A. Phillips, *From Neurons to Neighborhoods: The Science of Early Childhood Development* (Washington: National Academy Press, 2000).

38. Baydar and Brooks-Gunn, "Effects of Maternal Employment and Child-Care Arrangements"; Blau and Grossberg, "Maternal Labor Supply and Children's Cognitive Development"; Desai, Chase-Lansdale, and Michael, "Mother or Market?"; Han, Waldfogel, and Brooks-Gunn, "The Effects of Early Maternal Employment on Later Cognitive and Behavioral Outcomes"; Hill and others, "Maternal Employment and Child Development."

39. Rebekah Levine Coley and others, "Maternal Functioning, Time, and Money: The World of Work and Welfare," *Children and Youth Services Review*, vol. 29 (2007), pp. 721–41; Rand D. Conger and others, "A Family Process Model of Economic Hardship and Adjustment of Early Adolescent Boys," *Child Development*, vol. 63 (1992), pp. 526–41.

40. Rachel Dunifon, Ariel Kalil, and Sheldon K. Danziger, "Maternal Work Behavior under Welfare Reform: How Does the Transition from Welfare to Work Affect Child Development?" *Children and Youth Services Review*, vol. 25 (2003), pp. 55–82; Johnson, Kalil, and Dunifon, *Mothers' Work and Children's Lives*; Kalil, Dunifon, and Danziger, "Does Maternal Employment Mandated by Welfare Reform Affect Parenting Behavior?" in *For Better or Worse: Welfare Reform and the Well-Being of Children and Families,* edited by Duncan and Chase-Lansdale; Kalil and Ziol-Guest, "Single Mothers' Employment Dynamics and Adolescent Well-Being"; Secret and Peck-Heath, "Maternal Labor Force Participation and Child Well-Being"; Hirokazu Yoshikawa and Edward Seidman, "Multidimensional Profiles of Welfare and Work Dynamics: Development, Validation, and Associations with Child Cognitive and Mental Health Outcomes," *American Journal of Community Psychology*, vol. 29, no. 6 (2001), pp. 907–36.

41. Coley and Lombardi, "Long-Term Effects of Early Maternal Employment."

42. Johnson and Corcoran, "The Road to Economic Self-Sufficiency: Job Quality and Job Transition Patterns after Welfare Reform"; Sheldon Danziger and others, "Barriers to the Employment of Welfare Recipients," in *Prosperity for All*, edited by Cherry and Rodgers.

43. Rebecca Blank, "Economic Change and the Structure of Opportunity for Less-Skilled Workers," in *Changing Poverty*, edited by Maria Cancian and Sheldon Danziger (New York: Russell Sage Foundation, 2009).

44. Rebecca Ray, Janet C. Gornick, and John Schmitt, "Parental Leave Policies in 21 Countries: Assessing Generosity and Gender Equality" (Washington: Center for Economic and Policy Research, 2008).

3

Family Joblessness and Child Well-Being in Australia

MATTHEW GRAY AND JENNIFER BAXTER

While the Australian economy has experienced an extended period of strong growth since the mid-1990s and the unemployment rate is low compared with that in most other OECD countries, Australia has a relatively high proportion of jobless families—that is, families in which no adult is employed. In 2007, 14.8 percent of Australian children less than 15 years of age were living in a jobless family; the corresponding figure for U.S. children was 8.0 percent, and the OECD average was 8.7 percent.[1] One of the reasons for the high rates of joblessness in families with children in Australia is the relatively low employment rate of lone mothers and the relatively high proportion of children living in lone-mother families.[2]

Family joblessness is the most important single cause of child poverty in Australia,[3] and there are concerns about its impact on children's developmental trajectories.[4] Indeed, one of the six priority areas for the Australian Social Inclusion Agenda is "helping jobless families with children by helping the unemployed into sustainable employment and their children into a good start in life."[5]

In the middle of the first decade of the 2000s, the poverty rate in Australia for households with children was 10 percent, similar to the OECD average of 11 percent and much lower than the rate in the United States, which was 18 percent. There were large differences in poverty rates for two-parent and

The Longitudinal Study of Australian Children Project was initiated and is funded by the Australian Government Department of Families, Housing, Community Services, and Indigenous Affairs and is undertaken in partnership with the Australian Institute of Family Studies and the Australian Bureau of Statistics. The views expressed in this chapter are those of the authors and may not reflect those of the Australian Institute of Family Studies or the Australian government. We are grateful to Peter McDonald and the editors of this book for comments on an earlier version of the chapter.

lone-parent families. The mid-decade poverty rate (the share of all children living in households with an equivalized income of less than 50 percent of the median) in Australia was 6.5 percent for two-parent families and 38.3 percent for lone-parent families, while the poverty rate in the United States was 13.6 percent for two-parent families and 47.5 percent for lone-parent families. The OECD average poverty rate at that time was 9.0 percent for two-parent families and 30.9 percent for lone-parent families.[6]

It has been well established that unemployment (and joblessness) typically has negative effects on economic well-being as well as on the mental and physical health of individuals and that those effects can flow to other family members.[7] Of particular concern is the potential effect of parental joblessness on children's development and well-being.

Concerns over the potential harmful effects of joblessness have led to the development of policies that attempt to both reduce levels of joblessness and improve the living standards of the jobless. With regard to the latter, in Australia the income support system provides government benefits that help jobless families meet their financial needs; with regard to joblessness, various government programs and supports aim to address barriers to employment and encourage labor force participation.

There is surprisingly little research on the direct impact of parental job loss on child well-being, although there is a great deal of research on the impact of poverty on child well-being, and poverty rates are higher in jobless families than employed families. An excellent summary of the literature is provided by Ariel Kalil, who identifies the following three mechanisms by which parental joblessness might have a negative impact on children's developmental outcomes:[8]

— *"Investments" perspective:* Lack of paid employment limits a family's economic resources; the family therefore spends less on things such as education, food, housing, and so on, which can result in a child not doing as well as he or she would have otherwise.[9]

— *"Family stress" perspective:* Lack of paid employment is psychologically stressful.[10] The stress can have an adverse impact on the quality of parenting provided, which can in turn have a negative impact on a child's well-being. The stress may also have an adverse effect on a couples' relationship and increase the chance of relationship breakdown.[11]

— *"Role model" perspective:* Children without an employed parent as a role model do not learn the skills required to find and retain a job and may have diminished motivation to succeed in education.

Much of the existing research in this area is based on U.S. data, including research that has found that parental joblessness can have a negative impact on children's school achievement.[12] There is limited empirical evidence for Australia about the direct effects of parental unemployment and joblessness on child well-being. One study, also using the Longitudinal Study of Australian Children (LSAC) data, finds that family joblessness has an effect on a range of developmental outcomes for children 5 to 10 years of age.[13] Given the very different rates of poverty among jobless families in the United States and Australia, it is important to have Australian evidence on the effect of joblessness on Australian children's developmental outcomes.

The impact of family joblessness on children's developmental outcomes is likely to depend, at least in part, on how long the joblessness lasts. However, there is little Australian evidence on the persistence of family or household joblessness. We are aware of only two existing Australian studies that provide estimates of the persistence of household joblessness using longitudinal data.[14] We are not aware of any Australian research that has explored how child well-being is associated with the length of time that the child experiences family joblessness.[15]

This chapter uses a new source of longitudinal data on Australian children and their families, *Growing Up in Australia: The Longitudinal Study of Australian Children (LSAC)*, to document the extent to which Australian children experience persistent joblessness (that is, live in a jobless family for an extended period of time); to estimate the impact of living in a jobless family on children's developmental outcomes; and to estimate the extent to which effects differ between children who are living in a persistently jobless family and those who have experienced relatively short periods of family joblessness.

The chapter next provides an overview of the data used in the chapter, followed by descriptive information on the extent and the persistence of joblessness in Australian families with young children and how those factors vary according to family type. The characteristics of jobless families are described and compared with those of families that do not experience joblessness, and the relationship between joblessness and child developmental outcomes is analyzed. How the financial well-being of families varies with the experience of joblessness also is described. The final discussion deals with some of the implications of the material presented in the chapter for the development of child and family policies in Australia.

The Longitudinal Study of Australian Children

The LSAC survey is a nationally representative large-scale longitudinal survey that is following two cohorts of children for 14 years (and possibly longer). When the first wave of interviews was conducted in 2004, the cohorts of children were aged 0–1 years (B cohort) and 4–5 years (K cohort).[16] In this chapter, for the sake of simplicity, only data from the K cohort are used. The survey collects detailed information on a range of measures of child well-being and parental labor force status, thereby allowing construction of a measure of family joblessness, as well as on socioeconomic, demographic, and parenting-style characteristics of the study child's parents. The children were selected from the enrollment database of Medicare (Australia's national public health insurance scheme); the sampling unit is "the child." The sample is broadly representative of Australian children in the birth cohorts from which the sample was selected.[17]

Wave 1 collected data on 4,983 children four to five years of age and their parents. The second wave was conducted in 2006, at which time the children were six to seven years of age, and the third wave was conducted in 2008, when they were eight to nine years of age. As in all longitudinal studies, not all of the original wave 1 sample participated in subsequent waves. The response rate for wave 3 was 86 percent of the originally recruited sample, yielding a total of 4,330 participants in the K cohort. The rates of nonresponse to waves 2 and 3 were higher for lone-parent and jobless families. The dataset includes sample weights that are designed to take into account the effects of nonrandom sample attrition, and the weights were applied in analyses of characteristics of families according to the persistence of family joblessness.[18] The analysis in this chapter is restricted to respondents who participated in all three waves and who were living in a lone- or two-parent family at the time of each interview.

The higher rate of attrition among families that were jobless at wave 1 means that estimates of the prevalence of joblessness based on the LSAC data underrepresent the number of persistently jobless families. The higher rate of attrition among those families is strongly associated with being a lone parent at the time of the wave 1 interview. However, to the extent to which the higher rate of attrition is explained by factors that are measured on the dataset (such as family type), the estimates of the impact of joblessness on child well-being will be unbiased by the nonrandom sample attrition.

The survey asked parents to identify which parent knew the most about the child ("primary carer"). In the vast majority of cases, the primary carer is the mother. The primary carer then provides the most extensive set of data about the child and about her- or himself and also, on some items, about the other parent. In two-parent families, the other parent is also asked to complete a questionnaire; this questionnaire collects information on a range of topics, including parenting practices and styles and the parents' well-being.

The measure of family joblessness used in this analysis is lack of paid employment of either a lone parent or both parents in two-parent families living in the same household as the child at the time of the interview.[19] It is not possible using the LSAC data to derive a measure of whether families were jobless between interviews.[20]

Box 3-1. *Measures Contributing to LSAC Outcome Indices for Eight-to-Nine-Year-Old Children at Wave 3*[a]

Learning/cognitive outcome index incorporates measures of language and literacy:
—Peabody Picture Vocabulary Test
—Wechsler Intelligence Scale for Children: Matrix Reasoning Subscale
—Academic Rating Scale: Language and Literacy and Mathematical Thinking

Social/emotional outcome index incorporates measures of internalizing and externalizing problems and social competence:
—Strengths and Difficulties Questionnaire: Emotional, Conduct, Hyperactivity, Peer Problems, and Prosocial Behaviour scales

Physical outcome index incorporates measures of health and motor skills:
—Overall rating of child's health: a single, parent-rated item
—Special Health Care Needs Indicator: a single derived yes-or-no item based on six component items indicating whether the child needed medication or more health care than the average child due to a condition that had lasted or was expected to last twelve months or more
—Health Problems Index: a derived item based on the number of health problems that the child was reported to be experiencing around the time of the main interview
—Weight status: a score reflecting deviation from normal weight status, based on the physical measurements of the child taken at the time of the interview
—Gross Motor Coordination Scale: a three-item, parent-rated scale asking how well the child can run, jump, and balance on one leg compared with his or her peers
—Pediatric Quality of Life Inventory: Physical health: an eight-item, parent-reported measure, largely assessing motor coordination but also containing two items about more general health.

---

a. A detailed description of the derivation of these indexes is provided by Sebastian Misson and others, "Tracking Children's Development over Time: The Longitudinal Study of Australian Children Outcome Indices, Waves 2 and 3," AIFS Research Paper 50 (Melbourne: Australian Institute of Family Studies, 2011).

In this chapter the well-being of children is measured at wave 3 (at age eight to nine years) by using composite measures of how children are developing in three broad areas (domains): learning and cognitive development; social and emotional functioning; and physical development. The LSAC outcome indexes incorporate both strengths and weaknesses. The three domains covered by the outcome indexes were chosen by those who developed the indexes as the "major components of current well-being and the future capability to be a successful civic and economic participant."[21] The outcome index for each of the domains has a mean of 100 and a standard deviation of 10. Box 3-1 provides information on the individual measures used to construct each of the outcome indices.

Table 3-1. *Persistence of Joblessness, 2004–08*[a]

Percent

	Number of waves jobless					
Family type	*Never jobless*	*One wave*	*Two waves*	*Three waves*	*Total*	*Sample size*
Lone-parent family	42.7	22.2	17.4	17.7	100.0	3,487
Two-parent family	92.2	4.6	1.8	1.4	100.0	568
Total	84.0	7.5	4.4	4.1	100.0	4,055
Proportion of lone-parent families	8.4	48.5	65.6	71.0	16.4	

Source: Longitudinal Study of Australian Children, Waves 1–3, K Cohort.

a. Family type was measured at the time of the wave 3 interviews (2008). Percentages may not total 100 percent due to rounding.

The Extent and Persistence of Joblessness in Families with Young Children

Here we provide an overview of the prevalence and persistence of family jobless-ness experienced by Australian children between the ages of four to five years and eight to nine years and analyze the differences in the experiences of family joblessness between lone- and two-parent families. In order to simplify the analysis, we use family type at the time of the wave 3 interviews.

Overall, 84 percent of the LSAC study children were not living in a jobless family at any of the first three waves of interviews and 16 percent were living in a jobless family at the time of at least one interview (table 3-1). Overall, 7.5 per-cent of families were jobless at the time of one interview, 4.4 percent were job-less at the time of two of the interviews, and 4.1 percent were jobless at the time of all three interviews.

Many more children in lone-parent families experienced parental joblessness (57 percent) than those living in two-parent families (8 percent). Furthermore, lone-parent families that experienced joblessness were more likely to be persist-ently jobless (61 percent) than were two-parent families (41 percent). ("Persis-tently jobless" is defined as jobless at two or three of the waves.)

The link between family type and joblessness can be clearly illustrated by examining the proportion of lone-parent families according to their experience of joblessness. Overall, 16 percent of eight-to-nine-year-old children were living in a lone-parent family. However, just 8 percent of families that were never job-less were lone-parent families while 49 percent of families that were jobless at one wave were lone-parent families; 66 percent of those jobless at two waves were lone-parent families; and 71 percent of those jobless at three waves were lone-parent families.

As discussed above, while the LSAC study does not allow the joblessness status of the families between interviews to be identified, it does provide information on whether either parent living in the household at the time of the interview had been employed at all since the previous interview. That allows identification of families that were jobless for the entire four-year period (2004–08) between the wave 1 and wave 3 interviews. In total, 4 percent of children were living in families in which no parent had engaged in any paid employment between waves 1 and 3. Of the families reported to be jobless at all three waves, 71 percent also reported that no parent had been employed between waves. Among the persistently jobless families, even if employment between waves was reported, it was of relatively short duration—an average of less than two months a year for mothers employed at some time and less than seven months a year for fathers employed at some time.

Characteristics of Jobless Families

Here we provide an overview of how human capital, demographic characteristics, parenting style, and financial well-being vary according to family joblessness. We highlight those characteristics that are likely to contribute to family joblessness (for example, relatively low levels of education of parents). We also examine characteristics that are likely to affect children's developmental outcomes and that the "family stress model" suggests that joblessness may have an impact on. Examples of such characteristics are parental mental health and parenting style, both of which joblessness may have a negative impact on and which then have a negative impact on children's developmental outcomes.

There were 3,557 families in the K cohort that were never jobless across the three waves of LSAC. Another 258 were jobless at one wave, 128 at two waves, and 112 at three waves. When the numbers are disaggregated into lone- and two-parent families, 79 lone-parent and 33 two-parent families were jobless at three waves. These sample sizes are too small to provide statistically reliable estimates, so for the descriptive analyses, those who were jobless at two or three waves are combined into a single category (termed "persistently jobless"). This results in the sample sizes as shown in table 3-2.

There is a clear link between joblessness and a low level of parental educational attainment (table 3-3). The proportion of lone parents with an incomplete secondary education increased from 21 percent for those who were never jobless to 28 percent for those who were jobless at one wave and to 41 percent for those who were persistently jobless. Of mothers in two-parent families,

Table 3-2. *Sample Size by Experience of Family Joblessness and Family Type*[a]
Number

| | Number of waves jobless | | | |
Family type	Never jobless	One wave	Two or three waves	Total
Lone-parent family	278	125	165	568
Two-parent family	3,279	133	75	3,487
Total	3,557	258	240	4,055

Source: Longitudinal Study of Australian Children, Waves 1–3, K Cohort.
a. These sample sizes are for the entire sample with cross-wave data on joblessness. Sample sizes are smaller in other analyses because some data were missing for some of the family and parent characteristics.

20 percent of those who were never jobless, 42 percent of those who were jobless for one wave, and 57 percent of those who were persistently jobless had a low level of educational attainment. The proportion of never-jobless lone parents who had a low level of educational attainment was very similar to that for mothers in two-parent families; however, lone parents who were jobless for one wave or two or three waves were less likely to have a low level of educational attainment than jobless mothers in two-parent families. Of fathers in two-parent families, those who were in a jobless family were more likely to have a low level of educational attainment (34 percent) than those who were in a never-jobless family (16 percent).

With respect to physical health, lone parents were about twice as likely to assess their health as being fair or poor than were mothers and fathers in two-parent families. Of fathers in two-parent families, the proportion having fair or poor health increased from 8 percent of those who were in a never-jobless family to 30 percent of those who were in a persistently jobless family. Similarly, parents in jobless families had lower levels of mental health than those who lived in never-jobless families.

Parents who experienced persistent family joblessness were somewhat more likely to speak a main language other than English at home than those who were in a never-jobless family or in a family that was jobless for only one wave. The average number of children in jobless families was higher than in families that were never jobless.

Two aspects of parenting that are important influences on children's developmental outcomes are consistency and hostility of parenting, here measured on a scale of angry parenting.[22] More consistency and less angry parenting are associated with better developmental outcomes. Table 3-4 shows that both mothers and fathers in jobless families displayed less consistent parenting of their child

Table 3-3. *Human Capital and Demographic Characteristics of Parents,*
by Persistence of Joblessness and Family Type[a]

| | Number of waves jobless | | | |
| | | | | |
Characteristic	Never jobless	One wave	Two or three waves	Total
Low level of educational attainment (percent)				
Lone parents	20.8	28.0*	40.8***	29.4
Two-parent mothers	19.6	41.7***	57.0***	21.8
Two-parent fathers	15.8	33.5***	33.7***	17.2
Fair or poor self-reported physical health (percent)				
Lone parents	13.9	20.1	23.1*	18.4
Two-parent mothers	7.4	17.4***	13.9	8.0
Two-parent fathers	8.3	17.5 ***	29.8***	9.2
Mental health (mean)				
Lone parents	4.22	4.02*	4.01*	4.10
Two-parent mothers	4.46	4.20***	4.21***	4.44
Two-parent fathers	4.48	4.32 **	4.42	4.48
Main language spoken at home not English (percent)				
Lone parents	10.3	12.4	18.5	13.6
Two-parent mothers	16.0	14.9	28.4**	16.4
Two-parent fathers	15.4	12.9	22.1	15.5
Number of resident children (mean)				
Lone-parent families	2.28	2.48	2.69***	2.47
Two-parent families	2.67	3.16***	3.49***	2.72

Source: Longitudinal Study of Australian Children, Waves 1–3, K Cohort.

a. Mental health is measured on the Kessler K6 depression scale (1 to 5, higher = better). Main language refers to language spoken by each parent at home, so it can be different for mothers and fathers. Characteristics were measured at wave 3. Significance tests indicate differences from the never-jobless group. Distributions were tested using chi-square and means using t tests. *$p < .05$, **$p < .01$, ***$p < .001$.

than those who were never jobless. In lone-parent families, a higher level of angry parenting was apparent for those who were jobless at two or three waves than for those who were never jobless.

The nature of the neighborhood in which children grow up can affect how children develop.[23] One measure of neighborhood socioeconomic status is the proportion of the neighborhood working-age population that is employed. For both lone- and two-parent families there were only relatively small differences in average employment rates, with neighborhoods (postcodes) in which jobless families lived having slightly lower employment rates than those in which never-jobless families lived (table 3-5). Nevertheless, the differences are statistically sig-

Table 3-4. *Parenting Style, by Persistence of Joblessness and Family Type*[a]
Mean

| Style | Number of waves jobless | | | |
	Never jobless	One wave	Two or three waves	Total
Consistent parenting				
Lone parents	4.09	4.04	3.81***	3.99
Two-parent mothers	4.19	4.09*	3.80***	4.17
Two-parent fathers	4.09	3.96*	3.83***	4.08
Angry parenting				
Lone parents	2.12	2.19	2.28*	2.19
Two-parent mothers	2.14	2.23	2.14	2.14
Two-parent fathers	2.16	2.34	2.21	2.17

Source: Longitudinal Study of Australian Children, Waves 1–3, K Cohort.

a. Characteristics were measured at wave 3. Parenting style was rated on a scale of 1 to 5, with 5 = more consistent/more angry parenting. Significance tests indicate differences from the never-jobless group. Distributions were tested using chi-square and means using t tests. *$p < .05$, **$p < .01$, ***$p < .001$.

nificant, and local area employment was lowest for persistently jobless two-parent families.

Another aspect of the nature of the neighborhood in which families live is parents' perception of its safety. The parent-reported data on whether the neighborhood was safe also show that persistently jobless families, whether lone- or two-parent, were least likely to report that their neighborhood was safe.

Table 3-5. *Neighborhood Employment and Safety of Surroundings, by Persistence of Joblessness and Family Type*[a]

| Measure | Number of waves jobless | | | |
	Never jobless	One wave	Two or three waves	Total
Percentage of postcode employed (mean)				
Lone-parent family	62.1	60.5*	60.1**	61.1
Two-parent family	63.1	60.1***	58.9***	62.8
Neighborhood is safe (percent)				
Lone-parent family	91.8	83.0*	78.4***	85.2
Two-parent family	95.7	91.5	83.5***	95.1

Source: Longitudinal Study of Australian Children, Waves 1–3, K Cohort.

a. Characteristics were measured at wave 3. Percentage of postcode employed is from the Australian census; neighborhood safety statement is based on those agreeing or strongly agreeing that their neighborhood is safe. Significance tests indicate differences from the never-jobless group. Distributions were tested using chi-square and means using t tests. *$p < .05$, **$p < .01$, ***$p < .001$.

A very important factor is that, in many families, joblessness is likely to be accompanied by financial hardship. The measures of financial well-being used to examine that possibility are objective measures of equivalent parental income and number of financial hardships experienced in the previous year.[24]

Equivalized parental income varies considerably according to the persistence of family joblessness. Further, differences between two-parent and lone-parent families are apparent, although they are less so for persistently jobless families. Not surprisingly, given the differences in income, lone-parent families were much more likely to report having experienced one financial hardship or more in the previous year (20.6 percent) than were two-parent families (3.4 percent). (See table 3-6.)

For both lone- and two-parent families, the proportion experiencing one or more financial hardships was higher among families that experienced joblessness than it was among those that were never jobless. However, even among families that were persistently jobless, a majority had not experienced any financial hardship in the previous year (72 percent of lone-parent families and 82 percent of two-parent families). In general, families that experienced joblessness were more likely to have experienced each of various types of financial hardship than those who did not experience joblessness. For example, of lone-parent families, 5.8 percent of the never-jobless families sought assistance from a welfare or community organization while 19.5 percent of families that were jobless for two or three waves did so. Of two-parent families, 0.9 percent of the never-jobless families but 12.2 percent of the families that were jobless for two or three waves sought assistance from a welfare or community organization.

Joblessness and Children's Developmental Outcomes

Here we analyze the associations between family joblessness and children's developmental outcomes at age eight to nine years. Figure 3-1 clearly shows that on all developmental outcome measures, longer exposure to family joblessness was associated with poorer outcomes. While there is a clear and strong association between joblessness and developmental outcomes for all three domains, the association is strongest for the learning/cognitive domain, next-strongest for the social/emotional domain, and weakest for the physical domain. For the learning/cognitive index, the difference between children who were not in a jobless family at any of the three waves and those in a jobless family at all waves is about 1 standard deviation (10 points).

Of course, these associations may reflect many underlying factors besides joblessness. As demonstrated above, children in jobless families (particularly persistently jobless families) have, on average, mothers with much lower levels of educational attainment and live in more disadvantaged neighborhoods, factors that

Table 3-6. *Equivalized Income and Experience of Financial Hardship, by Family Joblessness and Family Type*[a]

| | Number of waves jobless | | | |
| | Never jobless | One wave | Two or three waves | Total |
Family type				
	Equivalized parental income (mean AU$ per week)			
Lone-parent family	489	309***	238***	362
Two-parent family	820	487***	283***	788
		Experienced financial hardship in previous 12 months (percent)		
Lone-parent family				
Experienced one or more hardships	11.5	27.5***	27.5***	20.6
Type of hardship				
Adults or children have gone without meals	4.5	10.4*	8.4*	7.2
Unable to heat or cool home	3.1	4.7	8.6*	5.4
Pawned or sold something	3.4	8.9*	9.1**	6.6
Sought assistance from a welfare or community organization	5.8	16.8**	19.5***	13.0
Two-parent family				
Experienced one or more hardships	2.3	14.8***	18.0***	3.4
Type of hardship				
Adults or children have gone without meals	0.6	3.3***	1.6	0.8
Unable to heat or cool home	0.5	3.8***	2.4**	0.7
Pawned or sold something	1.0	8.0***	7.1***	1.5
Sought assistance from a welfare or community organization	0.9	6.3***	12.2***	1.5

Source: Longitudinal Study of Australian Children, Waves 1–3, K Cohort.

a. Characteristics were measured at wave 3. Significance tests indicate differences from the never-jobless group. Distributions were tested using chi-square and means using t tests. *$p < .05$, **$p < .01$, ***$p < .001$.

are associated with lower levels of child well-being and development. Statistical techniques can be used to allow the association between joblessness and child well-being to be estimated while holding constant the effects of observable characteristics that are related to both the likelihood of living in a jobless family and child developmental outcomes.

Statistical Method

The effects of living in a jobless family on children's developmental outcomes at eight to nine years of age can be estimated using statistical techniques that allow

Figure 3-1. *Child Outcome Indices at Wave 3, by Joblessness at Waves 1–3, K Cohort*[a]

Mean score

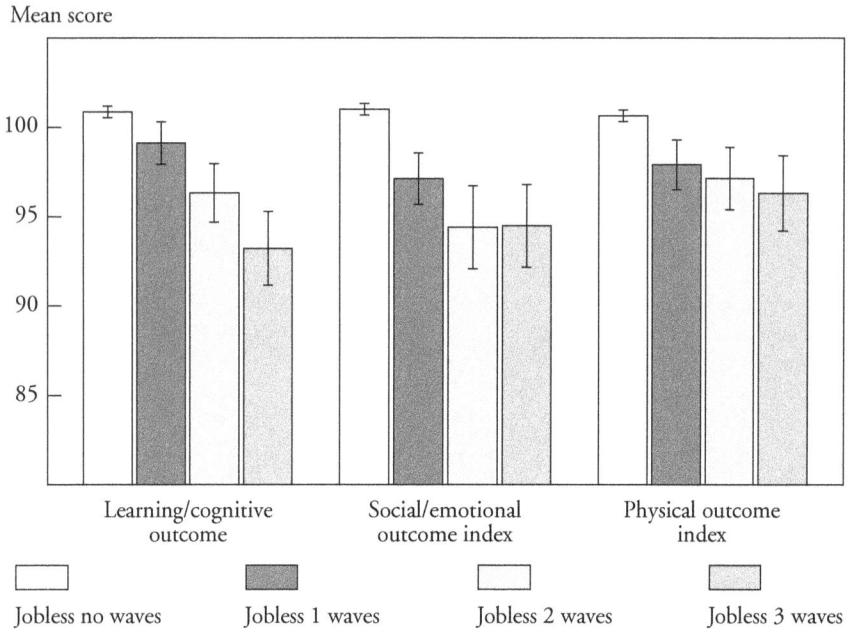

Source: Longitudinal Study of Australian Children, Waves 1–3, K Cohort.
a. 95 percent confidence interval shown.

the effects of other factors affecting children's developmental outcomes to be held constant. Because the measures of child developmental outcomes analyzed in this chapter are continuous variables, ordinary least squares (OLS) regression is an appropriate statistical technique. Family joblessness is analyzed through the inclusion of a set of dummy variables that capture having never been in a jobless family and having been jobless for one wave, for two waves, or for three waves. The omitted category is never having been jobless.

For each of the developmental domains, four models are estimated. The first model (model 1) includes only the measures of family joblessness. This model provides an estimate of the association between living in a jobless family, according to persistence of joblessness, and developmental outcomes. The second model (model 2) includes a range of control variables that attempt to capture the key factors that affect developmental outcomes. This model provides an estimate of the extent to which the associations between joblessness and developmental outcomes can be explained by a range of other factors that are associated with both parental joblessness and children's developmental outcomes. The third model (model 3) includes equivalized parental income in addition to all of the control variables included in model 2. The income measure is included in an attempt to understand how much of the impact of family joblessness can be explained by the effects of income. The fourth model (model 4) allows the effects of joblessness to vary between single- and couple-parent families by interacting family type with the joblessness indicators.

The selection of the control variables included in models 2 and 3 was informed by current theoretical frameworks of child developmental outcomes. Important factors include characteristics of the child and the family, including parents' human capital, and demographic and social characteristics of the environment in which they live.[25] The control variables included in the regression analysis were family type (whether child was living in a lone-parent family); highest level of parental educational attainment (of the parent or parents with whom the child was living); parenting style (measured as the higher of mothers' and fathers' level of angry parenting and the lower of mothers' and fathers' level of parenting consistency); having no parent whose main spoken language was English; parent having his or her first child when the parent was less than 25 years of age; primary carers' mental health status; parents' reports that their neighborhood was safe; gender of the child; age of the child (months); whether the child was indigenous; whether the child had a low birth weight; number of siblings; and whether the child had attended preschool.

Multivariate Estimates of the Relationship between Family Joblessness and Children's Developmental Outcomes

Here we discuss first the results for the measures of joblessness and then the results for family type (lone- or two-parent) and parental income. The results pertaining to the other control variables, the full regression results, and the descriptive statistics are provided in appendix 3A.

The results of estimating model 1 reveal that for all three measures of developmental outcomes examined, having lived in a jobless family is associated with poor outcomes for children at eight to nine years of age (table 3-7). The greater the number of waves at which the child was living in a jobless family, the greater the negative effects. The results are not discussed in detail because they are very similar to those presented previously.

For all three measures of developmental outcomes, the inclusion of the demographic and parenting control variables (model 2) reduces the estimated effects of living in a jobless family on children. Once the control variables are included, the estimates suggest that having been in a jobless family for only one or two waves does not have a negative and statistically significant independent impact on children's learning/cognitive developmental outcomes, although statistically significant

Table 3-7. *Ordinary Least Squares Estimates of the Impact of Living in a Jobless Family on Child Well-Being*[a]

Item	Learning/cognitive			Social/emotional			Physical		
	Model 1	Model 2	Model 3	Model 1	Model 2	Model 3	Model 1	Model 2	Model 3
Never jobless (omitted category)									
Jobless 1 wave	-2.3**	-0.9	-0.6	-4.3***	-1.9*	-1.7*	-3.4***	-2.0*	-1.7
Jobless 2 waves	-3.4**	-1.8	-1.3	-7.4***	-4.0***	-3.7**	-5.1***	-3.2**	-2.9**
Jobless 3 waves	-8.1***	-5.4***	-4.9***	-6.6***	-2.7*	-2.4*	-5.8***	-3.3*	-3.0*
Lone parent		2.6***	2.8***		-0.7	-0.5		0.2	0.4
Equivalized parental income (AU$00 per week)			0.2***			0.1***			0.1**
Includes demographic and parenting controls	No	Yes	Yes	No	Yes	Yes	No	Yes	Yes

Source: Data are from the Longitudinal Study of Australian Children, Waves 1–3, K Cohort.

a. The estimation of the models takes account of the initial stratification and clustering in the LSAC sample. The standard errors are robust to heteroskedasticity. The control variables included in models 2 and 3 are parent education, English language proficiency, age at first birth, and mental health; whether neighborhood is safe; whether child attended preschool; child's age, sex, and birth weight; number of siblings; parenting consistency; and angry parenting. The full set of coefficient estimates and t statistics are provided in appendix 3A. * $p < .05$, ** $p < .01$, *** $p < .001$.

differences remain for social/emotional and physical outcomes. Having been in a jobless family at two waves is estimated to have a negative and statistically significant impact on social/emotional and physical developmental outcomes. Having lived in a jobless family for three waves has a statistically significant negative impact on all three measures of children's outcomes.

Generally, the negative effects of parental joblessness on children are larger the greater the number of interviews during which the child was living in a jobless family. This finding is consistent with research on the effects of poverty on children's outcomes, which generally has found that it is the experience of persistent poverty rather than more transient experiences of poverty that has the greatest impact.[26] The exception to these results was for social/emotional outcomes, in which the coefficient was actually higher for those jobless at two waves than at three waves (although there was not a statistically significant difference between these two coefficients).

The independent effects of family joblessness on developmental outcomes were largely unchanged by the inclusion of equivalized parental income as an explanatory variable (model 3). However, higher equivalized parental income was estimated to have a positive effect on each of the developmental domains, meaning that poorer child outcomes were associated with lower parental income. Thus, joblessness contributes to outcomes for children through the independent effects described above as well as through effects of lower income.[27]

The outcome indices of children's development are derived in such a way that 1 standard deviation is equal to 10 points on the scale. The effects of joblessness that we have found in these analyses are quite large, being between one-third and one-half of a standard deviation. One way of assessing the size of the effects of persistent joblessness is to compare the coefficients with those of other variables included in the model. The estimated effects of parental joblessness on children are greater than those estimated for most other controls included in the models (see the tables in appendix 3A).

The results for the inclusion of an indicator of living in a lone-parent family (compared with a two-parent family) are shown in table 3-7. The estimated effects of being in a lone-parent family on child well-being are the estimated additional effects of being in a lone-parent family, holding constant the impact of parental joblessness and holding constant the impact of the other control variables. When interpreting the estimates it is important to bear in mind that many of the lone-parent families were jobless and differed from couple families on a range of characteristics, such as parental education and mental health. That may contribute to the unexpected result for learning/cognitive outcomes, which shows a higher score for lone-parent families. Similar associations are not apparent for the other outcomes, which did not vary according to family type, holding constant other factors.

Given the much higher rate of joblessness among lone-parent families, an important policy-relevant question is whether the negative effects of parental joblessness on children's developmental outcomes differ between lone- and two-parent families. This question can be tested by extending the statistical models used previously to include a set of interactions between the measures of joblessness and family type (lone-parent family). These results are also shown in the tables in appendix 3A as model 4. When the full set of control variables is included, none of the interactions between joblessness and family type are statistically significant (at the 5 percent confidence level) for learning/cognitive outcomes and physical outcomes. That suggests that for these outcomes the effects of parental joblessness on children's developmental outcomes do not differ between lone- and two-parent families.

However, for social/emotional outcomes, the interaction between being a lone parent and being jobless for one wave is positive and statistically significant. This indicates that the negative effects on children's social/emotional development of living in a jobless family for one wave (compared with living in a never-jobless family) are larger for children living in a two-parent families than for those living in a lone-parent family.

We briefly refer now to findings regarding the control variables that are of greatest relevance to the question of how parental joblessness might matter to children's outcomes. In particular, the variables that were very important in predicting better outcomes for children were better parental mental health and more positive parenting practices. These variables were especially important in explaining the variation in children's social/emotional outcomes and also physical outcomes. The earlier descriptive analyses showed some differences on these measures according to parental joblessness. This therefore suggests that another pathway by which children with jobless parents might have more negative outcomes is through their having parents who have poorer mental health and who exhibit less positive parenting practices.

Implications for Public Policy and Concluding Comments

With the release of data from the third wave of LSAC, Australia now joins a number of other OECD countries in having a nationally representative longitudinal study of child development. This chapter uses this new source of longitudinal data to better understand children's experience of growing up in families in which there is no employed parent and the impacts of that experience on their developmental outcomes. The previous lack of data that would allow family joblessness and the persistence of joblessness to be linked to measures of children's development and well-being meant that very little evidence existed to inform related policy areas. Rather, existing research has focused on questions for which the necessary data have been available, such as the impacts associated with family joblessness on government expenditure and taxation revenue as well as adult physical and mental health.

A key finding is that although a significant minority of children spend time living in a jobless family, about half of the children living in a jobless family at one or more of the first three waves of LSAC were in a jobless family at only one of the waves. From a policy perspective, an important question is whether the effects of shorter-term family joblessness on children's developmental outcomes differ from the impacts of longer-term or persistent family joblessness.

The analysis in this chapter reveals that children who spend time living in a jobless family have poorer developmental outcomes across the learning/cognitive, social/emotional, and physical domains than children who do not spend time in jobless families. The longer the period spent living in a jobless family, the poorer the developmental outcomes are. Parents in jobless families have, on average, lower levels of human capital than those who do not experience joblessness, and they also exhibit poorer parenting skills. Once those differences are taken into account, there remain negative effects of persistent joblessness on children's outcomes, although in these analyses being jobless for only one wave was no longer statistically significant in the analyses of learning/cognitive outcomes.

For all outcomes, the size of the effect of being jobless for one wave declined substantially with the inclusion of the control variables. That means that the negative association between living in a jobless family for one wave and children's developmental outcomes is explained in part by other characteristics, such as parental educational attainment, parental mental health, and the quality of parenting. It is likely that joblessness, even at only one wave, works its effect on children's outcomes through those factors. The different family and environmental circumstances of jobless families are especially relevant when considering links between joblessness and children's outcomes. While not the primary focus of this chapter, many of the control variables included in the regression models are important in explaining variation in children's outcomes. In fact, some of these factors, such as parenting style, mental health, and neighborhood disadvantage, had especially strong associations with children's outcomes.[28] While this chapter focuses on joblessness in relation to children, it is important to note that policy and program development in a broad range of other areas is also relevant.

Joblessness and persistent joblessness are much more prevalent in lone-parent families than in two-parent families. The finding that joblessness has a negative impact on children's outcomes is therefore relevant to lone-parent families in particular. In general, the effects of family joblessness did not differ between lone- and two-parent families. The exception was for social/emotional outcomes, in which we found that being jobless for one wave had a greater impact on couple families than on single-parent families. Regardless of family form, the broad issue of joblessness and persistent joblessness is important to address in relation to children's outcomes.

The data presented in this chapter provide information that is relevant to the development of social and economic policy. The findings suggest that the current Australian policy focus on jobless families is sensible and that most effort should be put into assisting longer-term jobless families and preventing shorter-term jobless families from becoming jobless over the long term. The findings of this research provide further support for the importance of developing policies aimed at improving the employment rate of jobless lone parents (who are mostly lone mothers).

The mechanism by which joblessness affects children's well-being is unclear and needs further research. Possibilities include that the effects are driven by low income, although this research has shown that joblessness has an effect beyond that of income. Another possibility is that joblessness leads to social isolation and mental health problems that can affect children.

A range of government policies are relevant to increasing the employment rate of jobless parents. These include making receipt of social security payments dependent on the recipient actively seeking employment or participating in training (that is, implementing a form of conditionality of benefits); ensuring that the social security and tax systems interact to produce financial benefits for those who engage in paid employment (making work pay); and providing job search assistance and training to the jobless. In addition, it is important to provide more intensive support for the long-term jobless, who often face multiple barriers to finding paid employment and for whom the broader macro-policy settings and job search system may be less effective.

Programs that aim to improve the quality, effectiveness, and accessibility of social services in disadvantaged communities may also have a role in improving parenting skills, reducing parental joblessness, and improving the well-being of children. A significant finding emerging from evaluations of area-based parenting programs in Australia (Communities for Children) and England (Sure Start)[29] is that these programs can have positive effects on children and are associated with a reduction in parental joblessness.[30] Further work is required to understand exactly how these programs could reduce parental joblessness. Currently they primarily attempt to create "child family communities" by improving the quality and coordination of local services aimed at helping families with children living in disadvantaged areas and by providing assistance with parenting skills. While there are a number of possible mechanisms, it is likely that helping jobless parents to address factors such as mental and physical health issues enhances their ability to parent effectively and also enhances their ability to find and sustain employment. Likewise, programs that build parents' confidence and improve their social networks can be important in helping them find and sustain employment. The evaluation of Communities for Children (CfC) suggests that better coordination of services at the local level and having these services "wrapped around" vulnerable families may be especially important to their success. Another factor that was important to the success of CfC was allowing considerable flexibility at the local level regarding which services to provide and how to provide them.[31]

Further research and evaluation are needed to assess the effectiveness of area-based parenting programs in addressing the multiple and overlapping issues faced by many jobless families. It is also important to understand which aspects of these programs are most effective and to test how effectively they can be scaled up in order to be one part of the policy response to family joblessness at the national level.

Australia has a higher rate of family joblessness than many other OECD countries. A range of policy approaches and responses is required to help parents move into employment and thereby help improve outcomes for children. Approaches include those at the macro level, such as ensuring that receipt of benefits is subject to appropriate work requirements, making work pay through the design of the social security and taxation systems, and supporting a strong labor market combined with more intensive, individualized assistance to long-term jobless families, which all too often face multiple barriers to finding and sustaining employment. Given the negative impacts of long-term family joblessness on young children's developmental outcomes, there is an important role for social and community services such as mental health, education, drug and alcohol, and family relationship services to assist parents in overcoming the factors that prevent them from maintaining employment and to ameliorate the impacts of joblessness on children's developmental outcomes.

Notes

1. Data on joblessness are from the OECD Family Database, table LMF1.1.A., February 13, 2011 (www.oecd.org/els/social/family/database).

2. In 2007, 5.5 percent of children under 15 years of age living in a two-parent family were in jobless families and 54.5 percent living in lone-parent families were in jobless families. The corresponding U.S. figures were 2.8 percent of children in two-parent families and

26.6 percent of children in lone-parent families. The OECD averages were 5.0 percent for two-parent families and 36.1 percent for lone-parent families. Data are from the OECD Family Database.

3. Peter Whiteford, *Family Joblessness in Australia* (Canberra: Social Inclusion Unit, Department of the Prime Minister and Cabinet, 2009).

4. For example, Peter Dawkins, "The Distribution of Work in Australia," *Economic Record*, vol. 72, no. 218 (1996), pp. 272–86; Patrick McClure, *Participation Support for a More Equitable Society: The Report of the Reference Group on Welfare Reform* (Canberra: Department of Family and Community Services, 2000).

5. Australian Government, *Social Inclusion Priorities* (2010) (www.socialinclusion.gov.au/SIAgenda/Priorities/Pages/default.aspx).

6. Data are from Whiteford, *Family Joblessness in Australia*.

7. For a discussion of this literature, see Peter Saunders, "Introduction: The Reality and Costs of Unemployment," in *The Price of Prosperity: The Economic and Social Costs of Unemployment,* edited by Peter Saunders and Richard Taylor (University of New South Wales Press, 2002), pp. 1–12.

8. Ariel Kalil, "Joblessness, Family Relations, and Children's Development," *Family Matters*, vol. 83 (2009), pp. 15–22.

9. See, for example, Greg Duncan and Jeanne Brooks-Gunn, *Consequences of Growing Up Poor* (New York: Russell Sage Foundation, 1997); Tytti Solantaus, Jenni Leinonen, and Raija-Leena Punamäki, "Children's Mental Health in Times of Economic Recession: Replication and Extension of the Family Economic Stress Model in Finland," *Developmental Psychology*, vol. 40 (2004), pp. 412–29.

10. See, for example, Andrew Clark, "Unemployment as a Social Norm: Psychological Evidence from Panel Data," *Journal of Labor Economics*, vol. 21 (2003), pp. 323–51; Karsten Paul and Klaus Moser, "Unemployment Impairs Mental Health: Meta-Analyses," *Journal of Vocational Behavior*, vol. 74, no. 3 (2009), pp. 264–82.

11. See Rand Conger and Glen Elder, *Families in Troubled Times: Adapting to Change in Rural America* (Hawthorne, N.Y.: Aldine Transaction, 1994); Rand Conger, Martha Rueter, and Glen Elder, "Couple Resilience to Economic Pressure," *Journal of Personality and Social Psychology*, vol. 76 (1999), pp. 54–71; Glen Elder, *Children of the Great Depression: Social Change in Life Experience*, 25th anniversary ed. (University of Chicago Press, 1999); Kornelius Kraft, "Unemployment and the Separation of Married Couples," *Kyklos*, vol. 54 (2001), pp. 67–88; Jeffrey Liker and Glen Elder, "Economic Hardship and Marital Relations in the 1930s," *American Sociological Review*, vol. 48, no. 3 (1983), pp. 343–59; Silvia Mendolia and Denise Doiron, *The Impact of Job Loss on Family Dissolution* (University of New South Wales, School of Economics, January 2008).

12. Ariel Kalil and Kathleen M. Ziol-Guest, "Parental Employment Circumstances and Children's Academic Progress," *Social Science Research*, vol. 37, no. 2 (2008), pp. 500–15; Michael B. Coelli, "Parental Job Loss, Income Shocks, and the Educational Enrolment of Youth," Research Paper 1060 (University of Melbourne, 2009).

13. A recent example is Matthew Taylor, Ben Edwards, and Matthew Gray, "Unemployment and the Well-Being of Australian Children Aged 5 to 10 Years," Benevolent Society Background Paper (Sydney: 2010).

14. Roger Wilkins, Diana Warren, and Markus Hahn, *Families, Incomes, and Jobs,* vol. 4, *A Statistical Report on Waves 1 to 6 of the HILDA Survey* (Melbourne: Melbourne Institute of

Applied Economic and Social Research, 2009); Trevor Breusch and Deborah Mitchell, "Australian Family Income Dynamics: Preliminary Evidence from the NLC Project, 1997 and 2000," Negotiating the Life Course Discussion Paper 14 (Australian National University, 2003).

15. See Deborah A. Cobb-Clark and Anastasia Sartbayeva, "The Relationship between Income Support History Characteristics and Outcomes of Australian Youth," Youth in Focus Project Discussion Paper 2 (Australian National University, 2007); Deborah A. Cobb-Clark and Anastasia Sartbayeva, "The Relationship between Income Support History Characteristics and Outcomes of Australian Youth: Outcomes of Wave 2 of the Youth in Focus Survey," Youth in Focus Project Discussion Paper 9 (Australian National University, 2010). This research examined the links between parental income support payment history and young people's well-being (at the ages of 18 and 20 years). While income support history and family joblessness are different measures, they are closely linked. Cobb-Clark and Sartbayeva showed that there were links between persistent parental reliance on income support payments and how the children were doing at 18 and 20 years of age.

16. Matthew Gray and Diana Smart, "Growing Up in Australia: The Longitudinal Study of Australian Children Is Now Walking and Talking," *Family Matters*, vol. 79 (2008), pp. 5–13.

17. Children in some remote parts of Australia were excluded because of the extremely high data collection costs in those areas.

18. LSAC Project Operations Team, *The Longitudinal Study of Australian Children Data Users Guide* (Melbourne: Australian Institute of Family Studies, 2009).

19. Employment status is collected only for parents in LSAC, so it is not possible to take the employment of other family members into account.

20. While LSAC provides information on the number of months each parent was not in paid employment between waves, it does not collect information on the exact months in which the parents were not employed; therefore, it is not possible to determine whether there were months in which neither parent in a two-parent family was employed (that is, whether the family was jobless).

21. Ann Sanson and others, "Summarising Children's Well-Being: The LSAC Outcome Index," LSAC Technical Paper 2 (Melbourne: Australian Institute of Family Studies, 2005).

22. See, for example, Diana Smart and others, *Home-to-School Transitions for Financially Disadvantaged Children* (Sydney: Smith Family, 2008). These items are derived from a series of questions asking each parent about how often they exhibit certain parenting styles while interacting with their child. Each item is scored on a five-point scale. Parental consistency is the mean of five related items and angry parenting is the mean of four related items.

23. Ben Edwards and Leah M. Bromfield, "Neighborhood Influences on Young Children's Conduct Problems and Pro-Social Behavior: Evidence from an Australian National Sample," *Children and Youth Services Review*, vol. 31, no. 3 (2009), pp. 317–24.

24. Equivalized parental income was calculated from each parent's income and the number of people in the family up to 15 years of age. The modified OECD equivalence scales were used. This equivalence scale gives a weight of 1 to the first adult, 0.5 to the second and subsequent adults, and 0.3 to all dependent children. For the measure of financial hardship, the primary carer was asked whether any of the following had occurred in the previous twelve months due to shortage of money: the carer not been able to pay gas, electricity, or telephone bills on time; the carer could not pay the mortgage or rent on time; adults or children had

gone without meals; the carer been unable to heat or cool the home; the carer had pawned or sold something; or the carer had sought assistance from a welfare or community organization. Following Bray (2001), the first two of these occurrences were said to constitute cash flow problems and the other four were said to constitute financial hardships. Families were said to have experienced either one of these if they reported having experienced at least one of the underlying events. Here we use the data on financial hardship only. J. Rob Bray, "Hardship in Australia: An Analysis of Financial Stress Indicators in the 1998–99 Australian Bureau of Statistics Household Expenditure Survey," Occasional Paper 4 (Canberra: Department of Family and Community Services, 2001).

25. While a range of theoretical frameworks are used to explain the determinants of child developmental outcomes, two that are currently influential are the risk and resiliency framework (Garbarino 1995; Rutter 1999), and the bioecological developmental systems perspective (Bronfenbrenner and Morris 2006). James Garbarino, *Raising Children in a Socially Toxic Environment* (San Francisco: Jossey-Bass Publishers, 1995); Michael Rutter, "Resilience Concepts and Findings: Implications for Family Therapy," *Journal of Family Therapy*, vol. 21, no. 2 (1999), pp. 119–44; Urie Bronfenbrenner and Pamela A. Morris, "The Bioecological Model of Human Development," in *Handbook of Child Psychology*, 6th ed., vol. 1, *Theoretical Models of Human Development*, edited by William Damon and Richard M. Lerner (Hoboken, N.J.: Wiley), pp. 793–828.

26. For example, Kerry E. Bolger and others, "Psychosocial Adjustment among Children Experiencing Persistent and Intermittent Family Economic Hardship," *Child Development*, vol. 66, no. 4 (1995), pp. 1107–29; Greg J. Duncan, Jeanne Brooks-Gunn, and Pamela Kato Klebanov, "Economic Deprivation and Early Childhood Development,"*Child Development*, vol. 65, no. 2 (1994), pp. 296–318.

27. These analyses resulted in the unexpected finding that children's cognitive outcomes were higher in lone-parent than two-parent families, after we controlled for joblessness, income, and a range of other important variables; however, no differences in socioemotional or physical outcomes were apparent for children in lone-parent families. Given that our focus here is on joblessness rather than family type per se, we do not explore this result further in this chapter.

28. See also Smart and others, *Home-to-School Transitions for Financially Disadvantaged Children*.

29. Communities for Children (CfC) is a large-scale, area-based initiative designed to enhance the development of children in forty-five disadvantaged community sites around Australia. The CfC initiative, which was implemented in 2004, aimed to improve coordination of services for children 0–5 years of age and their families, identify and provide services to address unmet needs, build community capacity to engage in service delivery, and improve the community context in which children grow up. Decisions about which services to provide and how to provide them were made by nongovernment organizations at the local level. The program had an explicit focus on service coordination, and cooperation in communities was a novel aspect of the initiative. Sure Start was implemented in England in 1999 with the objectives of reducing child poverty and improving child and family services. The program targets all children under 4 years of age and their families living in relatively small areas of marked deprivation. Each local program had extensive local autonomy in terms of the services that were developed.

30. Ben Edwards and others, "Early Impacts of Communities for Children on Children and Families: Findings from a Quasi-Experimental Cohort Study," *Journal of Epidemiology*

and Community Health, vol. 65, no. 10 (2011); National Evaluation of Sure Start Team, "The Impact of Sure Start Local Programmes on Five-Year-Olds and Their Families: Report of the Longitudinal Study of Five-Year-Old Children and Their Families," Research Report DFE-RR067 (Institute for the Study of Children, Families, and Social Issues, Birkbeck University of London, 2010).

31. Ilan Katz and others, "The National Evaluation of the Communities for Children Initiative," *Family Matters*, vol. 84 (2010), pp. 35–42.

Table 3A-1. *Descriptive Statistics*[a]

Variables	Mean	Standard deviation
Experience of joblessness (percent)		
Never jobless (omitted category)	89	
Jobless at one wave	6	
Jobless at two waves	3	
Jobless at three waves	2	
Lone-parent family	13	
Equivalized parental income (AU$ per week)	$773	$521
Highest parental educational attainment (percent)		
Bachelor's degree or higher (omitted category)	37	
Completed secondary education or diploma-level qualification	56	
Incomplete secondary education	7	
Parenting style		
Angry parenting style (1 to 5, higher = more angry)	2.33	0.61
Consistent parenting style (1 to 5, higher = more consistent)	4.36	0.55
No parent whose main language spoken was English (percent)	9	
Primary carer's first birth at age < 25 (percent)	23	
Primary carer's mental health (1 to 5, higher = better)	4.42	0.60
Parent-reported safe neighborhood (percent)	95	
Boy (percent)	51	
Age of child (months)	105.5	2.8
Indigenous child (percent)	2	
Low birth weight (percent)	6	
Number of siblings (percent)		
No siblings (omitted category)	8	
One sibling	46	
Two or more siblings	46	
Child had attended preschool (percent)	95	
Number of observations	3,256	

Source: Longitudinal Study of Australian Children, Waves 1–3, K Cohort.

a. These statistics are based on the unweighted data from the sample with non-missing values on the learning outcome index and non-missing variables contributing to model 3.

Table 3A-2. *Ordinary Least Squares Estimates of the Impact of Living in a Jobless Family on Child Well-Being: Learning/Cognitive Outcomes*

Variables	Model 1		Model 2		Model 3		Model 4	
	Coefficient	t statistic	Coefficient	t statistic	Coefficient	t statistic	Coefficient	t statistic
Joblessness (reference category = never jobless)								
Jobless at one wave	-2.3	-2.9	-0.9	-1.1	-0.6	-0.7	-1.0	-0.9
Jobless at two waves	-3.4	-3.2	-1.8	-1.6	-1.3	-1.2	-2.5	-1.7
Jobless at three waves	-8.1	-5.8	-5.4	-3.9	-4.9	-3.6	-6.2	-3.6
Lone-parent family			2.6	4.0	2.8	4.4	2.2	3.0
Lone parent and jobless at one wave							1.4	0.9
Lone parent and jobless at two or three waves							2.4	1.4
Equivalized parental income (AU$00 per week)					0.2	4.4	0.2	4.4
Highest parental educational attainment (reference category = bachelor's degree or higher)								
Completed secondary education or diploma-level qualification			-4.0	-10.3	-3.5	-8.4	-3.5	-8.4
Incomplete secondary education			-5.4	-8.0	-4.8	-6.9	-4.8	-6.9

(continued)

73

Table 3A-2. *Ordinary Least Squares Estimates of the Impact of Living in a Jobless Family on Child Well-Being: Learning/Cognitive Outcomes (Continued)*

Variables	Model 1		Model 2		Model 3		Model 4	
	Coefficient	t statistic	Coefficient	t statistic	Coefficient	t statistic	Coefficient	t statistic
Parenting style								
Angry parenting (1 to 5, higher = more angry)			−0.3	−0.9	−0.2	−0.9	−0.3	−0.9
Consistent parenting (1 to 5, higher = more consistent)			2.3	6.6	2.3	6.6	2.3	6.6
No parent whose main language spoken was English			0.6	0.9	0.7	1.2	0.7	1.2
Primary carer's first birth at age < 25			−2.0	−4.5	−1.9	−4.3	−1.9	−4.2
Primary carer's mental health (1 to 5, higher = better)			0.2	0.7	0.1	0.5	0.1	0.4
Parent-reported safe neighborhood			0.2	0.2	0.1	0.2	0.2	0.2
Boy			−0.9	−2.5	−0.9	−2.5	−0.9	−2.5
Age of child (months)			0.0	0.4	0.0	0.3	0.0	0.3
Indigenous child			−2.5	−2.3	−2.4	−2.2	−2.3	−2.2
Low birth weight			−3.5	−5.0	−3.4	−4.9	−3.4	−4.9
Number of siblings								
One sibling			−0.7	−1.0	−0.5	−0.7	−0.6	−0.8
Two or more siblings			−1.2	−1.7	−0.9	−1.2	−1.0	−1.3
Child had attended preschool			2.3	2.5	2.2	2.4	2.1	2.4
Constant	101.5	403.8	90.6	13.6	90.0	13.5	89.9	13.5
Number of observations	3,256		3,256		3,256		3,256	
R^2	0.03		0.13		0.14		0.14	

Source: Longitudinal Study of Australian Children, Waves 1–3, K Cohort.

74

Table 3A-3. *Ordinary Least Squares Estimates of the Impact of Living in a Jobless Family on Child Well-Being: Social/Emotional Outcomes*

	Model 1		Model 2		Model 3		Model 4	
Variables	Coefficient	t statistic	Coefficient	t statistic	Coefficient	t statistic	Coefficient	t statistic
Joblessness (reference category = never jobless)								
Jobless at one wave	-4.3	-5.1	-1.9	-2.5	-1.7	-2.2	-3.0	-3.0
Jobless at two waves	-7.4	-5.2	-4.0	-3.6	-3.7	-3.3	-3.8	-2.9
Jobless at three waves	-6.6	-4.7	-2.7	-2.3	-2.4	-2.0	-2.5	-1.9
Lone-parent family			-0.7	-1.1	-0.5	-0.8	-1.2	-1.7
Lone parent and jobless at one wave							3.2	2.3
Lone parent and jobless at two or three waves							0.8	0.4
Equivalized parental income (AU$00 per week)					0.1	4.0	0.1	3.9
Highest parental educational attainment (reference category = bachelor's degree or higher)								
Completed secondary education or diploma-level qualification			-1.7	-5.4	-1.3	-3.9	-1.3	-3.9
Incomplete secondary education			-2.3	-3.7	-1.9	-3.0	-1.9	-3.0

(continued)

Table 3A-3. *Ordinary Least Squares Estimates of the Impact of Living in a Jobless Family on Child Well-Being: Social/Emotional Outcomes (Continued)*

Variables	Model 1		Model 2		Model 3		Model 4	
	Coefficient	t statistic	Coefficient	t statistic	Coefficient	t statistic	Coefficient	t statistic
Parenting style								
Angry parenting (1 to 5, higher = more angry)			-5.8	-19.3	-5.8	-19.3	-5.8	-19.2
Consistent parenting (1 to 5, higher = more consistent)			2.3	6.7	2.2	6.7	2.2	6.6
No parent whose main language spoken was English			0.4	0.7	0.5	0.9	0.5	0.8
Primary carer's first birth at age < 25			-0.5	-1.2	-0.5	-1.1	-0.4	-1.1
Primary carer's mental health (1 to 5, higher = better)			3.2	10.7	3.2	10.6	3.2	10.6
Parent-reported safe neighborhood			1.9	2.5	1.9	2.5	2.0	2.6
Boy			-2.4	-7.7	-2.4	-7.7	-2.4	-7.7
Age of child (months)			0.0	0.7	0.0	0.6	0.0	0.6
Indigenous child			-1.6	-1.4	-1.6	-1.3	-1.5	-1.3
Low birth weight			-1.0	-1.5	-0.9	-1.4	-0.9	-1.3
Number of siblings								
One sibling			0.2	0.4	0.3	0.6	0.3	0.5
Two or more siblings			0.5	0.8	0.7	1.2	0.7	1.1
Child had attended preschool			0.4	0.4	0.3	0.3	0.3	0.3
Constant	101.1	465.3	86.3	14.4	85.9	14.5	86.3	14.5
Number of observations	3,258		3,258		3,258		3,258	
R^2	0.04		0.33		0.34		0.34	

Source: Longitudinal Study of Australian Children, Waves 1–3, K Cohort.

Table 3A-4. *Ordinary Least Squares Estimates of the Impact of Living in a Jobless Family on Child Well-Being: Physical Outcomes*

Variables	Model 1		Model 2		Model 3		Model 4	
	Coefficient	t statistic	Coefficient	t statistic	Coefficient	t statistic	Coefficient	t statistic
Joblessness (reference category = never jobless)								
Jobless at one wave	-3.4	-3.7	-2.0	-2.0	-1.7	-1.7	-2.2	-1.5
Jobless at two waves	-5.1	-4.6	-3.2	-2.9	-2.9	-2.6	-4.5	-2.9
Jobless at three waves	-5.8	-4.0	-3.3	-2.2	-3.0	-2.0	-4.6	-2.5
Lone-parent family			0.2	0.4	0.4	0.7	-0.5	-0.6
Lone parent and jobless at one wave							1.7	0.9
Lone parent and jobless at two or three waves							3.2	1.5
Equivalized parental income (AU$00 per week)					0.1	2.8	0.1	2.7
Highest parental educational attainment (reference category = bachelor's degree or higher)								
Completed secondary education or diploma-level qualification			-1.0	-2.8	-0.7	-1.7	-0.6	-1.6
Incomplete secondary education			-1.0	-1.3	-0.6	-0.8	-0.6	-0.8

(continued)

Table 3A-4. *Ordinary Least Squares Estimates of the Impact of Living in a Jobless Family on Child Well-Being: Physical Outcomes (Continued)*

Variables	Model 1 Coefficient	Model 1 t statistic	Model 2 Coefficient	Model 2 t statistic	Model 3 Coefficient	Model 3 t statistic	Model 4 Coefficient	Model 4 t statistic
Parenting style								
Angry parenting (1 to 5, higher = more angry)			-1.8	-6.0	-1.8	-6.0	-1.8	-6.1
Consistent parenting (1 to 5, higher = more consistent))			1.5	4.8	1.5	4.7	1.5	4.7
No parent whose main language spoken was English			-1.1	-1.5	-1.0	-1.4	-1.0	-1.4
Primary carer's first birth at age < 25			-0.3	-0.8	-0.3	-0.7	-0.3	-0.6
Primary carer's mental health (1 to 5, higher = better)			2.1	6.5	2.1	6.4	2.1	6.3
Parent-reported safe neighborhood			1.4	1.3	1.4	1.3	1.4	1.3
Boy			-0.5	-1.2	-0.5	-1.2	-0.5	-1.2
Age of child (months)			-0.0	-0.4	0.0	-0.5	-0.0	-0.4
Indigenous child			-0.9	-0.7	-0.8	-0.7	-0.8	-0.7
Low birth weight			-2.5	-3.8	-2.4	-3.7	-2.5	-3.8
Number of siblings								
One sibling			1.1	1.6	1.2	1.7	1.2	1.6
Two or more siblings			1.7	2.3	2.0	2.6	1.9	2.5
Child had attended preschool			1.5	1.4	1.4	1.3	1.4	1.3
Constant	101.0	471.9	89.0	11.7	88.6	11.7	88.4	11.7
Number of observations	3,260		3,260		3,260		3,260	
R^2	0.03		0.10		0.10		0.10	

Source: Longitudinal Study of Australian Children, Waves 1–3, K Cohort.

4

The Way Families Work: Jobs, Hours, Income, and Children's Well-Being

LYNDALL STRAZDINS, MEGAN SHIPLEY, LIANA LEACH, AND
PETER BUTTERWORTH

Australia faces two potentially conflicting policy imperatives: maximizing the labor force participation of all working-age adults, including parents, as the population ages and improving children's mental health and well-being by giving them a good start in life. We argue that to succeed over the long term, each policy goal depends on the other. Together, these goals raise the issue of how to combine working with caring for children in an equitable and sustainable way.

Compared with the labor force participation rate among mothers in Canada, Finland, Sweden, France, and the United States, the rate among Australian mothers is low; in 2006 two-thirds of mothers in couple households and 59 percent of lone mothers with children under the age of 14 years were employed.[1] Of employed mothers, the majority worked part-time (59 percent of couple mothers and 60 percent of lone mothers in 2006).[2] There is a small but significant proportion of jobless families in Australia (about 12 percent of all families with children under 15 years of age,[3] most of which are lone-parent families headed by mothers). Conversely, most Australian fathers are fully employed, with the exception of a small number of jobless fathers. Ninety-two percent of Australian fathers with children less than 15 years of age are employed, with many fathers working long hours (an average of 52 hours per week).[4] Thus, in

Megan Shipley is currently employed as a senior researcher in the Commonwealth Department of Families, Housing, Community Services and Indigenous Affairs. The opinions, comments, and/or analysis expressed in this chapter are those of the authors and do not necessarily represent the views of the Minister for Families, Housing, Community Services and Indigenous Affairs and cannot be taken in any way as expressions of government policy.

79

terms of increasing workforce participation, it is mothers' employment and work hours that are a potential target of future policy efforts.

A parallel policy imperative giving all children the best start in life and developing their capabilities is also critical to Australia's social and economic future. Having adequate family resources, especially income, is central to how children fare. The evidence on the benefits of income for children is incontrovertible: studies of poverty and of jobless families show that greater parent workforce participation generates more income and that more income can in turn improve children's outcomes.[5] Consequently, it would seem that increasing the hours that mothers spend in paid work could address productivity concerns *and* improve children's well-being. However, such an approach involves a trade-off between family time (especially mothers' time) and family income. The majority of Australian children are currently growing up in households in which both parents have jobs, typically with fathers working long hours and mothers working part-time. The consequences to these families of shifting from a one-and-a-half job arrangement to two full-time jobs are not clear, nor is there current evidence to support the assumption that additional income outweighs the time costs to families.

Work Hours, Income, and Children's Well-Being

This chapter focuses on families in which both parents are employed and considers the trade-off between time and income in terms of children's well-being. Our previous research has shown that in terms of children's well-being, not all jobs are "family friendly."[6] A series of studies have analyzed the nature of jobs to determine how employment can support (or undermine) parent and child health and identify which aspects of jobs matter for families. These studies consider the extent to which mothers' or fathers' work conditions—such as security, control, flexibility, paid leave, and work at unsociable times (evenings, nights, and weekends)—showed associations with children's emotional and behavioral difficulties.

This chapter extends that research by considering whether parents' combined work time influences children's well-being. We start with a brief review of the links between mothers' and fathers' jobs and child well-being and then outline the Australian labor market context and our own research on jobs and parent and child well-being. We then present a preliminary longitudinal analysis of children in dual-earner households, comparing the well-being of children in households with different work-hour arrangements at four to five, six to seven, and eight to nine years of age.

Mechanisms Connecting Jobs to Children's Well-Being

Because work usually takes place outside of the home, connections between jobs and children are not obvious. Yet several strands of research reveal how parents' work conditions and the quality of family life are interconnected. Stress transmission is one mechanism linking work to family, whereby negative mood generated in one setting can cross to the other, affecting relationships and interactions. Parents with stressful jobs are more likely to be tense at home, and their tension can translate into withdrawing from or arguing with their spouse and children.[7] After a high-workload day, for example, fathers tended to withdraw from their children and, if angry or distressed from work, reported more irritable parent-child interactions.[8]

Health transmission is another potential mechanism. Developmental research highlights the critical influence of both mothers' and fathers' health, especially depression, on children's development and mental health.[9] Epidemiological research has long recognized the significant, independent contribution of work conditions to adverse health in employed adults, including ischemic heart disease, depression, anxiety, absence because of sickness, and poor self-rated health.[10] The associations between work conditions and adult mental health are not trivial: job insecurity and low job control show cross-sectional and longitudinal associations comparable with key risk factors such as adverse life events, bereavement, and relationship disruption.[11] Indeed, holding a poor-quality job (one combining an array of negative conditions) may be as bad for mental health as being unemployed.[12] Because the lives and health of parents and children are so closely linked, jobs that affect parent health also have the potential to affect children.

Contemporary Work in Australia: Conditions and Work Time

The globalized economic landscape, structural changes to the labor market, and the shift to a service economy that operates twenty-four hours a day, seven days a week ("24/7") are reshaping the way that contemporary Australian families live and work. There is now a discernable split in the Australian labor market between well-paid, high-skilled jobs with good conditions and a growing pool of unskilled, insecure, and low-paid jobs. Economic growth has been accompanied by deregulation of work hours, downsizing, work intensification, and a striking increase in insecure employment. Casual employees, who constituted 16 percent of the Australian workforce in 1984, now constitute 28 percent,[13] and many workers report heightened concerns about job security and diminished job control. Australian trends mirror those of other developed nations. Temporary and casual work has risen steadily in the European Union (EU), up from 3.9 percent of the workforce in 1983 to 9.3 percent in 1991 and 13.3 percent in 2004.[14]

Furthermore, the pace and time demands of work have increased, with Australian full-time employees working among the longest hours of workers in countries belonging to the Organization for Economic Cooperation and Development (OECD).[15] About two-thirds of those who regularly work overtime do not receive any extra pay.[16] Relative to the labor market in other OECD countries, the Australian labor market is characterized by a gendered polarization of work time, with a relatively high incidence of very short weekly hours (fifteen or less) among employed women and very long weekly hours (fifty or more) among employed men.[17] Short-hour jobs are much more likely to be poor quality, aligning the gender differences in work hours with gender inequity in the quality of work.[18]

The split of the labor market into good and bad jobs has occurred in tandem with the shift to a 24/7 economy. As jobs move offshore, the Australian labor market is in direct competition with the labor markets in developing countries. Along with these pressures, domestic demands have also led to expanded business hours.[19] The working week has been reshaped, profoundly affecting when people work and how work time is structured.[20] More than half of the Australian labor force works some or most work hours outside a standard nine-to-five weekday.[21] Employees in the United States are even more likely to work unsociable hours, with 40 percent working on the weekends, evenings, or nights.[22] These changes are likely to continue with the employment growth expected in 24/7 services such as retail, health care, and hospitality, in which workers typically are female.

The Australian labor market is therefore characterized by a high rate of insecure work, a growing pool of poor-quality jobs, long work-hour expectations for full-time jobs, and growth in jobs with nonstandard and unsociable work times. These structural characteristics form the backdrop to increasing parents' (largely mothers') work participation and shape parents' employment choices and opportunities. Some mothers will not be able to find a good-quality job, and some will be required to work at unsociable times. It is not clear how families would manage a shift toward full-time employment for both parents, especially if the long work hours of fathers persist.

Linking Parent Work Conditions to Children's Well-Being

In previous research we focused on four aspects of parents' jobs: security, control, flexible work hours, and access to paid family leave.[23] We developed a brief index of parent job quality as a first step in redefining family friendliness in the workplace. Good-quality jobs were those that offered a full array of positive conditions,[24] in contrast to jobs with poor conditions, such as insecurity, inflexible hours, lack of paid leave, and/or little employee control. Using this index, we investigated the cross-sectional associations between the quality of parents' work and their children's well-being.[25] That study was one of the first, to our knowledge, to test for links between the quality of work and child outcomes, including the extent to which parent mental health was an explanatory mechanism.

We found that parents working in poor-quality jobs showed more psychological distress than those in good-quality jobs. Their children also showed more emotional and behavioral difficulties. Poorer parent mental health partially, but not fully, explained the pathway, and the associations held for both mothers' and fathers' jobs, after we adjusted for a wide range of confounders including income, parent education, and work hours. The findings confirmed other cross-sectional and longitudinal Australian studies on the mental health risk to adults from bad jobs.[26] Our study added evidence for an intergenerational transfer of risk from bad-quality jobs to children.

Given the changes in the timing of work, we have also investigated possible implications of work at unsociable times for children's well-being.[27] This study used survey data from the Canadian National Longitudinal Survey of Children and Youth (cycle 2, 1996–97) because it contained detailed information on both mothers' and fathers' work schedules, along with measures of parents' and children's well-being (comparable Australian data were not available at the time). Cross-sectional data were used to compare child outcomes in dual-earner households in which one or both parents usually worked unsociable hours (regularly worked weekends, evenings, or nights) with child outcomes in families in which both parents worked within standard weekday hours.

We found elevations in children's emotional and behavioral difficulties when one or both of their parents regularly worked nonstandard hours, which mirrored the findings from the job-quality analysis. The association between nonstandard work schedules and child difficulties was partially explained (mediated) by parent depressive symptoms and by hostile and inconsistent parenting. The associations, which were net of family income and parent education, were stronger for two- to four-year-old children than for children aged five to eleven years. Furthermore, links to child outcomes were evident when mothers or fathers worked nonstandard times, indicating that the timing of fathers' (not just mothers') work matters.

Exploring the Links between Work Time and Children

Thinking about work time as an individual property misses the way that time operates as a household resource.[28] Within households, time and what it can achieve are calibrated and traded among household members.[29] When both parents work, time is shifted into the labor market and away from care and from domestic production and consumption. Purchasing child care and services may help displace some of the time costs if families can afford them, and the time demand of caring for children changes over the life course. Thus, family capacity to shift time to the labor market varies, depending on children's age and family income. Furthermore, the way that time is allocated within families is profoundly gendered. Gendered wage differentials mean that maximizing fathers' capacity to work usually makes the most financial sense; hence mothers' care work helps free fathers' time for employment but limits mothers' labor market outcomes. Considering both parents' work time therefore is critical to any analysis of the family time economy and children's well-being; however, the majority of studies tend to focus on mothers' employment alone. Most studies show few or modest associations between children's well-being and mother's employment, and when negative consequences of early maternal employment are detected, the impacts are usually confined to full-time employment and apparent only for infants and young children.[30] Fathers' work hours are absent from most of these analyses, raising important questions about the role of fathers' jobs.

This study is a preliminary investigation of the association between parent work-hour arrangements and children's well-being in dual-earner (couple) families. We examine four different combinations of parent work hours, arrayed from least to greatest total work time investments of mothers and fathers. Our aim is to tease out work-related time and income consequences for children's well-being in Australian dual-earner families, comparing families in which parents adopt a one-and-a-half-worker arrangement with families in which both parents work full-time. We consider the relationship between income, time, and child well-being, asking whether the benefits of greater family income from full participation in the labor market outweigh the family time costs. Although preliminary, these analyses represent an attempt to model work-hour distributions of both mothers and fathers against child well-being while also accounting for the important role of income.

Method

Three waves of data from *Growing up in Australia: The Longitudinal Study of Australian Children (LSAC)* were used to investigate parent work time and child well-being. LSAC is a cross-sequential longitudinal study of two representative cohorts of Australian children who were born in 2000 and 2004.[31] Approximately 5,000 children from each cohort were sampled in 2004 and will be followed every two years until late adolescence. Children were sampled through the Medicare Australia database (which includes all Australian citizens and permanent residents) using a two-stage clustered sample design, first selecting postcodes and then children. Sample selection was stratified to maintain the proportional geographic representation of states and territories.

Our study uses data on children born in 2000 (the K cohort, age four to five years at wave 1) because there are comparable child outcomes in all three waves of data. At wave 3, when the children were eight to nine years of age, 86 percent of families from wave 1 had been retained in the study[32] although response rates vary for the different instruments used during data collection.[33] More details on the study can be found in discussion papers for the study.[34]

The primary respondent of the study was the parent who knew the most about the child (97 percent of primary respondents were mothers), and data were also collected from the child's other parent (including nonresident fathers) using self-complete questions. LSAC includes data collected on a range of topics related to the child, the parent, the family, the school, and the community in which the child lived. Waves 1 to 3 include data on both mothers' and fathers' job conditions and work hours and the study child's emotional and behavioral adjustment, allowing unique insight into the interplay between mothers' and fathers' jobs and children's well-being. For this study, the sample was restricted to two-parent families in which both parents were employed at the time of data collection and for which complete data were available on the measures of interest. We considered the emotional and behavioral difficulties of children as our marker of child well-being. The children were four to five years old at wave 1 ($n = 1,970$), six to seven years at wave 2 ($n = 1,952$), and eight to nine years at wave 3 ($n = 1,915$).

Measures

Household work-hour arrangements were classified into four groups. Mothers' and fathers' work hours were cross-classified. Mothers' work hours were classified as either part-time (less than thirty-five hours) or full-time hours (thirty-five hours or more). Fathers' work hours were classified as either full-time (thirty-five to forty-five hours) or long hours (greater than forty-five hours). Very few fathers in LSAC work part-time (6 to 7 percent across the waves) and few mothers work long hours (7 to 9 percent across the waves), so these groups could not be considered separately. Families in which mothers worked part-time and fathers worked long hours were the most common arrangement at all three time points, and 60 percent of families maintained this arrangement for the next four years of available data. Given their stability and size, we used these families as the reference group in the multivariate analyses.

Child emotional and behavioral difficulties were measured with the Strengths and Difficulties Questionnaire (SDQ).[35] The SDQ was used to assess children's emotional distress ("Often unhappy, downhearted, or tearful"), conduct and oppositional behaviors ("Often has temper tantrums or hot tempers"), hyperactivity and inattention ("Restless, overactive, cannot stay still for long"), and peer problems ("Picked on or bullied by other children"). The SDQ was rated by the primary parent of the child, so this measure largely reflects mothers' report of children's well-being. An overall child difficulties score was formed by summing the twenty items (response categories 0 =*not true*, 1 = *somewhat true*, and 2 = *certainly true*), yielding a possible range of 0–40 points, with higher scores indicating more difficulties. SDQ scores decreased over the waves, indicating fewer emotional and behavioral problems as children age.

We used gross equivalized household income in analyses. Household income was topcoded to $130,000 and equivalized by dividing by the square root of the number of people in the household to represent income proportionate to family need.[36] Equivalized income was centered for all multivariate analyses.[37] Gross household weekly income and gross household banded income are used for descriptive purposes only.

Statistical Approach

Given that multi-wave data were available, we used generalized estimating equation (GEE) models to examine the averaged associations between work-hour arrangements and income with children's emotional and behavioral difficulties over time. The GEE approach meant that we could test for child age-specific effects by computing an interaction term (household work-hour arrangements by wave) to determine whether the association between hour arrangements differed by the age of the child. GEE models use a correlation structure that models the intercorrelations among repeated measures from the same child over time and can also accommodate time-dependent and time-varying covariates.

The primary goal of this study was to test for associations between household work-hour arrangements and child outcomes and to determine whether any association was consistent or varied across early and middle childhood. Due to data limitations, this study does not examine trajectories of child well-being linked to parent work-time arrangements (to do so requires more waves of data to draw robust conclusions).

Multivariate analyses adjusted for sociodemographic factors that might confound the associations between parents' work-hour arrangement, income, and their children's emotional and behavioral difficulties. Analyses are adjusted for gender of the child (1 = male, 2 = female), mothers' and fathers' years of education, age of youngest child (in years) in the household, and number of children in the household. Health selection may mean that parents with poorer health work shorter hours; we therefore also adjusted for mothers' and fathers' medical conditions (0 = no medical conditions, 1 = one medical condition or more that has lasted/is expected to last for six months or more).

Results

Our analyses used the following logic. First we assessed whether household income increased as combined parent work time increased and whether household income was associated with children's well-being (emotional and behavioral difficulties). The next analysis examined associations between children's well-being and combined parent work time. We considered children's well-being across four groupings of dual-earner work-hour arrangements to determine whether children in some arrangements fared better than others. These analyses also sought to tease out the role played by income, by first adjusting for family sociodemographics and covariates but not income and then adjusting for income. Finally, by interacting wave and parent work arrangements, we tested for age (wave) differences in the association between combined parent work hours and child well-being.

Families, Income, and Combined Work Time across the Three Waves

Table 4-1 presents descriptive statistics of the sociodemographic measures used. Approximately half the children in the sample were boys. Children's average SDQ scores decreased over time.[38] As expected, the age of the youngest child (not necessarily the study child) in the household increased in successive waves. Parents' years of education remained stable over the three waves, while mothers' work hours increased over time and fathers' hours did not.

Table 4-2 presents the average work hours of mothers, fathers, and the household across the four work-hour arrangements for the three waves. We find large differences in household work hours across the four work-time arrangements, especially when comparing families in which mothers work part-time to those in which mothers work full-time. For example, dual-earner families with the longest work-hour arrangement (mothers work full-time and fathers work long hours) worked thirty-five (wave 1), thirty-four (wave 2), or thirty-three (wave 3) more hours each week than families in which mothers worked part-time and fathers worked ordinary full-time hours.

Table 4-2 also confirms that long hours for fathers and part-time hours for mothers are the most common arrangement in LSAC. Across the three waves, almost half of the children lived in families in which mothers worked part-time (averaging between sixteen and nineteen hours a week) and fathers worked long hours (averaging fifty-five hours a week). The next-most-common arrangement (seen in about one-third of the families) involved mothers working part-time

Table 4-1. *Descriptive Statistics for Family Sociodemographics and Child Difficulties, by Wave*

Item	Wave 1 (4–5 years)	Wave 2 (6–7 years)	Wave 3 (8–9 years)
Child difficulties, mean (standard deviation)	8.50 (4.82)	7.89 (5.06)	7.50 (5.31)
Boys (percent)	49.3	50.5	51.1
Income, mean (standard deviation)[a]	$38,910.50 ($14,909.98)	$37,140.55 ($16,651.77)	$41,091.19 ($17,051.37)
Annual gross income, percent (number of families)			
$0–31,199	3.0 (60)	1.4 (27)	1.0 (19)
$31,200–51,999	15.9 (314)	7.4 (145)	4.6 (89)
$52,000–77,999	31.8 (627)	26.4 (516)	18.9 (362)
$78,000–114,399	31.5 (621)	37.4 (730)	36.2 (694)
$114,400+	17.6 (347)	27.3 (533)	39.2 (751)
Years of education, mean (standard deviation)			
Mother	15.02 (2.47)	14.56 (2.57)	14.76 (2.52)
Father	14.92 (2.41)	14.76 (2.52)	14.76 (2.54)
Age of youngest child (percent)			
0–1	18.4	8.2	4.8
2–5	70.6	32.6	15.2
6–9[b]	10.2	58.5	80.3
Medical conditions (percent)[c]			
Mother	23.4	11.2	6.0
Father	20.5	9.2	6.1
Work hours, mean (standard deviation)			
Mother	21.24 (11.56)	24.95 (14.29)	26.60 (13.96)
Father	48.51 (11.38)	46.78 (13.13)	47.69 (13.31)
Household	69.74 (14.94)	59.75 (23.38)	63.20 (24.07)
Sample size	N = 1,970	N = 1,952	N = 1,915

Source: Data are from the Longitudinal Study of Australian Children.

a. Equivalized household income is measured as the gross annual household income (topcoded to $130,000) divided by the square root of the number of people in the household. Income is in Australian dollars.

b. Nine is the maximum age of the youngest child in the household in wave 3.

c. The medical condition questions are not consistent across waves; consequently, proportions are not comparable across waves.

hours (between eighteen and nineteen hours a week) and fathers working "ordinary" full-time hours (averaging thirty-nine hours a week). Household work-hour arrangements in which mothers worked full-time were relatively uncommon at all three waves. Between 10 and 11 percent of families had mothers working full-time

Table 4-2. *Mothers', Fathers', and Combined Household Work Hours for Dual-Earner Couples, by Work-Hour Arrangement*[a]

Work-hour arrangement	Percent of sample	Average work hours		
		Mothers	*Fathers*	*Household*
K cohort, wave 1 (4–5 years)				
Mother PT/Father FT	32.9	18.23 (8.27)	39.34 (1.72)	57.57 (8.42)
Mother PT/Father LH	47.8	16.25 (8.72)	55.83 (10.67)	72.08 (13.19)
Mother FT/Father FT	10.4	38.62 (1.83)	39.07 (1.68)	77.68 (2.99)
Mother FT/Father LH	8.9	38.98 (2.06)	54.06 (9.78)	93.04 (10.34)
K cohort, wave 2 (6–7 years)				
Mother PT/Father FT	32.5	18.71 (8.21)	39.25 (1.72)	57.96 (8.34)
Mother PT/Father LH	47.1	16.40 (8.36)	55.33 (10.06)	71.97 (12.30)
Mother FT/Father FT	10.7	38.21 (2.02)	39.18 (1.92)	77.40 (3.06)
Mother FT/Father LH	9.7	38.41 (2.15)	53.89 (9.95)	92.29 (10.00)
K cohort, wave 3 (8–9 years)				
Mother PT/Father FT	32.5	19.87 (7.92)	39.40 (1.69)	59.27 (8.16)
Mother PT/Father LH	45.7	18.41 (8.39)	55.71 (10.27)	74.11 (13.20)
Mother FT/Father FT	11.3	38.51 (2.05)	39.13 (1.75)	77.64 (2.94)
Mother FT/Father LH	10.5	38.39 (2.31)	53.83 (8.89)	92.22 (10.25)

Source: Data are from the Longitudinal Study of Australian Children.
a. PT (part-time) refers to working less than thirty-five hours a week; FT (full-time), between thirty-five and forty-five hours a week; and LH (long hours), more than forty-five hours a week. Standard deviations are given in parentheses.

with fathers working "ordinary" full-time hours, and another 9 to 10 percent of families had mothers working full-time while fathers worked long hours.

Figure 4-1 shows the average gross weekly income for each wave across the four parent work-hour arrangements. As expected, household income increased over waves for each of the work arrangements—that is, families with mothers working full-time and fathers working long hours showed an average increase in gross (before tax) weekly income of AU$663 between wave 1 and 3. The figure also confirms that as parents' combined work time went up, so did family income. Dual-earner families working the longest combined weekly hours (mothers worked full-time and fathers worked long hours) grossed on average AU$479 more each week than families in which mothers worked part-time and fathers worked full-time hours (at wave 1). Table 4-2 shows that these families worked virtually an extra full-time job to earn considerably less than the national minimum wage (the national minimum wage in 2011 was AU$589.30, based on thirty-eight hours per week). Thus, income does increase as parent work time

Figure 4-1. *Average Weekly Income, by Household Work-Hour Arrangement and Wave*[a]

Average weekly income

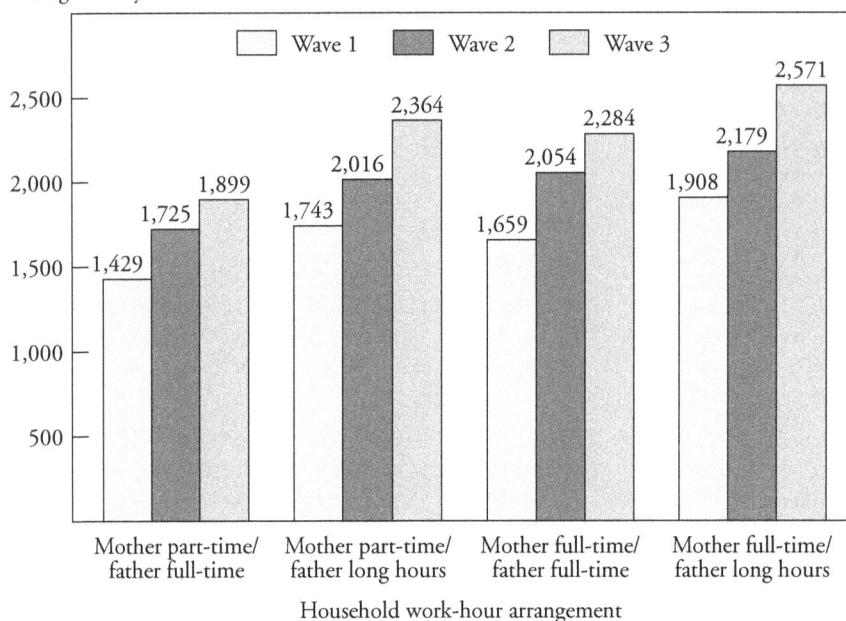

Source: Data are from the Longitudinal Study of Australian Children.
a. Approximately 12 percent of the data in wave 1 are missing because of the way that income questions were structured. Income is given in Australian dollars.

increases. However, in the context of the Australian labor market, large additional time investments from families do not deliver large increases in income.

A GEE analysis tested whether these differences in income across household work-hour arrangements (shown in figure 4-1) were statistically significant.[39] Families in which mothers worked part-time and fathers worked long hours were the reference group. Analyses confirm that families in which mothers worked part-time and fathers worked full-time had significantly lower equivalized income (*beta* = -0.338, standard error = 0.058, p < .001)[40] and that families in which both parents worked full-time (*beta* = 0.488, standard error = 0.089, p < .001) or mothers worked full-time and fathers worked long hours (*beta* = 0.826, standard error = 0.100, p < .001) had significantly higher equivalized household income than the reference group.

Although these analyses show that family income is higher when parents invest more time in employment, the increase in income was surprisingly modest relative to the extra time worked.

Table 4-3. *GEE Models for Income and Household Work-Hour Arrangements Predicting Children's Emotional and Behavioral Well-Being*[a]

Model	Estimate	Standard error	95 percent confidence interval
Model 1			
Income	–0.078**	0.026	–0.130 — –0.026
Model 2			
Work-hour arrangement			
Mother PT/Father FT	0.130	0.125	–0.114 — 0.374
Mother PT/Father LH	Reference	Reference	Reference
Mother FT/Father FT	0.550**	0.192	0.173 — 0.927
Mother FT/Father LH	0.371*	0.189	0.001 — 0.740
Model 3			
Income	–0.110***	0.030	–0.169 — –0.052
Work-hour arrangement			
Mother PT/Father FT	0.092	0.125	–0.151 — 0.336
Mother PT/Father LH	Reference	Reference	Reference
Mother FT/Father FT	0.577**	0.192	0.201 — 0.954
Mother FT/Father LH	0.434*	0.190	0.062 — 0.807

Source: Data are from the Longitudinal Study of Australian Children.

a. All analyses were adjusted for wave, child gender, number of children in the household, age of youngest child in the household, mother and father education, and mother and father medical conditions. PT (part-time) refers to working less than thirty-five hours a week; FT (full-time), between thirty-five and forty-five hours a week; and LH (long hours), more than forty-five hours a week. * $p < .05$, ** $p < .01$, *** $p < .001$.

Multi-Wave Modeling

The previous analyses confirm that parent work-hour arrangements and family income were associated, although the gains in income required parents to reallocate large amounts of time to the labor market. The next analyses seek to clarify the associations between income, combined parent work hours, and children's well-being.

Table 4-3 presents the results of the GEE models of children's emotional and behavioral difficulties (SDQ scores), adjusted for wave, child gender, number of children in the household, age of youngest child in the household, mother and father education, and mother and father medical conditions. Model 1 shows that as household income increased, outcomes for children were better. Even in this relatively affluent sample of dual-earner families, higher income is significantly associated with fewer child emotional and behavioral difficulties.

Model 2 considers whether children's difficulties varied by parent work-time arrangements, without adjusting for income. If the income benefits of higher work hours outweigh the family time costs, we would expect to see an effect size and direction of association similar to those with income in model 1. However, our analysis shows that household work-hour arrangements were associated with child SDQ scores in the opposite direction: that is, as work hours increased, child well-being decreased. Thus, despite higher income, children in families with mothers working full-time and fathers working full-time or long hours have significantly poorer emotional and behavioral well-being than children in families in which mothers worked part-time and fathers worked long hours. Note that there were no differences in outcomes between children whose mothers worked part-time and fathers worked full-time and those whose mothers worked part-time and fathers worked long hours.

Finally, to tease out any independent roles played by income and by work-hour arrangements, we modeled income and work arrangements together (model 3 in table 4-3). We observe only minor changes in coefficients, suggesting that income and household work hours have independent and opposing effects on the well-being of children aged four to nine years. Although we cannot directly compare nested GEE models, we wanted to further evaluate the importance of parent work hours for children. Therefore, we contrasted random intercept models and confirmed the significant contribution of parent work hours. The likelihood ratio test indicated that including work-hour arrangements in the model made for a better model fit than did just modeling the effect of income on children's well-being ($\chi^2 = 11.18$, $df = 3$, $p = .010$).

Does the association between combined parent work hours and well-being depend on children's age? An advantage of the GEE approach is that it allows testing for age effects. Most research on parent work hours or employment (which usually focuses on maternal employment) detects negative effects (if any) only for younger children. Therefore we expected to see a stronger association at wave 1, before children attended school. We found marginal support for that association, but only for children in families in which mothers worked full-time and fathers worked long hours (*beta* = –0.610, standard error = 0.336, $p < .07$). Consequently, we explored the relationship between parent work-hour arrangements and children's well-being separately for each wave.

Figure 4-2 presents the estimated marginal means, using adjusted analysis of variance (ANOVA) for children's emotional and behavioral difficulties by combined work-hour arrangement. The pattern for the younger children (ages four to five years and six to seven years) mirrors our GEE results. Children had significantly higher SDQ scores when their mothers worked full-time and their fathers worked full-time or long hours than they did when their mothers worked part-time and their fathers worked full-time or long hours. However, once children reached eight to nine years of age, the pattern appears to be

Figure 4-2. *Average Annual Income, by Household Work-Hour Arrangement*[a]

Average annual income

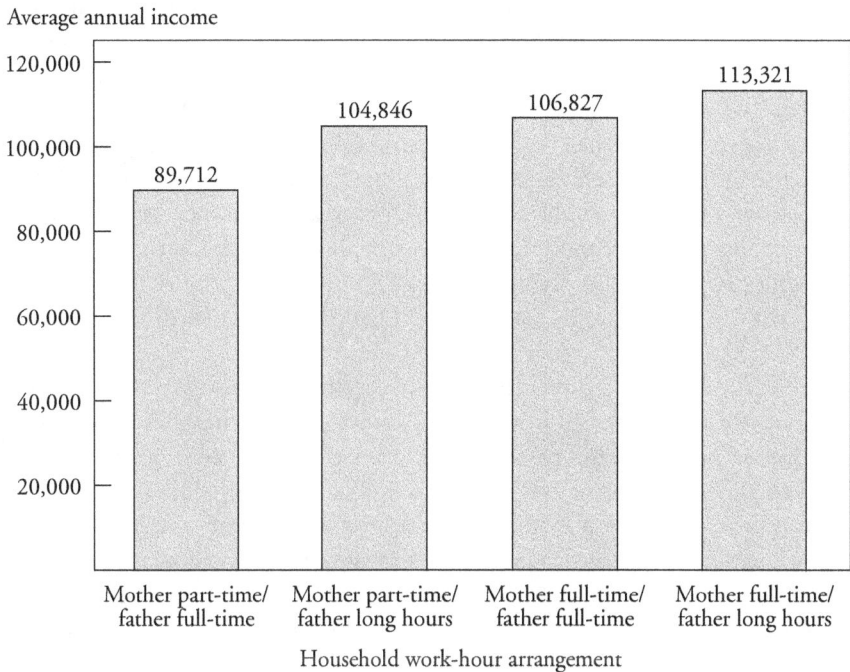

Source: Data are from the Longitudinal Study of Australian Children.

a. These data are from dual-earner households with complete data only. Annual household income rather than equivalized income is used. Income is given in Australian dollars.

weaker, suggesting little to no association between longer combined parent work hours and poorer child emotional and behavioral outcomes.

Discussion

We consider here the interplay between household income and combinations of parent employment hours in three waves of data on Australian children. Instead of finding that income trumped time in terms of children's outcomes—or vice versa—we find that family income and parent's joint work time show opposite and independent associations with children's well-being.

As expected, household income went up when parents invested more time in the labor market and greater income was associated with fewer child emotional and behavioral difficulties, even in these relatively affluent dual-earner families. However, the gains in income were relatively modest compared with the extra hours that parents worked. There were large increases in hours in families in which both parents worked full-time, compared with families where one parent (nearly always mothers) worked part-time. Even though family income was higher if both parents worked full-time, we found that children's well-being was worse when combined parent work time went up, and that association held whether we adjusted for income (among other confounders) or not. We also found suggestive evidence that any negative impact of combined parent work time may attenuate as children grow up, but we await further waves of data to robustly test for this possibility. Our findings reveal that in dual-earner families, full-time participation of mothers led to some income-related benefits for children but that the benefits did not outweigh the time costs.

Limitations

The elevations in child difficulties were observed in households with relatively long joint work hours, but it was hard to tease out separate roles for mothers' and fathers' hours. Although children did better in families in which mothers worked part-time (irrespective of fathers' full-time or long hours), we caution against the interpretation that it is mothers' work hours that matter. We cannot test a counterfactual that having *one* parent work part-time hours is protective for children's mental health because so few fathers in Australia work part-time. At most, our data suggest that long joint hours could pose a mental health risk to children between four and nine years of age.

Cell sizes limited our capacity to test for lagged effects of parent work-time arrangements on children, and LSAC currently does not have sufficient waves to test for trajectories. Therefore, these more complex and definitive analyses await further waves of data. In this analysis we did not consider the quality of jobs across work-hour categories or whether parents worked at unsociable hours. Our previous work indicated that job quality and the timing of work are important to children. This study finds that the quantity of time that parents devote to paid work also matters for child outcomes. Future work needs to consider how job quality, work schedules, and the quantity of hours worked may coalesce to influence children's well-being.

Furthermore, this study considers only couple families that were dual-earner households, which are not yet an explicit target of labor market participation policies. In Australia, the focus has largely been on the employment of lone parents; nearly half (48 percent) of all children under 15 years of age in Australia who live in lone-parent families are living with a parent, usually their mother, who is not employed.[41] The relatively small numbers of lone mothers in LSAC limited our capacity to consider associations with child well-being across varying work arrangements.

Participation, Well-Being, and Gender

As the economic pressures of population aging intensify, participation policy may consider encouraging all parents to be fully engaged in the labor market. The vast majority of lone parents and full-time caregivers are women, as are the vast majority of part-time workers. Within the families that we studied, the majority of mothers worked short part-time hours (less than twenty hours per week) and the majority of fathers worked very long hours, averaging around fifty-five hours a week. Therefore, there is a distinct gender dimension to increasing parent participation that requires careful consideration.

Working part-time and shouldering the major responsibility for unpaid work as caregivers locks many mothers out of influential, well-paid positions, embedding gender discrimination in the labor market and decision making. Helping address the economic problem of population aging by increasing work hours for all mothers might help advance gender equity objectives. However, full-time work hours in Australia already rank among the highest in the OECD countries[42] and the historical declines in work time observed over the past century appear to have halted and even begun to reverse in the United States, Australia, Canada, and the United Kingdom.[43] For example, one-third of men employed full-time worked fifty hours a week or more in 2005, while only 22 percent did so in 1985.[44] Because fathers in Australia already work long hours in paid employment, increasing mother's work hours may have profound implications for household time if fathers continue to work long hours. In both the United States and Australia, mothers who are employed full-time and have young children report poorer self-rated physical health and more psychological distress than do mothers working part-time.[45] Therefore, increasing the work hours of mothers without addressing the role played by fathers' work hours may inadvertently undermine gender equity because it erodes mothers' well-being.

Implications for Public Policy

In the next four decades, the Australian population pyramid will invert, doubling the ratio of people over 65 years of age to those of working age. If full parent labor market participation becomes a policy target (that is, both parents are encouraged to work full-time), interventions to minimize the time trade-offs faced by parents will be needed if both economic and child development policy goals are to be met.

Our previous studies on job quality and work-time scheduling demonstrate the potential importance of labor market conditions for children. These studies indicated that children fared better if their mothers or fathers worked in good-quality jobs (jobs with security, autonomy, flexible hours, and paid leave for family care) in which hours were largely standard (weekdays, between 8:00 a.m. and 6:00 p.m.). The current study adds the problem of long combined work hours for families and for children.

Within families, decisions about maternal labor force participation often are made in the context of fathers' work hours, yet the consequences of these intertwined and apparently private decisions may be far-reaching. For example, time-use studies indicate that as women increase their paid work time, men further increase their paid work hours (rather than increase unpaid work).[46] If that is the case, then this gendered mechanism will escalate long work-hour expectations for full-time jobs across the labor market, making them increasingly difficult for families to manage. Our findings suggest that for policy to address the triple objective of full participation, gender equity, and child well-being, fathers' work time (not mothers) may need to be addressed—a counterintuitive idea.

We have argued that workforce participation, gender equity, and child well-being policy objectives are interdependent rather than separate. To achieve all three requires a more complex and refined understanding of family-friendly work, of which legislated paid parental leave in Australia is a historic first step. Policymakers may need to address a broader range of work characteristics than just income, including autonomy, security, flexibility, scheduling of jobs, and full-time work-hour expectations to enable fuller participation of mothers without compromising their own or their children's well-being.

Paradoxically, policy responses to population aging could therefore have profound implications for children. This study underlines the complexity of any policy efforts to increase full-time employment for parents. Although who works what hours is negotiated within families, the real driver is the amount of hours expected for a full-time job, and that issue rests with national and workplace employment policies and culture. These polices and cultures are forces beyond the individual parent's control, and they will be challenging policy targets.

Notes

1. Australian Bureau of Statistics, "Families Week Facts and Figures" (Canberra: 2008).

2. Ibid.

3. Australian Bureau of Statistics, "Australian Labour Market Statistics," No. 6105.0 (Canberra: 2009).

4. Australian Bureau of Statistics, "Families Week Facts and Figures."

5. Robert H. Bradley and Robert F. Corwyn, "Socioeconomic Status and Child Development," *Annual Review of Psychology*, vol. 53 (2002), p. 371; Mary Corcoran and others, "How Welfare Reform Is Affecting Women's Work," *Annual Review of Sociology*, vol. 26 (2000), p. 241.

6. Lyndall Strazdins and others, "What Does Family Friendly Really Mean? Well-Being, Time, and the Quality of Parents' Jobs," *Australian Bulletin of Labour*, vol. 33 (2007), p. 202.

7. David M. Almeida and others, "Daily Transmission of Tensions between Marital Dyads and Parent-Child Dyads," *Journal of Marriage and the Family*, vol. 61 (1999), p. 49; David M. Almeida, "Using Daily Diaries to Assess Temporal Friction between Work and Family," in *Work-Family Challenges for Low-Income Families and Their Children*, edited by Ann C. Crouter and Alan Booth (Mahwah, N.J.: Lawrence Earlbaum, 2004), pp. 127; Rena L. Repetti, "Short-Term and Long-Term Processes Linking Job Stressors to Father-Child Interaction," *Social Development*, vol. 3 (1994), p. 1.

8. Repetti, "Short-Term and Long-Term Processes Linking Job Stressors to Father-Child Interaction," p. 1.

9. Geraldine Downey and James C. Coyne, "Children of Depressed Parents: An Integrative Review," *Psychological Bulletin*, vol. 108 (1990), p. 50; M. C. Lovejoy and others, "Maternal Depression and Parenting Behaviour: A Meta-Analytic Review," *Clinical Psychology Review*, vol. 20 (2000), p. 561; Vicky Phares and Bruce E. Compass, "The Role of Fathers in Child and Adolescent Psychopathology: Make Room for Daddy," *Psychological Bulletin*, vol. 111 (1992), p. 387.

10. Michael Marmot and others, "Health and the Psychosocial Environment at Work," in *Social Determinants of Health*, edited by Michael Marmot and Richard G. Wilkinson (Oxford University Press, 1999), p. 105.

11. Donald Cole and others, "Work and Life Stressors and Psychological Distress in the Canadian Working Population: A Structural Equation Modelling Approach to Analysis of the 1994 National Population Health Survey," *Chronic Diseases in Canada*, vol. 23 (2002), p. 91; Lyndall Strazdins and others, "Job Strain, Job Insecurity, and Health: Rethinking the Relationship," *Journal of Occupational and Health Psychology*, vol. 9 (2004), p. 296.

12. P. Butterworth and others, "The Psychosocial Quality of Work Determines Whether Employment Has Benefits for Mental Health: Results from a Longitudinal National Household Panel Survey," *Occupational and Environmental Medicine*, vol. 68 (2011), pp. 806–12.

13. Iain Campbell, "Casual Work and Casualisation: How Does Australia Compare?" *Labour and Industry*, vol. 15 (2004), p. 85.

14. Anni Weiler, "Annual Review of Working Conditions in the EU: 2004–2005" (Dublin, Ireland: European Foundation for the Improvement of Living and Working Conditions, 2005).

15. See OECD, "Clocking In and Clocking Out: Recent Trends in Working Hours," Policy Brief (2004) (www.oecd.org/dataoecd/42/49/33821328.pdf).

16. Australian Bureau of Statistics, "Working Time Arrangements," No. 6224.0 (Canberra: 2009).

17. Sangheon Lee and others, *Working Time around the World: Trends in Working Hours, Laws, and Policies in a Global Comparative Perspective* (London: Routledge, 2007).

18. Sara Charlesworth and others, "Parents' Jobs in Australia: Work Hours Polarisation and the Consequences for Job Quality and Gender Equality," *Australian Journal of Labour Economics*, vol. 14, no. 1 (2011), pp. 35–57.

19. Harriet B. Presser, *Working in a 24/7 Economy: Challenges for American Families* (New York: Russell Sage Foundation, 2003); Harriet B. Presser, "Toward a 24-Hour Economy," *Science*, vol. 284 (1999), p. 1778; Jennifer Glass, "Envisioning the Integration of Family and Work: Toward a Kinder, Gentler, Workplace," *Contemporary Sociology*, vol. 29 (2000), p. 129.

20. Ian Watson and others, *Fragmented Futures: New Challenges in Working Life* (Sydney: Federation Press, 2003).

21. Ibid.

22. Presser, "Toward a 24-Hour Economy," p. 1778.

23. Strazdins and others, "What Does Family Friendly Really Mean?" p. 202.

24. Most definitions include a measure of pay, although this index focuses on job conditions only.

25. Lyndall Strazdins and others, "Job Quality and Inequality: Parents' Jobs and Children's Emotional and Behavioural Difficulties," *Social Science and Medicine*, vol. 70 (2010), p. 2052.

26. Dorothy H. Broom and others, "The Lesser Evil: Bad Jobs or Unemployment? A Survey of Mid-Aged Australians," *Social Science and Medicine*, vol. 63 (2006), p. 575; Peter Butterworth and others, "Psychosocial Job Adversity and Health in Australia: Analysis of Data from the HILDA Survey," *Australian and New Zealand Journal of Public Health*, forthcoming; Liana S. Leach and others, "No Magic Bullet: The Limitations of Employment as a Tool for Social Inclusion Policy," October 2010 (www.ncbi.nlm.nih.gov/pmc/articles/PMC2972242).

27. Lyndall Strazdins and others, "Unsociable Work? Nonstandard Work Schedules, Family Relationships, and Children's Well-Being," *Journal of Marriage and the Family*, vol. 68 (2006), p. 394.

28. Jerry A. Jacobs and Kathleen Gerson, *The Time Divide: Work, Family, and Gender Inequality* (Harvard University Press, 2004).

29. Gary S. Becker, "A Theory of the Allocation of Time," *Economic Journal*, vol. 75 (1965), p. 493.

30. Jeanne Brooks-Gunn and others, "Maternal Employment and Child Cognitive Outcomes in the First Three Years of Life: The NICHD Study of Early Child Care," *Child Development*, vol. 73 (2002), p. 1052; Paul Gregg and others, "The Effects of Mothers' Return-to-Work Decision on Child Development in the UK," *Economic Journal*, vol. 115 (2005), p. 48.

31. Carol Soloff and others, "Sample Design," LSAC Technical Paper 1 (Melbourne: Australian Institute of Family Studies, 2005).

32. Mark Sipthorp and Sebastian Misson, "Wave 3 Weighting and Non-Response" (Melbourne: Australian Institute of Family Studies, 2009).

33. For example, more data are missing in the parent self-complete questionnaires than in the face-to-face interview with the primary caregiver.

34. Anne Sanson and others, "Introducing the Longitudinal Study of Australian Children," LSAC Discussion Paper 1 (Melbourne: Australian Institute of Family Studies, 2002); Carol Soloff and others, "Proposed Study Design and Wave 1 Data Collection," LSAC Discussion Paper 2 (Melbourne: Australian Institute of Family Studies, 2002).

35. Robert Goodman, "The Strengths and Difficulties Questionnaire: A Research Note," *Journal of Child Psychology and Psychiatry*, vol. 38 (1997), p. 581.

36. Anthony B. Atkinson and others, "Income Distribution in OECD Countries: Evidence from Luxembourg Income Study," Social Policy Studies 18 (Paris: OECD, 1995).

37. Sensitivity analyses were conducted and patterns of results were similar when income was not topcoded or centered.

38. Robert Goodman, "Using the Strengths and Difficulties Questionnaire (SDQ) to Screen for Child Psychiatric Disorders in a Community Sample," *British Journal of Psychiatry*,

vol. 177 (2000), p. 534; Robert Goodman and others, "Predicting Type of Psychiatric Disorder from Strengths and Difficulties Questionnaire (SDQ) Scores in Child Mental Health Clinics in London and Dhaka," *European Child and Adolescent Psychiatry*, vol. 9 (2000), p. 129.

39. The model was adjusted for wave, child gender, number of children in the household, age of youngest child in the household, mother and father education, and mother and father medical conditions.

40. An interaction between work-hour arrangements and income on children's well-being was also modeled. We used families in which mothers worked part-time and fathers worked full-time as the comparison group. We found that income had a significant impact on the well-being of children in families in which mothers worked part-time and father worked full-time (which tended to have the lowest household income), but not in families in which mothers worked full-time and fathers worked full-time or long hours.

41. Australian Bureau of Statistics, "Working Time Arrangements."

42. OECD, "Clocking In and Clocking Out: Recent Trends in Working Hours."

43. Jonathan Gershuny, "Increasing Paid Work Time? A New Puzzle for Multinational Time-Diary Research," *Social Indicators Research*, vol. 101 (2011), p. 207.

44. Australian Bureau of Statistics, "Australian Social Trends 2006," No. 4102.0 (Canberra: 2006).

45. Jennifer Baxter and others, "Mothers and Fathers with Young Children: Paid Employment, Caring, and Well-Being," Social Policy Research Paper 30 (Canberra: Australian Government Department of Families, Community Services, and Indigenous Affairs, 2007); Jason Schnittker, "Working More and Feeling Better: Women's Health, Employment, and Family Life 1974–2004," *American Sociological Review*, vol. 72 (2007), p. 221.

46. Gershuny, "Increasing Paid Work Time?" pp. 207–13.

5

The Impact of Child Care Subsidies on the Quality of Care that Two-Year-Old Children Receive

ANNA JOHNSON AND REBECCA RYAN

A large literature suggests that high-quality child care in the first five years of life can improve low-income children's readiness for school.[1] However, low-income parents struggle to afford high-quality care, spending a greater proportion of their income on child care than their middle- and upper-income counterparts[2] and experiencing lower-quality arrangements on average than their more affluent peers.[3] To help low-income families afford child care, the U.S. federal government provides child care subsidies through the state-administered Child Care and Development Fund (CCDF), now among the federal government's largest child care programs.[4] Although subsidies reduce families' cost of care[5] and facilitate parental employment,[6] it is less clear whether parents use subsidies to purchase higher-quality care than they would otherwise. Of particular interest is whether subsidies elevate child care quality for children under three years of age, for whom other publicly funded care options are more limited and on whom caregiving environments may exert their greatest developmental influence.[7]

This study addresses that issue, asking whether families who receive a child care subsidy choose higher-quality care for their two-year-old children than comparable families who do not. Studies of preschool children suggest that subsidy receipt can elevate the quality of care that low-income children receive under certain conditions.[8] To date, no studies have examined whether that association holds for toddlers. Given that nearly one-third of the approximately 2 million children served by the CCDF in 2008 were age two or younger,[9] it is especially important to consider how subsidy receipt may impact the child care environments of the youngest children. In this study, we used newly available, nationally representative data from the Early Childhood Longitudinal Study–Birth Cohort (ECLS-B) to examine that question. The ECLS-B is an ideal data source for this inquiry; it is the first and only nationally representative U.S. dataset designed to collect information on children's early home and learning environments from birth through kindergarten entry. The ECLS-B includes information on subsidy receipt, child care arrangements, and child care quality as well as rich data on child and family background characteristics, all collected prospectively. Moreover, data are collected from multiple sources, including parents and child care providers, allowing us to construct a more reliable measure of subsidy receipt than one based on parent report alone. And, unlike many national studies, the ECLS-B includes direct, observational measures of child care quality. Together, these unique features of the ECLS-B permit us to address our analytic goal of assessing the impact of subsidy receipt on quality in a way that no other dataset could.

The Child Care Subsidy Program

The primary goal of the CCDF subsidy program, enacted as part of the 1996 welfare reform legislation, is to support the economic independence of low-income parents by reducing out-of-pocket child care costs, thereby facilitating parental employment. Child care subsidies are most often provided as vouchers that eligible parents can use to purchase nearly any kind of nonparental child care that fits their needs. Some states also use their CCDF dollars to fund a portion of subsidized care through contracts negotiated directly with child care providers.[10] Families who receive welfare and low-income families who meet state-determined income and work requirements are eligible for subsidies.

Although recent evidence suggests that the CCDF program is achieving its primary aim of supporting economic self sufficiency,[11] less is known about whether subsidies impact the quality of care that parents choose. Theoretically, parents with a child care subsidy should purchase higher-quality child care than comparable families without one because subsidies decrease income constraints and increase purchasing power, multiplying child care options. That theory could be supported only if high-quality child care—or at least options that range in quality—were available in recipients' child care markets and subsidies were generous enough to cover the cost of such care. However, research suggests that the supply of regulated care is limited and that often the average quality of care is quite poor in low-income communities, where subsidy recipients typically reside.[12] It is also possible that certain features of the subsidy program itself may undermine recipients' ability to purchase high-quality care. Adams and

Rohacek explain that given limited funding and high demand for subsidies, many states (understandably) choose to cover more families instead of increasing the value of subsidies.[13] As a result, subsidies are often not generous enough to cover the cost of high-quality care. Moreover, subsidies reimburse providers (or pay parents) at providers' average rates, with the aim of increasing access to existing providers.[14] For these reasons, parents may use subsidies to purchase the same quality of care that they would otherwise purchase but pay less (or nothing) for it, making child care subsidies an effective work support for parents and a potentially useful cash transfer but not a support for early child development.

Previous Research

Prior studies have investigated the broad question of associations between child care subsidy use and child care quality. In addition to focusing almost exclusively on preschool-aged children, this body of work suffers from methodological problems that limit understanding of the subsidy–quality association. First, much of the earlier work has compared the types of care that recipients and nonrecipients use to proxy quality, or they have used maternal reports of child care quality rather than observed quality itself. The consensus from those studies is that parents who use subsidies are more likely to choose center- versus home-based care than demographically similar parents who do not use subsidies[15] and are more likely to choose licensed care—both center- and home-based—than comparable nonrecipients.[16] Studies that have used maternal reports of child care quality or satisfaction with care find evidence that subsidy recipients use higher-quality care,[17] but a separate body of research has found that parental ratings of child care quality tend to be inconsistent with ratings by professional observers trained to monitor developmental quality.[18] Although many infer from those studies that subsidies allow parents to purchase more developmentally enriching care than they would otherwise, the studies do not provide empirical evidence that that is the case. To conclude that subsidies lead to higher-quality care, direct, observational measures of developmental quality are needed.

Second, due to the limitations of available data, previous research has not been able to address the two levels of selection bias that plague nonexperimental work on this topic: not all families are eligible for subsidies, and among eligible families, not all choose to use or are granted subsidies. Comparing the quality of care used by subsidy recipients to that used by a heterogeneous population of nonrecipients, some of whom may not be eligible for subsidies, can produce misleading estimates of the effect of subsidies on quality if unobserved characteristics that determine subsidy eligibility also influence parents' selection of their child care arrangement. For example, some studies have found that centers serving larger proportions of subsidized children are lower in quality than those serving none or fewer.[19] However, because subsidies are reserved for low-income families, it is not surprising that centers serving subsidized children are of lower quality on average than those serving nonsubsidized children. The latter group is probably more affluent, and more affluent families tend to purchase higher-quality care.[20] Although these analyses demonstrate that subsidies do not elevate low-income families' quality of care to equal that of relatively affluent families, they do not identify whether subsidies elevate low-income families' quality of care above that of socioeconomically comparable, unsubsidized families. To answer the latter question, it is important to compare families who are equally eligible for and likely to obtain child care subsidies.

A study by Weinraub and colleagues[21] did directly compare the quality of preschool child care used by subsidy recipients and nonrecipients in a sample of low-income African American families living in Philadelphia. They found that quality did not differ between the groups even though recipients were more likely to use licensed, center-based care, suggesting that even if receiving a subsidy allows families to move to center-based care, it does not necessarily allow them to choose care of higher quality than they would otherwise. This study's sample was ethnically and geographically homogenous, so it is not clear that its findings generalize to the broader population of subsidy recipients. Most important, however, the authors were not able to account for differences in use of subsidies by eligible parents. We know that not all eligible families received subsidies, as the take-up rate of subsidies among likely eligible households ranges between 14 percent and 40 percent.[22] Moreover, studies comparing the characteristics of subsidy recipients with those of eligible nonrecipients find that they differ on demographic characteristics that are associated with subsidy receipt, such as maternal age, race/ethnicity, and education level.[23] It is important to account for this apparent differential selection into subsidy receipt among eligible families when estimating the effect of subsidy receipt on child care choices.

In previous work, we attempted to address these limitations by using observational measures of child care quality, limiting our sample to families who are likely to be eligible for subsidies, and statistically adjusting for differences between the recipients and eligible nonrecipients of subsidies. Overall, we have found relatively consistent positive effects of subsidy receipt on child care quality for preschoolers across two datasets: the Fragile Families and Child Well-Being Study (FFCWS) Child Care Supplement (CCS)[24] and the preschool wave of the ECLS-B.[25] In the first study, we found that subsidies lead to higher-quality care but that recipients' greater use of center-based care accounted entirely for that positive main effect. Moreover, in subgroup analyses we found that subsidies led to higher-quality care among children using home-based care but not among children using center-based care. Regarding the latter finding, we suspected that some eligible nonrecipients in center-based care may have been using high-quality, publicly funded programs such as Head Start or public prekindergarten and that our comparison may have masked a positive effect of subsidy receipt among those using community-based centers. However, we were not able to formally test that theory because of sample size limitations. We were also unable to investigate whether subsidies were associated with quality for toddlers, as all children in the FFCWS CCS were three years old.

In the second study, Johnson and colleagues found support for the latter hypothesis. Specifically, subsidy receipt led parents to use higher-quality care for their preschool-aged children when the comparison group was limited to likely eligible nonrecipients who used some form of unsubsidized care. However, subsidy recipients received *lower-quality* care than likely eligible nonrecipients who used another form of publicly funded care such as Head Start or public prekindergarten. Further analyses suggested that, as Ryan and others found, the positive effect of subsidies when compared with unsubsidized care was explained by greater use of center-based care and by use of higher-quality home-based care. Although this study did not examine effects for younger children, its findings raised questions about what the association between subsidy receipt and child care quality would be for two-year-olds who have far more limited public alternatives available to them.

Hypotheses

Our hypotheses build on our prior work in this area, which suggests that for preschoolers, subsidy recipients use higher-quality care than eligible nonrecipients who use either home-based care or no other form of subsidized care. We hypothesize that the effect of subsidy receipt on quality will be positive overall and across care types among two-year-olds. Unlike low-income preschoolers, who have the option of Head Start or public prekindergarten as well as community-based centers and home-based care, choices for low-income toddlers are limited to community-based centers and various forms of home-based care.[26] Thus, subsidies are the only publicly funded care option for low-income toddlers, with the exception of Early Head Start, which is not widely available. Because subsidies are associated with the use of higher-quality care for preschoolers who receive unsubsidized or home-based care and toddlers are limited to these scenarios, we expect that subsidy receipt will be associated with the use of higher-quality care by parents of two-year-olds, that this association will not be accounted for entirely by greater use of center-based care among subsidy recipients, and that this association will hold across center- and home-based care arrangements.

Method

To test these hypotheses, we draw data from the nationally representative ECLS-B, the first and only nationally representative U.S. dataset that contains information on child care subsidy receipt and observed child care quality during early childhood. We reduce the full ECLS-B sample to those families that are likely to be eligible for subsidies and employ two analytic strategies to address the selection of eligible families into subsidy receipt. These data and methods are described below.

Data Source

The ECLS-B was designed to capture detailed information on children's early home and educational environments as well as their cognitive and social development from birth through kindergarten entry.[27] To that end, the ECLS-B gathered data from multiple sources, across multiple time points, on a representative cohort of children born in the United States in 2001. Approximately 14,000 birth certificates were sampled from ninety-six geographic areas that included counties or clusters of counties.

From the sample of birth certificates, approximately 10,700 children participated in the first wave of ECLS-B data collection, in 2001, when study children were approximately nine months old. Three subsequent waves of data collection followed: wave 2, in 2003, when children were approximately two years old; wave 3, in 2005–06, when children were in preschool; and wave 4, in 2006-07, when children were in kindergarten. The current study uses data from the nine-month (wave 1) and two-year (wave 2) waves. Response rates across both waves were high (ranging from 74 percent to 93 percent), and weights were created to account for sampling and survey nonresponse; once applied, the weights adjust the sample to be representative of all children born in the United States in 2001.

Across all waves of data collection, the child's primary caregiver (almost always the child's biological mother) was interviewed and the child's cognitive, social, and physical growth was assessed. In the two-year and preschool waves, child care providers completed phone interviews in which they responded to questions about their program type and funding sources, number of children served, licensing or regulation status, and policies on accepting subsidized children. Also, direct observational assessments of children's care settings were conducted with a subsample (by design) of children in the two-year and preschool waves ($N \approx 1,500$ for the two-year wave). Those observational assessments, designed to measure the developmental quality of the care arrangements, were conducted in both center- and home-based settings. For center-based arrangements, center directors completed questionnaires about program characteristics, including program funding source and type, enrollment of subsidized children, and program location type. The provider and director interviews and observations were all conducted with the child's primary care provider, defined as the provider with whom the child spent the greatest amount of time each week.

Analytic Sample

Analyses were restricted to families who were likely to be eligible for subsidies and who also had valid data on the key treatment variable, subsidy receipt, as well as on the outcome variable, child care quality. To identify families who were likely to be eligible for subsidies, we used data from the parent and child care provider interviews. In most states, subsidy recipients are required to demonstrate their eligibility regularly; eligibility is based on welfare receipt or income and employment information. Therefore, we assumed that welfare, income, and employment data collected in the preschool parent interview reflected ongoing eligibility status. Using mothers' reports of welfare receipt, household income, and work status and applying state CCDF rules from the 2003 state plan[28] (the year of wave 2 ECLS-B data collection),[29] we simulated subsidy eligibility in three steps. At the start, families who used no nonparental care in preschool were excluded as they were not eligible for subsidies. For other families, state eligibility rules were applied.

All states guaranteed child care subsidies to families currently receiving or transitioning off of welfare in 2003; thus, in the first step we coded all parents who reported receiving welfare in the last year as *welfare eligible*. For families who were not receiving welfare, we compared a family's reported annual income with the annual income threshold for each state for a family of its size; if the family's annual income was equal to or below the maximum for a family of that size in the state of residence, then the family was deemed *income eligible*. Finally, families were classified as *employment eligible* if the mother was working, in school or in job training, or looking for work. A number of states had minimum weekly work hour requirements for two-parent households, so mothers who reported having a partner in the home were considered employment eligible if they reported working and worked hours equal to or in excess of their state's minimum hour requirement. Families were classified as *subsidy eligible* if they were either welfare eligible or both income and employment eligible according to these rules.

When we cross-categorized subsidy-eligible families with subsidy recipients (see "Measures," below, for a definition of *subsidy recipient*), approximately

175 subsidy recipients were misclassified as ineligible. Because we do not have administrative data on families' welfare receipt, income, or employment and because the information that we used to simulate eligibility was collected at a single time point, it is not surprising that our eligibility estimates did not match families' eligibility status in all cases.[30] We recoded subsidy recipients in center-based care as eligible if the family was receiving at least one other means-tested public benefit (for example, food stamps, Medicaid) or if their household income was below 185 percent of the poverty line. Subsidy recipients in home-based care were recoded as eligible if they appeared income eligible (they were receiving at least one other means-tested public benefit or their household income was below 185 percent of the poverty line) and we could be reasonably certain that their care was subsidized (that is, the provider was regulated, was affiliated with a family child care network, and accepted subsidies). This recoding produced a sample of approximately 2,800 families who were likely eligible for subsidies in the two-year wave.[31]

From the likely eligible sample, we then further reduced the analytic sample by excluding cases missing data on child care quality or subsidy receipt. As mentioned earlier, for cost reasons the ECLS-B observed only child care settings for a subsample of children from the full ECLS-B ($N \approx 1,500$ child care observations out of $N \approx 9,800$ respondents in the two-year wave). We applied National Center for Education Statistics replicate weights W22P1-W22P90, which produced a final analytic sample of 550 subsidy-eligible children with data on child care quality in the two-year wave. Missing data on covariates were negligible in the two-year wave; nonetheless, we did use the imputation by chained equations (ICE) procedure for multiple imputation in Stata Version 10 to impute five datasets using all variables included in the analytic models, and we then used Stata's MIM program to conduct the analyses.[32] However, models that were run with and without multiply imputed data did not differ. Therefore, results from models run without MIM are presented here.

Measures

SUBSIDY RECEIPT. To construct the measure of subsidy receipt, we used information from the parent interview and the child care provider and director interviews. Following prior studies,[33] families who indicated that the child's primary nonparental care arrangement was with a center were coded as receiving a subsidy if the parent reported receiving assistance in paying for child care from a government or social welfare agency or if the parent reported using center-based care and that care was free.[34] Parents who indicated that their child's primary nonparental care arrangement was home-based were coded as receiving a subsidy if the parent reported receiving assistance in paying for care from a government or social welfare agency or if the parent reported that there was no charge for the care *and* the provider reported that he or she was licensed or was part of a family child care network, provided care in his or her home, and cared for four or more unrelated children. Families not meeting these conditions were coded "0" on the dichotomous subsidy receipt variable.

Of the approximately 2,800 families who were likely eligible for subsidies in the two-year wave, approximately 25 percent ($n \approx 700$) received a subsidy.[35] In 2003, the year of the two-year-wave data collection, the national estimate for subsidy receipt among eligible families was 28 percent.[36] The closeness of our estimates of subsidy receipt among eligible families to national estimates from the same years increases our confidence in both the measure of subsidy receipt and the identification of likely eligible families.

CHILD CARE QUALITY. Global child care quality, which includes space, materials, and activities that the caregiver engages in with the child, was assessed with two commonly used observational measures: the Infant-Toddler Environment Rating Scale (ITERS)[37] for center-based settings and the Family Day Care Rating Scale (FDCRS)[38] for home-based settings. Both measures have good reliability and validity, and they have been widely used in studies of child care quality.

The ITERS and FDCRS rate child care quality on a range of factors understood to augment children's early learning. Items on the parallel measures relate to nutrition, safety, cleanliness, furnishings, equipment, child-centered wall display, and activities and materials for play and learning in language, cognitive, and social domains. All items are scored on a seven-point scale on which 1 = *inadequate,* 3 = *minimal,* 5 = *good,* and 7 = *excellent.* The quality variable in this study represents the setting's average quality score, according to either the ITERS or the FDCRS.

Process quality—a dimension of child care quality that focuses on the relationship between caregivers and children—was assessed using the Arnett Caregiver Interaction Scale,[39] which measures the quality of interactions between caregivers and children, such as the caregiver's warmth and engagement with children, sensitivity, responsiveness, and use of harsh discipline. Like the ITERS and the FDCRS, the Arnett scale has demonstrated good reliability and validity, and it has been used frequently in studies of child care quality.

CHILD CARE TYPE. To account for type of child care, we included a dichotomous variable representing whether the child attended center- or home-based care (1 = center).

Covariates. In all multivariate models, we included a rich set of covariates that are empirically or theoretically linked to the decision to use a subsidy, to the selection of a care arrangement, or to both. It is especially important to draw time variant characteristics from a wave earlier than the treatment wave to ensure that the treatment and covariates are not simultaneously determined; therefore all covariates were drawn from the nine-month wave of data collection.

Family background characteristics. To account for differential selection into subsidy receipt or child care setting, we controlled for variables that have been found to be associated with subsidy use or care quality. They included maternal race (three dummy variables for black, Hispanic, and Asian/other race, with "white" as the reference category); maternal education (three dummy variables for less than high school, high school diploma/GED, and some college, with "bachelor's degree or higher" as the reference category); maternal relationship status (one dummy variable for whether mother was single); age of mother at the focal child's birth (one dummy variable; 1 = mother was a teen); number of children in the home age six and younger (a continuous variable); number of children in the home age seven and older (a continuous variable); family's place of residence (one dummy variable; 1 = urban area); maternal employment (four dummy variables, for mother works part-time, is in an education or training program, is looking for work, or is not in the labor force, with "works full-time" as the reference category); household's income-to-needs ratio, the ratio of family income to the federal poverty level for a family of the same size; and food insecurity in the last year (one dummy variable; 1 = family experienced food insecurity). Finally, we included a dummy variable for maternal English proficiency. At the nine-month parent interview, mothers were asked how well they read, write, speak, and understand English, and responses were scored on a 4-point Likert scale (1 = *not well at all*; 4 = *very well*). After summing responses across the four items and assigning native-English-speaking mothers who skipped these questions a score of 4 on each item, mothers who achieved a total score of 12 or more on the composite score were deemed proficient in English (1 = proficient).

To account for parents' familiarity and comfort with the subsidy system, we included four separate dummy variables, for whether the mother had received other public benefits since the child's birth, including welfare, food stamps, WIC (Special Supplemental Nutrition Program for Women, Infants, and Children), and Medicaid. Finally, to account for the possibility that parents decide to use a subsidy or select their care arrangement because of child-level characteristics, we controlled for whether the child had a diagnosed disability (1 = child has a disability), a measure of the child's cognitive ability (continuous score on the Bayley Short Form Research Edition), and child gender (1 = male).

Parents' child care preferences. In addition to detailed family demographic information, we included variables for parents' preferences for features of child care because their preferences may explain their selection into subsidy use or care arrangement. The ECLS-B is unique in its inclusion of an ample set of child care preference questions. At the nine-month parent interview, mothers were asked whether a series of child care characteristics were very important, somewhat important, or not very important when they selected their child's primary care arrangement. Mothers who were not yet using nonparental care at the nine-month wave were asked to imagine what would be important to them if and when they had to select a nonparental care setting for the focal child. Mothers were asked about the importance of the following factors: reasonable cost of care; small number of children in child's group or class; provider who cares for child when child is sick; proximity of care provider to family's home; provider who had training in caring for young children; and provider who speaks English. Separate dummy variables for each item were included (1 = very important; 0 = somewhat or not very important).

Analytic Strategy

A key concern in estimating a causal effect of subsidy use on child care quality is the self-selection of individuals into subsidy use or care of higher or lower quality. To address this issue, we employed two methodological approaches to estimate the treatment effect of subsidy receipt on child care quality. First, we ran ordinary least squares (OLS) regression models predicting child care quality from subsidy receipt while controlling for the rich set of family background characteristics and parental preferences for child care outlined above. Four regression models were run: the first was run to predict quality among all subsidy-eligible families; the second, to determine (by including an indicator for center-based care as a control) whether, if an association between subsidy and quality was detected, it was driven by recipients' increased likelihood of using center-based care; the third, to predict quality just among families in center-based care; and the fourth, to predict quality just among families in home-based care. The last two models were run to test whether the impact of subsidies on quality varied by child care type.

Next, drawing on the same set of covariates, we replicated those analyses by using a propensity score matching approach. The purpose of the propensity score matching analyses was to check the robustness of the OLS estimates; to the extent that estimates from the two methods differ, bias may exist in the OLS models. The propensity score, which here represents the likelihood of receiving a subsidy, is a one-dimensional summary of the covariates; it is used to identify matches between each treated case and one or more than one control case.

Treated cases with no match on the propensity score were excluded from analysis because they were considered to be outside the region of common support, or the range of values within which treated cases have adequate matches among controls. Therefore, the resulting treatment effect considers only those cases for which reliable estimates of the effect of subsidy receipt can be made.

The matching model that we used, described in more detail below, generates an estimate of the average effect of the treatment on the treated (ATT). A regression-adjusted estimate of the ATT is then obtained by regressing the outcome on the treatment and all covariates, on a sample restricted to cases whose propensity scores fall within the region of common support, or treated cases with a match in the control group. The resulting ATT is comparable with the OLS coefficient estimated with a dummy variable for subsidy receipt; therefore, we can compare the ATT from the propensity score matching approach with the coefficient for subsidy receipt from the OLS estimates to assess possible bias in the latter models.

As with the OLS models, we ran models comparing the quality of care used by subsidy recipients with the quality of care used by all eligible nonrecipients and then ran models comparing the quality of care used by subgroups according to care type (center- or home-based care). It is not possible to include posttreatment variables, like child care type, in a propensity score matching framework; therefore the model including an indicator for center-based care was not tested in the propensity score matching analyses. For the other models, separate propensity scores were estimated and separate matching models were run for each comparison. All OLS and propensity score matching models were run first with global child care quality as measured by the ITERS/FDCRS and then with process quality as measured by the Arnett scale as outcomes.

Results

Results are summarized below. First, we describe results from bivariate analyses, comparing subsidy recipients and eligible nonrecipients on child care quality and all covariates. Second, we report results from multivariate OLS and propensity score models predicting child care quality from subsidy receipt.

Bivariate Associations

Mean differences between subsidy recipients and eligible nonrecipients on child care quality and all covariates are displayed in table 5-1. On average, subsidy recipients chose care that was *higher* in quality than the care used by eligible nonrecipients. However, this difference emerged only among those using home-based care, not those using center-based care. Moreover, differences between the two

Table 5-1. *Descriptive Statistics: Subsidy-Eligible Sample with Child Care Observation Data*[a]

Variable	Full sample Mean/standard deviation (percent)	Subsidy recipients Mean/standard deviation (percent)	Eligible nonrecipients Mean/standard deviation (percent)	Range
N		250	250	
Child care quality				
Global quality	3.41 (1.2)	3.90 (1.1)	3.10 (1.1)**	1.25–6.54
Center-based care	4.18 (1.0)	4.10 (1.1)	4.44 (1.03)	1.63–6.54
Home-based care	2.98 (1.0)	3.43 (1.0)	2.83 (0.9)	1.25–6.48
Process quality	58.93 (11.0)	61.13 (10.5)	57.27 (11.2)*	8–78
Center-based care	61.14 (10.6)	60.80 (10.5)	62.25 (10.7)	12–78
Home-based care	57.70 (11.1)	61.70 (10.5)	56.39 (11.0)	8–78
Family characteristic				
Maternal race				
Mother is white	32	32	33	0–1
Mother is black	32	42	25**	0–1
Mother is Hispanic	32	22	40**	0–1
Mother is Asian/other race	3	4	2	0–1
Maternal education				
Mother has < high school education	28	28	28	0–1
Mother has high school diploma or GED	41	43	40	0–1
Mother has some college	27	27	27	0–1
Mother has BA or higher	3	2	5	0–1
Mother is single	47	60	38**	0–1
Mother is proficient in English	90	94	87*	0–1
Mother was < age 20 at focal child's birth	22	23	21	0–1
Number of children in household ≤ age 6	0.9 (0.9)	1.0 (1.1)	0.8 (0.9)*	0–6
Number of children in household ≥ age 7	0.6 (1.0)	0.5 (0.9)	0.7 (1.0)	0–6
Family lives in an urban area	67	68	67	0–1
Maternal employment				
Mother works full-time	39	32	45*	0–1
Mother works part-time	21	22	20	0–1
Mother participates in work-related activity	10	14	7	0–1
Mother is looking for work	16	18	15	0–1
Mother is not in labor force	13	14	13	0–1

(continued)

Table 5-1. *Descriptive Statistics: Subsidy-Eligible Sample with Child Care Observation Data*[a] *(Continued)*

Variable	Full sample Mean/standard deviation (percent)	Subsidy recipients Mean/standard deviation (percent)	Eligible nonrecipients Mean/standard deviation (percent)	Range
Household income-to-needs ratio	1.3 (1.0)	1.3 (1.0)	1.3 (1.0)	0–9.0
Family received welfare	22	28	16**	0–1
Family received food stamps	48	60	41**	0–1
Family received WIC	87	93	83**	0–1
Family received Medicaid	70	76	66*	0–1
Family experienced food insecurity	38	41	36	0–1
Child has a diagnosed disability	6	6	6	0–1
Child Bayley mental development index	77.1 (10.6)	75.5 (10.1)	79.2 (11.0)	34.3–131.2
Child is male	53	55	51	0–1
Child care preference				
Cost is very important	77	78	77	0–1
Class/group size is very important	71	71	71	0–1
Sick care is very important	80	77	82	0–1
Proximity is very important	70	70	70	0–1
Caregiver training is very important	91	90	91	0–1
Caregiver speaks English is very important	78	81	75	0–1

Source: ECLS-B Nine-Month–Kindergarten Restricted Use Data File.

a. All Ns are rounded to the nearest 50 per NCES requirements. All estimates were weighted by replicate weights W22P1-W22P90; standard errors are jackknife standard errors.

$*p < .05, **p < .01.$

groups in family background characteristics and parents' child care preferences suggest that selection issues may bias the association between subsidy receipt and care quality. Subsidy recipients were more likely to be black, less likely to be Hispanic, more likely to be single and proficient in English, more likely to have more children age six and younger in the home, and less likely to work full-time. Subsidy recipients were also more likely to have received other public benefits including welfare, food stamps, WIC, and Medicaid. No differences emerged, however,

Table 5-2. *Type of Care Used by Subsidy Recipients and Eligible Nonrecipients for Two-Year-Old Children*[a]

Percent

Type of care	Subsidy recipient	Eligible nonrecipient	National average
Center	63	15	31
Home	37	85	69

Source: ECLS-B Nine-Month–Kindergarten Restricted Use Data File.

a. National average represents estimates based on analyses of the full ECLS-B dataset at the two-year wave. All estimates were weighted by replicate weights W22P1-W22P90.

Differences between recipients and eligible nonrecipients were significant at $p < 0.001$.

in child care preferences. Overall, these differences suggest that subsidy recipients are generally more socioeconomically disadvantaged than nonrecipients but that parents are not selecting into the program with fundamentally different goals for child care.

We also conducted a chi-square test to determine whether the type of care chosen differed significantly between subsidy recipients and nonrecipients (table 5-2). Subsidy recipients were more likely to use center-based care than were the eligible nonrecipients. In addition, the rate of use of center-based care by subsidy recipients is higher than the national average for two-year-olds (see table 5-2). These findings are consistent with results from our analyses using Fragile Families and Child Wellbeing Study Child Care Supplement data, in which we found that subsidy receipt was associated with increased use of center-based care.[40] We should also note that analyses comparing the quality of care in center- and home-based care settings revealed that center-based care was higher in quality (results not shown).

OLS Regression Models

To test whether subsidy receipt when children are two years old is associated with child care quality at age two, we first regressed global child care quality on the dichotomous subsidy receipt variable in a model that controlled for all covariates (see table 5-3). The value of the coefficient on subsidy receipt can be interpreted as the difference (in points on the 7-point quality rating scale) between global care quality for subsidy recipients and quality for all eligible nonrecipients. Here, subsidy receipt was associated with higher global quality of care by nearly a full point (*beta* = 0.91; standard error = 0.12).

Next, to explore whether the positive coefficient on subsidy receipt was partially or fully explained by the fact that subsidy recipients are more likely to use center-based care, we entered an indicator for center-based care into the regres-

Table 5-3. *OLS and Propensity Score Matching Models Predicting Child Care Quality*[a]

Model	Global quality		Process quality	
	Beta	Standard error	Beta	Standard error
OLS regression				
Subsidy receipt, full sample	0.91***	0.12	4.02***	1.42
Subsidy receipt, full sample with type as control	0.32**	0.15	2.20	1.55
Subsidy receipt, center-based care only	−0.33	0.22	−1.67	2.34
Subsidy receipt, home-based care only	0.63***	0.18	3.38*	1.94
	ATT	Standard error	ATT	Standard error
Propensity score matching				
Subsidy receipt, full sample	0.92***	0.12	4.10***	1.42
Subsidy receipt, center-based care only	−0.32	0.33	−1.76	3.74
Subsidy receipt, home-based care only	0.58***	0.18	3.31*	1.94

Source: ECLS-B Nine-Month–Kindergarten Restricted Use Data.

a. Covariates (all drawn from the nine-month wave) include maternal race, education, and relationship status; maternal English language proficiency; mother's age at focal child's birth; number of children in household age six years and under; number of children in household age seven years and older; urbanicity; mother's work status; household income-to-needs ratio; whether the family received welfare, WIC, food stamps, and Medicaid; food insecurity; child disability status; child score on Bayley mental development index; child gender; and indicators for whether the mother considered the following features of care to be very important: cost, number of children, provision of sick care, proximity of care to home, caregiver training, and a caregiver who speaks English. All estimates were weighted by replicate weights W22P1-W22P90; standard errors are jackknife standard errors.

*p < .10, **p < .05, ***p < .01.

sion model (table 5-3). The inclusion of the indicator for child care type reduced the size of the subsidy estimate by nearly two-thirds, but the sign and significance of the coefficient remained the same.

While those results imply that the impact of subsidy on quality came from the increased use of center-based care by subsidy recipients, it could also be that the association between subsidy receipt and child care quality varies by child care type. To test that possibility, we repeated the first regression but on two separate subgroups: once on a sample restricted to families who used center-based care and once on a sample restricted to families who used home-based care. Interestingly, the positive and significant effect of subsidy receipt on global care quality persisted only among families using home-based care, whose use of a subsidy increased global quality of care by approximately one half of a standard deviation (*beta* = 0.63; standard error = 0.18). Among families using center-based care, subsidy receipt was not significantly associated with global care quality; moreover, the sign of the coefficient on subsidy receipt among families using centers was negative (*beta* = -0.33; standard error = 0.22).

As an extension of the forgoing analyses, we ran an identical set of logistic regression models predicting "good" quality care as defined by the ITERS/FDCRS (that is, care that received a score of 5 or above). Small cell sizes prohibited us from running models on subgroups by type of care; nevertheless, in the full sample, subsidy recipients were more likely to receive "good" quality care than were nonrecipients (odds ratio = 2.58; standard error = 0.95; *p* = 0.01; results not shown).

We then repeated the OLS analyses with our measure of process quality as the outcome. The pattern was nearly identical to that found for global quality. In the full sample, subsidy receipt at age two was associated with higher process quality at age two by about one-third of a standard deviation (*beta* = 4.02; standard error = 1.42). When an indicator for child care type was included in the model, the association between subsidy receipt and process quality was reduced to nonsignificance. When the sample was divided by the type of care that families used, the positive effect of subsidy receipt on process quality persisted only among families who used home-based care (although the significance of this association was reduced to the trend level; *beta* = 3.38; *standard error = 1.94*). Among families who used center-based care, the association between subsidy receipt and process quality was negative and nonsignificant (*beta* = –1.67; standard error = 2.34).

Propensity Score Matching Models

To check the robustness of the results from the OLS models, we replicated the series of OLS analyses using a propensity score matching technique. Propensity score matching requires three steps. First, a propensity score for each family is generated from a probit regression model predicting the treatment (subsidy receipt) from a set of covariates theoretically or empirically linked to subsidy receipt, child care quality, or both. The predicted propensity score represents each family's likelihood of using a subsidy. Results from the probit models used to estimate the propensity score (appendix 5A) suggest that relatively few family characteristics or child care preferences were significantly associated with subsidy receipt. Mothers who were Asian/other race were more likely to use subsidies than white mothers, those with a high school diploma or less were more likely to use subsidies than those with a bachelor's degree or more, and those who were single were more likely to use subsidies than those who were married or cohabiting. Mothers with more young children in the home, those with a higher income-to-needs ratio, and those who gave priority to cost of care when selecting a child care arrangement also were more likely to use subsidies.

Next, propensity scores generated from these probit models were used to match "treated" subjects (those who received subsidies) with "control" subjects (those who appeared similar to subsidy recipients on all characteristics except subsidy receipt). We employed a nearest neighbor matching with replacement algorithm, matching each treated case with the control case with the closest propensity score. Treated cases with matches in the control group were considered to fall within the region of common support; as mentioned earlier, this region includes only those treated cases with matches in the control group. Treated cases with no match in the control group were excluded from analysis.

In the comparison of subsidy recipients to all nonrecipients, sixteen treated cases were dropped because they were outside the region of common support, with propensity scores of 0.8 or higher. Balance on the means of all covariates across the two groups was inspected before and after matching (not shown). Results suggest that balance was improved markedly by matching. Whereas before matching ten of the covariates were statistically significantly different for the treatment and control groups, after matching the means on all variables were statistically equivalent for both groups.

The third and final step in our propensity score matching analysis was to replicate the OLS analyses by generating a regression-adjusted estimate of the ATT, which, as mentioned earlier, is analogous to the coefficient on the indicator for subsidy receipt in the OLS models. We generated our ATT by regressing child care quality on the dichotomous subsidy receipt variable in a model that included all covariates used for matching on observations that fell within the region of common support. The resulting ATT theoretically estimates the effect on quality of receiving a subsidy when subsidy recipients are compared with families that are identical to subsidy recipients on all characteristics except subsidy receipt.

Results from the propensity score matching model comparing subsidy recipients to nonrecipients on global care quality in the full sample are presented in the bottom section of table 5-3. As with the OLS models, the results of the propensity score analysis suggest that subsidy receipt leads to care that is nearly a full point higher in global quality than the care used by eligible nonrecipients. Indeed, the size of the coefficient on subsidy receipt was nearly identical to that from the comparable OLS model (ATT = 0.92, standard error = 0.12, versus *beta* = 0.91, standard error = 0.12).

Turning to the subgroup analyses, in which separate propensity scores were estimated for families in center-based care and families in home-based care, again we see that the results substantiate those from the OLS models. Among families who use center-based care, the effect of subsidy receipt on global quality is nonsignificant (ATT = -0.32; standard error = 0.33), whereas among families who use home-based care, the positive and significant effect of subsidy receipt on global quality persists (ATT = 0.58; standard error = 0.18). However, it should be noted that when propensity scores were generated and models were estimated just among families in center-based care, approximately ninety treated cases (all with propensity scores in the uppermost part of the distribution) were off-support and were dropped from analysis.

We ran the same propensity score models predicting process quality from subsidy receipt and found highly similar results. Subsidy receipt led to higher process quality in the full sample (ATT = –4.10; standard error = 1.42), an effect that persisted only among families who use home-based care and only at the trend level (ATT = 3.31; standard error = 1.94). Among families who use center-based care, the effect of subsidy receipt on process quality is negative and nonsignificant (ATT = –1.76; standard error = 3.74).

Discussion

This study investigates the effect of subsidy receipt on child care quality for toddlers. We hypothesized that subsidy receipt would lead parents to purchase higher-quality care than the care purchased by eligible nonrecipients regardless of the type of care used. This hypothesis was partially supported; using both OLS regression models with rich control variables as well as propensity score matching, we found that subsidy receipt when children are two years of age does lead to higher-quality care but that this effect was driven partially by care type. Specifically, we found that subsidy receipt led to increased use of center care, which was higher in quality than home-based care, and to the use of higher-quality home-based care. It would seem, then, that the coefficient on subsidy receipt at age two for the full sample actually represents the simultaneous effect of subsidies leading to increased use of center-based care and to higher-quality home-based care among those families using home-based care.

This study set out to determine whether child care subsidies could go beyond supporting parental employment to also serving child development goals. Our findings suggest that under the current subsidy system this aim *is* being met for toddlers, yet the story is somewhat complicated. Although we hypothesized that subsidies would elevate care quality for both center- and home-based care, our findings suggest that subsidy receipt does not increase quality of care for toddlers receiving center-based care. It is possible that the supply of quality center-based care for very young, low-income children is simply too low for most recipients to benefit from the increased purchasing power that subsidies afford.[41] Center-based care for infants and toddlers also tends to be more expensive than care for older children, largely because younger children need more supervision and attention, requiring more staff. If higher-quality infant-toddler center care is unaffordable even with the subsidy, then a subsidy would not elevate care quality among families in center-based care. The next generation of studies in this area should investigate these explanations to determine *why* subsidies improve care quality only among families who use home-based care. One possible approach would be to merge geo-coded data on center care availability and cost with rich survey data like that of the ECLS-B to compare the effects of these supply-side variables.

Although subsidies did not increase care quality among those using center-based care, we did find that subsidy receipt led to increased use of center-based care, which was higher in quality than home-based care. Indeed, among children in our sample whose primary care arrangement was with a center, the vast majority were subsidy recipients (76 percent), and among subsidy recipients, most used center-based care (63 percent). These patterns suggest that a greater number of children receive care in a center-based setting with the aid of a subsidy than without one. To the extent that a switch from home- to center-based care represents a switch to higher-quality care, a difference that we identified, there *are* positive effects of subsidies across recipients.

Subsidies also elevated the quality of home-based care that parents of toddlers used. Among home-based care users, subsidies may elevate quality because families using home-based care face a different set of options than those facing parents using center care. Whereas subsidies may not cover the cost of high-quality center-based care, they may cover the cost of most family child care providers, who tend to charge less than centers. Therefore, mothers looking for higher-quality home-based care may use subsidies to switch from more informal, lower-quality family, friend, and neighbor (FFN) arrangements to formal, licensed, family child care providers. Alternatively, states may drive parents' home-based choices by encouraging parents receiving subsidies to use regulated care. In the case of home-based care, subsidies may direct mothers away from using FFN providers and toward family child care providers, who are more likely to be licensed. In either scenario, subsidies may enable families to choose the higher-quality home-based option for their toddler.

Our study has several limitations that should be considered before drawing policy conclusions. First, the subsample of likely eligible families for whom data on child care quality were available was small. As is to be expected when using nationally representative survey data, cell sizes of particular subgroups that were not purposely oversampled were modest. Additional cases were lost as a result of implementing common support conditions. As mentioned earlier, we matched treated cases with control cases with the nearest propensity score but discarded treated cases with no matches in the control group. Although this technique may reduce bias, it may also reduce the precision of estimates. This is of particular concern in the subgroup analyses of children in center-based care, where nearly ninety treated cases were dropped. Our attempts to achieve better balance across treated and control samples by including higher-order terms and interactions and by excluding treated cases who may have been receiving free care from a source other than a subsidy (for example, a church or synagogue) were not successful. The repercussion for small subgroups is that statistically significant differences between groups may be difficult to detect; however, that did not appear to be a problem.

Another issue that warrants concern is possible measurement error in the key treatment variable (subsidy receipt) and in the identification of the subsidy-eligible families. Without administrative data on subsidy receipt, parental employment status, and household income, it is impossible to be certain that individuals in the current study were correctly identified as subsidy recipients and that subsidy-eligible families were, in fact, subsidy eligible. Indeed, as mentioned in the "Method" section, in the initial cross-categorization of subsidy recipients with the larger group of eligible families, a substantial number of recipients appeared ineligible. That could point to a problem with the identification of subsidy recipients or of subsidy-eligible families. Although it is difficult to know the magnitude and effect of possible misclassifications, we note that the estimated rate of subsidy receipt among likely eligible families was nearly identical to national estimates for subsidy receipt among eligible families in the same year.[42] Nonetheless, future studies examining this question ideally should merge administrative data that contain economic and employment information as well as information on the sources and amounts of child care assistance with rich survey data on family characteristics and child care quality.

Finally, we recognize that although OLS analyses with a comprehensive set of control variables and propensity score matching do approximate a causal estimate of the effects of subsidy receipt on quality, both methods assume that all characteristics driving selection into subsidy use and care arrangements are observable and have been included in statistical models. That is not a testable assumption, and if additional covariates that are confounded with selection into subsidy use or care setting were excluded, results could be biased.

Policy Implications

Despite this study's limitations, its findings have important implications for policy and future research. Most broadly, our findings suggest that under the current subsidy system, subsidy recipients use higher-quality care and are more likely to use "good" quality care than eligible nonrecipients. Therefore, making subsidies available to more families so that all those who are eligible have the opportunity to shift their children to centers or to higher-quality home-based care should be a future aim of subsidy policy. At the same time, more research is needed to understand why subsidies do not increase care quality among center-based care users. For instance, if future studies find that higher-quality center-based care options *do* exist in low-income communities but that the subsidies are simply not generous enough to cover the cost, then a policy recommendation might be to increase the subsidy so that families can purchase the highest-quality care available to them. However, if future studies find that too few high-quality centers exist in low-income communities for recipients to use, then efforts should focus on elevating the quality of existing programs.[43] In addition, if future studies find that subsidy administration officials encourage subsidy recipients who use home-based care to use licensed family child care instead of more informal FFN arrangements because licensed providers offer the highest-quality care to subsidy-eligible families using home-based care, then one policy implication could be to ensure that this advice is given in the referral process.

Future research should also explore whether subsidy receipt at age two shifts children into higher-quality care settings as they approach school entry age. For example, if the subsidy recipients in our sample who used center-based care for their children at age two are more likely than eligible nonrecipients to use Head Start or public prekindergarten for them at age four—two center-based programs that offer the highest quality of care available to subsidy-eligible preschoolers—the positive effects of subsidies may extend longitudinally. Such a finding, in turn, would suggest that shifting subsidy funds to cover more toddlers who have few other publicly funded care options may be a promising strategy for enhancing the development of low-income children.

Although our analyses cannot identify which policy changes to enact, our results stress the importance of integrating a stronger developmental focus in the CCDF, which is now the federal government's largest child care program and one that stands to impact thousands of the nation's youngest and most vulnerable children every day.

Notes

1. Frances A. Campbell and Craig T. Ramey, "Effects of Early Intervention on Intellectual and Academic Achievement: A Follow-up Study of Children from Low-Income Families," *Child Development*, vol. 65 (1994), pp. 684–98; Janet Currie, "Early Childhood Education Programs," *Journal of Economic Perspectives,* vol. 15 (2001), pp. 213–38; Fong-Ruey Liaw and Jeanne Brooks-Gunn, "Patterns of Low Birth Weight Children's Cognitive Development and Their Determinants," *Developmental Psychology*, vol. 29 (1993), pp. 1024–35; Kathleen McCartney and others, "Quality Child Care Supports the Achievement of Low-Income Children: Direct and Indirect Pathways through Caregiving and the Home Environment," *Journal*

of Applied Developmental Psychology, vol. 28 (2007), pp. 411–26; Lawrence Schweinhart and others, *Lifetime Effects: The High/Scope Perry Preschool Study through Age 40* (Ypsilanti, Mich.: High/Scope Educational Research Foundation, 2005); Elizabeth Votruba-Drzal, Rebekah Levine Coley, and P. Lindsay Chase-Lansdale, "Child Care Quality and Low-Income Children's Development: Direct and Moderated Effects," *Child Development*, vol. 75 (2004), pp. 296–312.

2. David M. Blau, *The Child Care Problem: An Economic Analysis* (New York: Russell Sage Foundation, 2001); Lynda Laughlin, "Who's Minding the Kids? Child Care Arrangements: Spring 2005/Summer 2006" (U.S. Census Bureau, 2010).

3. National Institute for Child Health and Human Development Early Child Care Research Network, "Familial Factors Associated with the Characteristics of Nonmaternal Care for Infants," in *Child Care and Child Development: Results from the NICHD Study of Early Child Care and Youth Development* (New York: Guilford, 2005), pp. 109–26; Deborah Phillips and others, "Child Care of Children in Poverty: Opportunity or Inequality?" *Child Development*, vol. 65 (1994), pp. 472–92.

4. Administration for Children and Families, *Child Care and Development Fund (CCDF) Fiscal Year 2008 State Spending from All Appropriation Years* (U.S. Department of Health and Human Services, 2008) (www.acf.hhs.gov/programs/ccb/data/expenditures/08acf696/overview.htm).

5. Nicole D. Forry, "The Impact of Child Care Subsidies on Low-Income Single Parents: An Examination of Child Care Expenditures and Family Finances," *Journal of Family and Economic Issues*, vol. 30 (2009), pp. 43–54; Lisa Gennetian and others, "Can Child Care Assistance in Welfare and Employment Programs Support the Employment of Low-Income Families?" *Journal of Policy Analysis and Management*, vol. 230 (2004), pp. 723–43.

6. David Blau and Erdal Tekin, "The Determinants and Consequences of Child Care Subsidies for Single Mothers in the USA," *Journal of Population Economics*, vol. 20 (2007), pp. 719–41.

7. Eric Knudsen and others, "Economic, Neurobiological, and Behavioral Perspectives on Building America's Future Workforce," *Proceedings of the National Academy of Sciences*, vol. 103 (2006), pp. 10155–62; Jack Shonkoff and Deborah Phillips, *From Neurons to Neighborhoods: The Science of Early Childhood Development* (Washington: National Academy Press, 2000).

8. Rebecca Ryan and others, "The Impact of Child Care Subsidy Use on Child Care Quality," *Early Childhood Research Quarterly*, vol. 26 (2011), pp. 320–31; Anna Johnson, Rebecca Ryan, and Jeanne Brooks-Gunn, "Child Care Subsidies: Do They Impact the Quality of Care Children Experience?" *Child Development* (forthcoming).

9. Administration for Children and Families, "FFY 2008 CCDF Data Tables" (U.S. Department of Health and Human Services, 2008) (www.acf.hhs.gov/programs/ccb/data/ccdf_data/06acf800/table1.htm).

10. Gina Adams and Monica Rohacek, "More Than a Work Support? Issues around Integrating Child Development Goals into the Child Care Subsidy System," *Early Childhood Research Quarterly*, vol. 17 (2002), pp. 418–40.

11. Blau and Tekin, "The Determinants and Consequences of Child Care Subsidies for Single Mothers in the USA"; Forry, "The Impact of Child Care Subsidies on Low-Income Single Parents: An Examination of Child Care Expenditures and Family Finances"; Gennetian and others, "Can Child Care Assistance in Welfare and Employment Programs Support the Employment of Low-Income Families?"; Erdal Tekin, "Child Care Subsidy Receipt,

Employment, and Child Care Choices of Single Mothers," *Economic Letters*, vol. 89 (2005), pp. 1–6; Erdal Tekin, "Single Mothers Working at Night: Standard Work and Child Care Subsidies," *Economic Inquiry*, vol. 45 (2007), pp. 233–50.

12. Rachel Gordon and P. Lindsay Chase-Lansdale, "Availability of Child Care in the United States: A Description and Analysis of Data Sources," *Demography*, vol. 38 (2001), pp. 299–316; Susanna Loeb and others, "Child Care in Poor Communities: Early Learning Effects by Type, Quality, and Stability," *Child Development*, vol. 75 (2004), pp. 47–65; Magaly Queralt and Ann Dryden Witte, "Influences on Neighborhood Supply of Child Care in Massachusetts," *Social Service Review*, vol. 72 (1998), pp. 17–46.

13. Adams and Rohacek, "More Than a Work Support? Issues around Integrating Child Development Goals into the Child Care Subsidy System."

14. Ibid.

15. Mark Berger and Dan Black, "Child Care Subsidies, Quality of Care, and the Labor Supply of Low-Income, Single Mothers," *Review of Economics and Statistics*, vol. 74 (1992), pp. 635–42; Fred Brooks, "Impacts of Child Care Subsidies on Child and Family Wellbeing," *Early Childhood Research Quarterly*, vol. 17 (2002), pp. 498–511; Danielle Crosby, Lisa Gennetian, and Aletha Huston, "Child Care Assistance Policies Can Affect the Use of Center-Based Care for Children in Low-Income Families," *Applied Developmental Science*, vol. 9 (2005), pp. 86–106; Julia Henly, Elizabeth Ananat, and Sandra Danziger, "Non-Standard Work Schedules, Child Care Subsidies, and Child Care Arrangements" (University of Michigan, Gerald Ford National Poverty Center, 2006) (www.fordschool.umich.edu/research/poverty/pdf/HenDanzAna_Mar2006.pdf); Tekin, "Child Care Subsidy Receipt, Employment, and Child Care Choices of Single Mothers"; Marsha Weinraub and others, "Subsidizing Child Care: How Child Care Subsidies Affect the Child Care Used by Low-Income African-American Families," *Early Childhood Research Quarterly*, vol. 20 (2005), pp. 373–92; Barbara Wolfe and Scott Scrivner, "Child Care Use and Parental Desire to Switch Care Type among a Low-Income Population," *Journal of Family and Economic Issues*, vol. 25 (2004), pp. 139–62.

16. Weinraub and others, "Subsidizing Child Care: How Child Care Subsidies Affect the Child Care Used by Low-Income African-American Families."

17. Berger and Black, "Child Care Subsidies, Quality of Care, and the Labor Supply of Low-Income, Single Mothers"; Brooks, "Impacts of Child Care Subsidies on Child and Family Wellbeing."

18. Debby Cryer, Wolfgang Tietze, and Holger Wessels, "Parents' Perceptions of Their Children's Child Care: A Cross-National Comparison," *Early Childhood Research Quarterly*, vol. 17 (2002), pp. 259–77; Debby Cryer and Margaret Burchinal, "Parents as Child Care Consumers," *Early Childhood Research Quarterly*, vol. 12 (1997), pp. 35–58.

19. Julie Jones-Branch and others, "Child Care Subsidy and Quality," *Early Education and Development*, vol. 15 (2004), pp. 329–41; H. Abigail Raikes, Helen Raikes, and Brian Wilcox, "Regulation, Subsidy Receipt, and Provider Characteristics: What Predicts Quality in Family Child Care Homes?" *Early Childhood Research Quarterly*, vol. 20 (2005), pp. 164–84.

20. Carollee Howes, Deborah Phillips, and Marcy Whitebook, "Teacher Characteristics and Effective Teaching in Child Care: Findings from the National Child Care Staffing Study," *Child and Youth Care Forum*, vol. 21 (1992), pp. 399–414; National Institute for Child Health and Human Development Early Child Care Research Network, "Familial Factors Associated with the Characteristics of Nonmaternal Care for Infants"; Ellen Peisner-Feinberg and others, "The Children of the Cost, Quality, and Outcomes Study Go to School: Executive Summary"

(University of North Carolina–Chapel Hill, Frank Porter Graham Child Development Center, 1999) (www.fpg.unc.edu/ncedl/PDFs/CQO-es.pdf); Phillips and others, "Child Care of Children in Poverty: Opportunity or Inequality?"

21. Weinraub and others, "Subsidizing Child Care: How Child Care Subsidies Affect the Child Care Used by Low-Income African-American Families."

22. Chris Herbst, "Who Are the Eligible Non-Recipients of Child Care Subsidies?" *Children and Youth Services Review*, vol. 30 (2008), pp. 1037–54; Bong Joo Lee and others, "Child Care Subsidy Use and Employment Outcomes of TANF Mothers during the Early Years of Welfare Reform: A Three-State Study" (University of Chicago, Chapin Hall Center for Children, 2004); Ann Dryden Witte and Magaly Queralt, "Take-Up Rates and Trade Offs after the Age of Entitlement: Some Thoughts and Empirical Evidence for Child Care Subsidies," Working Paper 8886 (Cambridge, Mass: National Bureau of Economic Research, 2002).

23. Herbst, "Who Are the Eligible Non-Recipients of Child Care Subsidies?"; Anna D. Johnson, "Who Uses Child Care Subsidies: Comparing Recipients to Eligible Non-Recipients on Family Background Characteristics and Child Care Preferences," *Children and Youth Services Review*, vol. 33 (2011), pp. 1072–83.

24. Ryan and others, "The Impact of Child Care Subsidy Use on Child Care Quality."

25. Johnson, Ryan, and Brooks-Gunn, "Child Care Subsidies: Do They Impact the Quality of Care Children Experience?"

26. National Institute for Child Health and Human Development Early Child Care Research Network, "Characteristics and Quality of Child Care for Toddlers and Preschoolers," in *Child Care and Child Development: Results from the NICHD Study of Early Child Care and Youth Development*, pp. 91–104.

27. Jodie Jacobson Chernoff and others, "Preschool: First Findings from the Third Follow-Up of the Early Childhood Longitudinal Study, Birth Cohort (ECLS-B)," NCES 2008-025 (National Center for Education Statistics, 2007).

28. CCDF state plans are published every other year; therefore eligibility rules from the 2003 state plan were used for the eligibility simulation at the two-year wave.

29. TRIM3 Project (http://trim3.urban.org).

30. See Herbst, "Who Are the Eligible Non-Recipients of Child Care Subsidies?" for a more thorough discussion of this issue. In addition, it is possible that household income reported in the ECLS-B was higher than income reported to the subsidy administration agency at the time of subsidy application. For instance, it may be that an unmarried mother applies for and receives a subsidy after presenting her pay stubs from her job, which would reflect her income only. When asked about the presence of a partner in the home and additional income from that partner, the mother may state that she lives alone because she knows that if her partner's income is counted she would be deemed ineligible for subsidies. However, in a survey interview, when asked about her total annual household income, the mother may report income from all householders.

31. All *N*s are rounded to the nearest 50, per NCES requirements.

32. Patrick Royston, "Multiple Imputation of Missing Values," *Stata Journal*, vol. 4 (2004), pp. 227–41; Patrick Royston, "Multiple Imputation of Missing Values: Update of ICE," *Stata Journal*, vol. 5 (2005), pp. 527–36.

33. Forry, "The Impact of Child Care Subsidies on Low-Income Single Parents: An Examination of Child Care Expenditures and Family Finances"; Linda Giannarelli, Sarah Adelman, and Stefanie Schmidt, "Getting Help with Child Care Expenses," Occasional Paper 62

(Washington: Urban Institute, 2003); Herbst, "Who Are the Eligible Non-Recipients of Child Care Subsidies?"

34. Only twenty-six children received free child care in an Early Head Start center, and they were coded as eligible nonrecipients of subsidies. However, results did not differ when they were excluded.

35. Note that this represents subsidy recipients among all eligible families before restricting the sample to families with child care quality observation data. The take-up rate for subsidies among eligible families with child care quality observation data is closer to 50 percent.

36. U.S. Department of Health and Human Services, Office of the Assistant Secretary for Planning and Evaluation, *Child Care Eligibility and Enrollment Estimates for Fiscal Year 2003* (July 2005) (http://aspe.hhs.gov/hsp/05/cc-eligibility/ib.pdf). The authors of this report note that these estimates do not necessarily reflect the proportion of families in need of assistance because information was not gathered on parents' use of other low- or no-cost care options.

37. Thelma Harms, Debby Cryer, and Richard Clifford, *Infant/Toddler Environment Rating Scale* (Teachers College Press, 1990).

38. Thelma Harms and Richard Clifford, *The Family Day Care Rating Scale* (Teachers College Press, 1989).

39. Jeffrey Arnett, "Caregivers in Day-Care Centers: Does Training Matter?" *Journal of Applied Developmental Psychology*, vol. 10 (1989), pp. 541–52.

40. Ryan and others, "The Impact of Child Care Subsidy Use on Child Care Quality."

41. Loeb and others, "Child Care in Poor Communities: Early Learning Effects by Type, Quality, and Stability"; Phillips and others, "Child Care of Children in Poverty: Opportunity or Inequality?"

42. U.S. Department of Health and Human Services, Office of the Assistant Secretary for Planning and Evaluation, *Child Care Eligibility and Enrollment Estimates for Fiscal Year 2003* (July 2005).

43. Robert C. Pianta and others, "The Effects of Preschool Education: What We Know, How Public Policy Is or Is Not Aligned with the Evidence Base, and What We Need to Know," *Psychological Science in the Public Interest*, vol. 10 (2009), pp. 49–88.

Appendix 5A.   *Probit Model Predicting Subsidy Receipt among All Eligible Families*[a]

Variable	Beta	Standard error
Family characteristic		
Mother is black	0.14	0.16
Mother is Hispanic	−0.37	0.21
Mother is Asian/other race	0.64	0.28*
Mother has < high school education	0.69	0.35*
Mother has high school diploma or GED	0.72	0.33*
Mother has some college	0.50	0.33
Mother is single	0.42	0.14**
Mother is proficient in English	0.01	0.32
Mother was < age 20 at focal child's birth	−0.21	0.17
Number of children in household ≤ age 6	0.15	0.17*
Number of children in household ≥ age 7	−0.08	0.07
Family lives in an urban area	0.00	0.14
Mother works part-time	−0.05	0.17
Mother participates in work-related activity	0.01	9.24
Mother is looking for work	−0.14	0.20
Mother is not in labor force	0.07	0.21
Household income-to-needs ratio	0.14	0.07*
Family received welfare	0.05	0.17
Family received food stamps	0.23	0.16
Family received WIC	0.31	0.21
Family received Medicaid	0.17	0.17
Family experienced food insecurity	−0.06	0.14
Child has a diagnosed disability	0.16	0.24
Child Bayley mental development index	0.00	0.01
Child is male	0.23	0.12
Child care preference		
Cost is very important	0.46	0.16*
Class/group size is very important	0.26	0.14
Sick care is very important	−0.17	0.15
Proximity is very important	−0.24	0.14
Caregiver training is very important	−0.23	0.23
Caregiver speaks English is very important	0.01	0.17
N	550	

Source: ECLS-B Nine-Month–Kindergarten Restricted Use Data File.

a. N = 250 subsidy recipients; all Ns are rounded to the nearest 50 per NCES requirements. All estimates were weighted by replicate weights W22P1-W22P90; standard errors are jackknife standard errors.
*$p < .05$, **$p < .01$.

6

Early Childhood Development and School Readiness

FRANK OBERKLAID, SHARON GOLDFELD, AND TIM MOORE

Healthy child development is the foundation for community and economic development because healthy, competent children grow up to fulfil their potential and contribute to society in a multitude of ways. Despite our knowledge of the importance of early childhood and the increasing policy interest in early childhood, only limited data have been available in Australia to either stimulate or evaluate local effort. In this chapter we report on the national implementation of the Australian Early Development Index (AEDI), a population measure of early childhood development completed by teachers for children in their first year of full-time schooling. In particular, we outline the reported national census results for children who are developmentally vulnerable (in the lowest 10th percentile of the total population) on one or more and on two or more domains (table 6-1 outlines all of the AEDI domains). We then discuss the broader early childhood policy challenges and opportunities within the Australian context that arise from the results.

Background

Over the past decade, public policy and service delivery to young children and their families have been informed by the rapidly growing body of research on the early years of life. The range of biological and environmental factors that pose a risk to the child's optimal development has been well described, and there is increasing interest in the mechanisms by which these factors affect the developing brain. What is clear is that by the time children begin formal schooling, many already are compromised in terms of their learning and developmental potential. The availability of national data about children's developmental status at school

127

entry creates a powerful argument for increasing the focus on the early years before the child starts school.

Importance of Early Childhood Development

A large and growing body of research points to the importance of the influence of the prenatal and early years on a range of health and developmental outcomes throughout the life course.[1] The brain is made up of integrated and interconnected sets of neural circuits that develop as a consequence of the complex continuous interplay between genes and experience. In the first few years of life, rapid and complex neural circuit development is dependent on, and very sensitive to, the quality and responsiveness of the caretaking environment.[2] Parents who are able to provide a consistently nurturing and responsive environment facilitate their child's optimal development. Brain development depends on environmental inputs at particular times—"sensitive periods" of development. Each period is associated with the formation of specific circuits that manifest as observable and predictable emerging developmental competencies in the young child. The development of more sophisticated neural circuits and more advanced skills builds on the neural circuits and skills developed earlier.[3] In this way, the foundation for future ongoing development and skill formation is established—it may be either a strong or a vulnerable foundation, depending on experiences in the first few years of life. Developmental competencies in the various domains—cognitive, social, and emotional—form the building blocks for success at school and beyond.[4]

Long-Term Effects of Early Experiences

Stressful and nonstimulating early environments interfere with optimal neural development, placing a child at risk for delays in cognitive, social, and emotional development.[5] A stressful pregnancy and subsequent stressful caretaking environments—harsh and inconsistent parenting, child abuse and neglect, exposure to violence, severe maternal depression, parental substance abuse—activate the body's stress management systems. There is an increase in levels of the stress hormone cortisol and alterations to physiological systems such as heart rate and blood pressure. This is a normal, adaptive part of the body's stress reaction that is usually short lived—the systems return to baseline when the stress is over. However, in situations in which a young child continues to experience his or her environment as stressful over a period of time, physiological stress responses do not return to normal but remain elevated. When that occurs, there can be significant disruption to neural circuit development and the architecture of the developing brain.[6]

A growing body of research suggests that such early experiences can have negative consequences throughout the life course.[7] They are thought to occur through two possible mechanisms: the cumulative deleterious effect over time on the child's developing brain of a poor caretaking environment and the resultant exposure to stressful situations and/or the biological embedding of adverse experiences and environmental events during sensitive periods of development in early childhood.[8]

It is thought that children who grow up in economically disadvantaged families and communities are especially vulnerable to biological embedding because of their greater exposure to stressful environments; that may account for the social gradient in health and developmental outcomes that has been well documented in many countries.[9] What is now established is that many conditions in adult life—obesity and its effects, hypertension, heart disease, mental health problems, criminality, family violence—have their origins in the adverse circumstances of children's early lives.[10] The experiences that children have in the years before they start formal schooling have significant impacts on their developmental trajectory and life course.

Early Emergence of Social Gradients

For many children, suboptimal developmental trajectories are well established or entrenched by the time they start school, and those trajectories become increasingly difficult to modify with the passage of time.[11] It has been shown that social and developmental gaps in children's functioning and achievement emerge as early as nine months and grow larger by 24 months of age.[12] These disparities exist across cognitive, social, behavioral, and health outcomes. By the time the children reach school, the gaps are even more significant.[13] As a result, children enter school with marked differences in the cognitive, noncognitive, and social skills needed for success in the school environment, and those differences are strongly predictive of later academic and occupational achievement.[14] Children who enter school not yet ready to take advantage of the learning environment tend to do less well academically and socially and have lower levels of education on leaving school than children who are ready. They also are more likely to become teenage parents, have poor employment records, become welfare recipients, engage in criminal activities, and have mental health problems.[15] These findings are consistent with the research described above linking early life experiences and environmental exposure with outcomes throughout the life course.

Defining School Readiness

In recent years the concept of "school readiness" has been broadened beyond cognitive achievement to include the child's social and emotional functioning, which is now understood to be equally important.[16] While a child's particular developmental skills in the various cognitive domains may be on track, whether the child is able to use those skills to take advantage of the learning opportunities of formal schooling is critical—concentration and application, peer relationships, confidence, adaptability and flexibility, and the ability to communicate needs and function independently are all important. School readiness in this context is not just a measurable set of skills that appear just before school entry but the cumulative outcome of the child's experiences in the first five years of life.[17] A number of factors have been shown to contribute to what has been termed the "school entry gap," or the differences in children's development when they begin school.[18] They include socioeconomic status and parental education level; family structure and functioning; child and parent health, including parent mental health; preschool attendance; cultural background; and parental involvement in literacy development. The gap can be considered social as well as developmental. Schools are faced with having to address the various social risk factors that affect learning as well as with attempting to flatten the developmental gap (which is often largely a consequence of the social gap).

Monitoring Progress

For the reasons discussed, school entry is an important time for capturing data on children's development and well-being. First, it reflects what happened in the years before school, and, when an ecological framework is applied, it represents an indirect measure of the child, family, and community factors that may have had an impact on children's development. Second, it acts as a natural baseline for measuring future school functioning in the cognitive, academic, and social-emotional domains. Finally, it is a good data capture point because all children go to school. From a population perspective there are only two points in time when we can sample all children: one is at birth, and the other is at school entry; in between there is great variability in attendance at out-of-home child care or preschool.

In Australia, there has been growing interest in data on the status of children during the preschool years, motivated primarily by widespread concern that too many children are falling behind before they reach school age. Therefore, in 2006 the Council of Australian Governments (COAG) released its human capital reform agenda, recognizing the importance of investing in early childhood development as a key plank for action.[19] This agenda flagged the development and subsequent release of the National Early Childhood Strategy, which noted the need for sufficient data to measure progress over time.[20] In response, the 2008 release of *Headline Indicators for Children's Health, Development and Well-Being*[21] and the subsequent data report, *A Picture of Australia's Children 2009*,[22] included a specific indicator (the proportion of children entering school with basic skills for life and learning) linking school entry to early childhood development. It was recognized that data on children's development at school entry would help inform policies, programs, and resource allocation at the national, state, regional, and local levels and greatly enhance efforts to support increased investment in the critical years before the child begins formal schooling and to evaluate the effects of that investment.

Method and Measures

The Australian Early Development Index is a relative population measure of early childhood development and an adaptation of the Canadian Early Development Instrument (EDI). It provides important data on children's development and well-being when they start school. The EDI was "conceived and designed to provide a simple, reliable and feasible proximal measure of the state of children's developmental health in communities. . . . The EDI reflects developmental outcomes and milestones children should be able to achieve under optimal circumstances in physical and socio-emotional health as well as in their cognitive development."[23] The adaptation of the EDI for Australia and the concurrent and construct validity of the AEDI and EDI have previously been described.[24]

The AEDI contains over 100 questions that map to five domains of children's development: physical health and well-being; social competence; emotional maturity; language and cognitive skills; and communication skills and general knowledge (table 6-1). Data are reported as the proportion of children who are developmentally vulnerable on each domain and who are vulnerable on one or more or on two or more domains. Each checklist also includes additional sociodemographic information such as birth date, first language, English as a second language status, language spoken at home, and Australian indigenous status. Geographic data include the child's suburb or town as well as the location of the school. The Australian Standard Geographic Classification (ASGC) of remote areas was applied to all geographic locations. Socioeconomic status (SES) was applied to individual children using the Australian census-based Index of Relative Socioeconomic Disadvantage score for the participant's home suburb.[25] Children's preschool attendance and care arrangements prior to school were based on teacher report. Preschool was defined as a separate program or a program within a child care center. The AEDI does not record any specific family-level variables.

Although the checklists are completed on individual children, data are not provided for each child or used for diagnostic purposes; rather, data are aggregated at the population level for the suburb or postcode where the child lives (not where he or she attends school). The AEDI results therefore emphasize the

Table 6-1. *AEDI Domain Descriptions*

Physical health and well-being	Social competence	Emotional maturity	Language and cognitive skills (school-based)	Communication skills and general knowledge
Physical readiness for the day	Overall social competence	Prosocial and helping behavior	Basic literacy, interest in literacy, numeracy, and memory	Communication skills and general knowledge
Physical independence	Responsibility and respect	Anxious and fearful behavior	Advanced literacy	
Gross and fine motor skills	Approach to learning	Aggressive behavior	Basic numeracy	
	Readiness to explore new things	Hyperactivity and inattention		

Source: Centre for Community Child Health and Telethon Institute for Child Health Research, "A Snapshot of Early Childhood Development in Australia: AEDI National Report 2009" (Canberra: Australian Government, 2009). Updated May 2011.

cumulative environmental influences on children's development in the years from birth until school entry rather than the influence of the school, and they allow comparisons between populations and geographic areas.

Following almost twelve months of planning, including broad and intensive consultation with federal and state governments, education departments, the various school systems (government, Catholic, and independent), teacher unions, and other stakeholders, the AEDI was completed nationwide for the first time in 2009. The AEDI was funded by the Australian government and conducted by the Centre for Community Child Health at the Royal Children's Hospital Melbourne/Murdoch Children's Research Institute, in partnership with the Telethon Institute for Child Health Research in Perth.

Between May 1 and July 31, information was collected on 261,203 children (97.5 percent of the estimated national five-year-old population)[26] through a secure, web-based data entry system. This involved 15,528 teachers from 7,423 government, Catholic, and independent schools around Australia. AEDI results were reported for the communities in which the children lived. The AEDI results were mapped to local communities (suburbs or towns) within larger communities (AEDI communities) with boundaries determined mainly at the local government level. Together with the previously described community profiles, these maps enable communities to see how local children are doing relative to or compared with other children in their community and across Australia. Since December 2009 these data and maps have been publicly available through the AEDI website (www.aedi.org.au).

The 2009 dataset was used to create national cut points on each of the AEDI domain scales. Children scoring below the 10th percentile on each domain are considered developmentally vulnerable.[27] The primary outcome measure reported in this study is children considered to be developmentally vulnerable on one or more or on two or more of the five AEDI domains.

Results

Table 6-2 shows the AEDI data for children who were developmentally vulnerable on one or more or on two or more domains analyzed by geography (state; major city; inner-regional area; outer-regional area; remote area; and very remote area); area-level socioeconomic status of communities where the children lived (in quintiles); gender; indigenous status; language diversity; and state or territory. Across Australia, 23.6 percent of children were rated as "developmentally vulnerable" (those falling below the 10th percentile compared with the national population) in one or more domains and 11.8 percent in two or more. Proportions of vulnerability varied considerably across population groups and geography. Children living in outer-regional, remote, or very remote areas were more likely to be developmentally vulnerable, and vulnerability rates of indigenous children (47.4 percent) were twice the national average. The proportion of children living in the most disadvantaged areas (32.0 percent) was higher than that of children in the least disadvantaged areas (16.2 percent), though the actual numbers of developmentally vulnerable children were more evenly distributed. The most disadvantaged areas accounted for only 27 percent of all vulnerable children, while 18 percent of developmentally vulnerable children lived in the least disadvantaged areas.

Data were also collected on children's use of preschool education and care. Overall, 80.9 percent of children had attended some type of early education program (kindergarten or child care) prior to starting school; there was considerable variability between states, ranging from 92.6 percent to 67.1 percent. Although there was a clear social gradient based on socio-economic status— only 75.6 percent of children in the most disadvantaged areas attended a preschool program in the year prior to starting school while 86.0 percent did so in the least disadvantaged area did so—a substantial majority of children living in disadvantaged areas attended preschool. Children living in very remote Australia as well as indigenous/Torres Strait Islander children and those from language

Table 6-2. *National AEDI Results: Children Developmentally Vulnerable in One or More or Two or More Domains*

Subgroups	Number of children[a]	Developmentally vulnerable on one or more domains (percent)	Developmentally vulnerable on two or more domains (percent)[b]
Australia	246,421	23.6	11.8
Socioeconomic status of communities where children live (SEIFA Index for Relative Disadvantage)[c]			
Quintile 1 *(most disadvantaged)*	52,087	32.0	17.5
Quintile 2	44,510	25.5	13.1
Quintile 3	42,388	23.5	11.5
Quintile 4	44,147	20.5	9.6
Quintile 5 *(least disadvantaged)*	60,130	16.2	7.2
Geographic location (ASGC Remoteness Areas)[c]			
Major cities of Australia	163,938	22.5	11.0
Inner-regional Australia	51,629	23.6	12.1
Outer-regional Australia	23,623	26.8	14.1
Remote Australia	4,557	29.5	16.0
Very remote Australia	2,648	47.1	30.5
Sex			
Male	124,249	30.2	16.2
Female	122,172	16.8	7.4
Indigenous			
Indigenous	11,190	47.4	29.6
Non-indigenous	235,231	22.4	11.0

(continued)

backgrounds other than English were also less likely to have attended a preschool program. Those children who had not attended a preschool program were developmentally more vulnerable in one or more domains, and that held true across all SES groups.[28]

Discussion

The AEDI results confirm that there is a great deal of variability in different communities with respect to sociodemographic profile, configuration of services, and needs. The considerable inter- and intra-community variability in the AEDI results suggests that any policy responses need to take into account the major differences between communities with respect to needs, demographics,

Table 6-2. *National AEDI Results: Children Developmentally Vulnerable in One or More or Two or More Domains (Continued)*

Subgroups	Number of children[a]	Developmentally vulnerable on one or more domains (percent)	Developmentally vulnerable on two or more domains (percent)[b]
Language diversity			
LBOTE[cd]	43,853	32.2	16.7
Proficient in English[cd]	35,435	21.8	9.6
Not proficient in English	6,334	93.7	59.0
English only[d]	202,568	21.7	10.8
Proficient in English	195,958	19.3	8.7
Not proficient in English	6,482	93.8	75.2
State/territory			
New South Wales	82,710	21.3	10.3
Victoria	57,277	20.3	10.0
Queensland	52,603	29.6	15.8
Western Australia	26,052	24.7	12.2
South Australia	15,009	22.8	11.5
Tasmania	5,699	21.8	10.8
Australian Capital Territory	4,180	22.2	10.9
Northern Territory	2,865	38.7	23.4

Source: Centre for Community Child Health and Telethon Institute for Child Health Research, "A Snapshot of Early Childhood Development in Australia: AEDI National Report 2009" (Canberra: Australian Government, 2009). Updated May 2011.

a. Results for children with special needs are not included in the results. In addition, children were omitted from domain analyses if the teacher answered an insufficient number of questions.

b. The denominator for this calculation may be lower than the denominator for "developmentally vulnerable on one or more domains" as there are fewer children with valid scores on more than one domain. For the total number of children for Australia (245,421), the denominator for "developmentally vulnerable on two or more domains" is lower by 134 children.

c. See relevant definition of terms in Centre for Community Child Health and Telethon Institute for Child Health Research, "A Snapshot of Early Childhood Development in Australia: AEDI National Report 2009."

d. The subsets of these categories do not equal the total because teachers selected the "Don't know" response.

and available resources; despite that, communities have little or no say in resource allocation or program development, and they are not accountable for outcomes. Accordingly, it is unlikely that a one-size-fits-all approach is likely to make a significant difference to all children and to all communities. The policy focus is beginning to shift toward building capacity within communities by facilitating and providing resources for community efforts to identify issues, determine needs, and develop local solutions.[29] In this context, the debate about how to improve outcomes in young children is now broader than before, and advocacy has moved from a focus on requesting more resources toward an understanding that government budgets are finite and an approach that seeks to determine how to get better value from existing services.

Australia is the first country in the world to have national data of this kind available for children soon after they start school. These data have contributed to a greatly increased awareness of the importance of early childhood development and thereby are helping to change the social discourse on early childhood development, at least at the policy and service-system level. The AEDI has also helped move policy discussions away from the traditional focus on new and additional programs (which are always difficult to scale up) and toward building capacity in communities, which is increasingly seen as offering the best chance of long-term sustainability.[30] The data confirm what educators and others already know: that large numbers of children, especially those from disadvantaged areas, are already in trouble by the time they get to school. From that point on, teachers are playing catch-up—attempting to address various developmental and social issues that prevent children from getting the most out of their school experience.

These national Australian results also support what has already been well documented in many other countries: that children living in disadvantaged areas are more likely to have poorer outcomes. Research has demonstrated that social gradients for children's developmental outcomes emerge early[31] and are either sustained or increase over the schooling years.[32] A number of these studies have been summarized recently in *Healthcare Quarterly*, which focuses specifically on the social determinants of child health within the construct of the broadest understanding of health and development.[33] In Australia, a number of recent studies and reports confirm social gradients for a range of outcomes. For example, Australian data show higher rates of low birth weight (<2,500 grams) for babies born into poorer families,[34] a significant risk factor for future health and development.[35] Australian longitudinal studies have similarly shown that social gradients for a range of health and developmental outcomes are already apparent in toddlers[36] and that measures of social disadvantage are significant predictors of poorer language skills by four years of age.[37] National education testing shows that socioeconomic status differences are still apparent at eight years of age and are either sustained or increase during the rest of schooling, particularly for indigenous children.[38] Finally, Australia's rating on country comparative data from the Organization for Economic Cooperation and Development's Program for International Student Assessment (PISA) for 15-year-old children show a relatively steep social gradient compared with other countries, with children from poorer backgrounds having far lower academic results than children from wealthier backgrounds.[39]

Implications for Public Policy

INTERVENING EARLY FROM A UNIVERSAL SERVICE PLATFORM. Despite the considerable government investment in universally available services (child care, preschool, primary health care), family support services, and social safety nets such as unemployment and other benefits, large numbers of children are already developmentally vulnerable and at risk by the time that they start school. That raises the question of the effectiveness of the existing service system in overcoming the damaging effects of disadvantage. We need to find ways of strengthening the capacity of the universal services to be more truly inclusive and to engage all families, especially the most vulnerable. There is good evidence that the most disadvantaged families—those who are likely to benefit most from services—are the least likely to use them because of various financial, logistical, and/or cultural barriers.[40] The outcome is the inevitable "inverse care law,"[41] whereby services are inequitably delivered, leading to a widening of the outcomes gap.[42] One approach being adopted to address these problems is a public health model known as *progressive universalism*[43] or *proportionate universalism*,[44] in which progressively more intensive support services are provided from a universal platform (that is, services are accessible and available for all) according to the needs of children and their families. This approach would need to be conceptualized centrally but delivered effectively at the local community level, with the specific model used matching the characteristics of the community.

There also are issues with the notion of targeting services to better meet need. Most programs that have been established to address emerging family issues and risk factors for child development are generally too narrow in scope—risk factors and problems cluster together. For example, substance abuse, family violence, and mental health problems—all of which may lead to dysfunctional parenting—are likely to coexist, yet relevant service programs are small in scale, act independently of universal systems, and are not oriented to the needs of adults as parents. Services at the community level tend to be fragmented, and there is little cooperation or coordination among them; this has led to duplication and inefficiencies in service delivery, creating pathways that are difficult for both parents and professionals to navigate.[45]

While the AEDI results demonstrate the negative impact of early disadvantage on children's development, they also illustrate another important point: children with developmental vulnerabilities are found at every socioeconomic level of society. While children living in disadvantaged communities were more likely to be developmentally vulnerable at school entry, they represent a minority of the total number of vulnerable children. In other words, most developmentally vulnerable children across the country did not live in disadvantaged areas. Clearly there is a strong case for increasing resources for disadvantaged communities, but that should not be done at the expense of maintaining a strong universal system if there is indeed to be a measurable shift in developmental outcomes for all children and an opportunity to intervene early and effectively.

THE IMPORTANCE OF EARLY DETECTION SYSTEMS. Early identification of children who are experiencing developmental problems is of paramount importance. Most developmental delays and social and emotional issues that are apparent in a child at school entry will have been evident well before then.[46] By the time children start school, many such problems have become entrenched and are much more difficult and complex to deal with. In other words, the longer we wait, the more difficult it becomes to change a child's developmental trajectory. It follows therefore that we need to be better at identifying and responding promptly to the emerging needs of young children and their families. This is self-evident, yet there are numerous challenges. Perhaps the foremost is that the service system in Australia generally has little or no contact with families in the toddler and preschool years—a time of rapid developmental change when we might detect the first emerging signs of delay or dysfunction. Although in most jurisdictions there is contact with most families in the antenatal and immediate postnatal period, the frequency of contact diminishes rapidly, especially with those who are most at risk. Contact may improve marginally in future years as the result of the government commitment to introduce universal preschool for four-year-olds across the country, but that is still fairly late in the child's developmental trajectory. To increase the capacity of the service system to respond promptly to the emerging problems of children and their families, it is important to find ways of maintaining continuous contact with them during the early years.

Another challenge is the training and expertise of service providers and the methods used to identify and respond to emerging problems. There is a major (re)training agenda for early-years service providers, but we need to ensure that we have the strong system of progressive universalism described above. In such a system, professionals with appropriate skills and expertise, using reliable methods of early identification, will have clearly identified referral sources for children and families that need further assessment or support. All of this requires the service system to become much more effectively integrated than it is currently.

Once children get to school, there needs to be a reliable, systemwide method of early detection and early intervention. We will need to develop more effective ways of catering to children with a wide range of needs—that is, with widely divergent degrees of "school readiness."

THE COMMUNITY AS A PLATFORM FOR CHANGE. Apart from changes to the service system, with an emphasis on improved coordination and integration, we need to ensure that communities are child and family friendly. We need to provide opportunities for parents to interact with others and avoid social isolation, and we need to ensure that they have access to information about their children's health and development; in particular, they must be able to access in a timely way the services and supports that they need to fulfill their obligations as parents. That in turn means paying attention to other services, such as transportation, parks and other community facilities, community drop-in centers, and so on. Service coordination is especially important for new housing developments and therefore requires a "whole-of-government" approach to ensure that it happens.

It is important to note that while the AEDI gives communities valuable information about how effectively children's early experiences have prepared them for the learning and social opportunities that schools provide, it does not tell them what to do. A major challenge is to understand more fully the factors that contribute to positive early experiences and how they can be best promoted. We also need to understand better how neighborhood affects outcomes—why some children in some areas are doing better than expected, or vice versa.[47] The conditions under which families are raising young children have altered dramatically over the past few decades. We are still in the process of trying to understand the impact of recent social and economic changes; some have been beneficial whereas others have had negative consequences. We need to understand how these changes have affected the capacity of parents to raise their children as they (and we) would wish, so that we can support them more effectively. Doing so will involve taking action to address the wider social and structural factors that affect family functioning—housing, employment, social support, and so forth. It would also involve reconfiguring the service system, which is still largely based on service models that for the most part have not evolved to meet the needs of contemporary families.

Conclusion

Just as no single factor is responsible for any particular developmental outcome, so no single form of intervention will produce sustainable improvements in outcomes. A multilevel ecological approach is required, involving simultaneous action at the macro level (involving larger structural factors such as policies and regulations), exo level (agencies, organizations, systems that affect individuals indirectly), meso level (social entities—peers, extended family, social service agencies—that affect individuals directly), and micro level (family, couple, kinship network). To develop and coordinate a community-based action plan incorporating all of these levels requires the combined efforts of governments, service providers, and communities. The substantial mechanisms and government structures needed to support this work are currently lacking and need to be built.

The implementation of the AEDI as a national census offers fertile ground for further rigorous policy and program testing against a solid and measurable early childhood development outcome. As data linkage emerges as a realistic and workable option in most states and territories in Australia, there is an opportunity to evaluate policy action against longitudinal population outcomes. It is only in this sort of evaluation-receptive environment that we will know whether Australian dollars are well spent, that no harm is done, and that the best systems to support young children and their families are in place.

Notes

1. Jack P. Shonkoff, Thomas W. Boyce, and Bruce McEwen, "Neuroscience, Molecular Biology, and the Childhood Roots of Health Disparities: Building a New Framework for Health Promotion and Disease Prevention," *Journal of the American Medical Association*, vol. 301, no. 21 (2009), pp. 2252–59.

2. National Scientific Council on the Developing Child, "Early Experiences Can Alter Gene Expression and Affect Long-Term Development," Working Paper 10 (Cambridge, Mass.: Center on the Developing Child, Harvard University, 2010).

3. National Scientific Council on the Developing Child, "The Timing and Quality of Early Experiences Combine to Shape Brain Architecture," Working Paper 5 (Cambridge, Mass.: Center on the Developing Child, Harvard University, 2007).

4. Leon Feinstein and Kathryn Duckworth, "Development in the Early Years: Its Importance for School Performance and Adult Outcomes." Wider Benefits of Learning Research Report 20 (London: Wider Benefits of Learning Research Centre, Institute of Education, 2006).

5. National Scientific Council on the Developing Child, "Early Experiences Can Alter Gene Expression and Affect Long-Term Development."

6. Robert F. Anda and others, "The Enduring Effects of Abuse and Related Adverse Experiences in Childhood: A Convergence of Evidence from Neurobiology and Epidemiology," *European Archives of Psychiatry and Clinical Neuroscience*, vol. 256, no. 3 (2006), pp. 174–86; Eamon McCrory, Stephane A. De Brito, and Essi Viding, "Research Review: The Neurobiology and Genetics of Maltreatment and Adversity," *Journal of Child Psychology and Psychiatry*, vol. 51, no. 10 (2010), pp. 1079–95; Jeniffer S. Middlebrooks and Natalie C. Audage, *The Effects of Childhood Stress on Health Across the Lifespan* (Atlanta, Ga.: Centers for Disease Control and Prevention, National Center for Injury Prevention and Control, 2008); National Scientific Council on the Developing Child, "Excessive Stress Disrupts the Architecture of the Developing Brain," Working Paper 3 (Cambridge, Mass.: Center on the Developing Child, Harvard University, 2005).

7. Shonkoff, Boyce, and McEwen, "Neuroscience, Molecular Biology, and the Childhood Roots of Health Disparities"; Neal Halfon and Miles Hochstein, "Life Course Health Development: An Integrated Framework for Developing Health, Policy, and Research," *Milbank Quarterly*, vol. 80, no. 3 (2002), pp. 433–79.

8. Daniel P. Keating and Clyde Hertzman, "Modernity's Paradox," in *Developmental Health and the Wealth of Nations: Social, Biological, and Educational Dynamics,* edited by Daniel P. Keating and Clyde Hertzman (New York: Guilford Press, 1999).

9. Clyde Hertzman and others, "Bucking the Inequality Gradient through Early Child Development," *British Medical Journal*, vol. 340 (February 10, 2010), p. c468; Richard G. Wilkinson and Kate E. Pickett, *The Spirit Level: Why More Equal Societies Almost Always Do Better* (London: Allen Lane, 2009).

10. National Scientific Council on the Developing Child, "Early Experiences Can Alter Gene Expression and Affect Long-Term Development."

11. Leon Feinstein, Kathryn Duckworth, and Ricardo Sabates, *Education and the Family: Passing Success across the Generations* (London: Routledge, 2008).

12. Tamara Halle and others, *Disparities in Early Learning and Development: Lessons from the Early Childhood Longitudinal Study—Birth Cohort (ECLS-B)*, report prepared for the Council of Chief State School Officers (Washington: Child Trends, 2009); Jan M. Nicholson and others, "Socioeconomic Inequality Profiles in Physical and Developmental Health from 0–7 Years: Australian National Study," *Journal of Epidemiology and Community Health*, vol. 1136 (2010).

13. Flavio Cunha and others, "Interpreting the Evidence on Life Cycle Skill Formation," in *Handbook of the Economics of Education*, edited by Eric Hanushek and Finis Welch (Amsterdam: North-Holland, 2006); Greg J. Duncan and others, "School Readiness and Later Achievement," *Developmental Psychology*, vol. 43, no. 6 (2007), pp. 1423–46; Leon Feinstein, "Inequality in the Early Cognitive Development of British Children in the 1970 Cohort," *Economica*, vol. 70 (2003), pp. 73–97; Vi-Nhuan Le and others, *School Readiness, Full-Day Kindergarten, and Student Achievement: An Empirical Investigation* (Santa Monica, Calif.: RAND, 2006).

14. Martha Boethel, *Readiness: School, Family, and Community Connections*, report prepared by the National Center for Family and Community Connections with Schools (Austin, Tex.: Southwest Educational Development Laboratory, 2004); Cunha and others, "Interpreting the Evidence on Life Cycle Skill Formation"; Feinstein, "Inequality in the Early Cognitive Development of British Children"; Le and others, *School Readiness, Full-Day Kindergarten, and Student Achievement.*

15. The Future of Children, "School Readiness: Closing Racial and Ethnic Gaps," Executive Summary (Spring 2005) (www.futureofchildren.org/futureofchildren/publications/docs/15_01_ExecSummary.pdf).

16. Charles Bruner, Cherie Floyd, and Abby Copeman, *Seven Things Policy Makers Need to Know about School Readiness* (Des Moines, Iowa: State Early Childhood Policy Technical Assistance Network, 2005); Cunha and others, "Interpreting the Evidence on Life Cycle Skill Formation"; Barry Zuckerman and Neal Halfon, "School Readiness: An Idea Whose Time Has Arrived," *Pediatrics*, vol. 111, no. 6 (2003), pp. 1433–36.

17. Edward C. Melhuish and others, "Effects of the Home Learning Environment and Preschool Center Experience upon Literacy and Numeracy Development in Early Primary School," *Journal of Social Issues*, vol. 64, no. 1 (2008), pp. 95–114.

18. Magdalena Janus and Eric Duku, "The School Entry Gap: Socioeconomic, Family, and Health Factors Associated with Children's School Readiness to Learn," *Early Education and Development*, vol. 18, no. 3 (2007), pp. 375–403.

19. Council of Australian Governments, *COAG Human Capital Reform: Report by the COAG National Reform Initiative Working Group* (Melbourne, Vic.: February 10, 2006).

20. Council of Australian Governments, *Investing in the Early Years—A National Early Childhood Development Strategy* (Melbourne, Vic.: July 2009).

21. Department of Human Services, Victoria, *Headline Indicators for Children's Health, Development and Well-being* (Melbourne, Vic.: 2006).

22. Australian Institute of Health and Welfare, *A Picture of Australia's Children 2009*, PHE 112 (Canberra, ACT: 2009).

23. Janus and Duku, "The School Entry Gap," pp. 375–403.

24. David Andrich and Irene Styles, *Final Report on the Psychometric Analysis of the Early Development Instrument (EDI) Using the Rasch Model*, technical paper commissioned for the development of the Australian Early Development Instrument (Melbourne, Vic.: 2004); Sally A. Brinkman and others, "Investigating the Validity of the Australian Early Development Index," *Early Education and Development*, vol. 18, no. 3 (2007), pp. 427–51; Sharon Goldfeld and others, "The Process and Policy Challenges of Adapting and Implementing the Early Development Instrument in Australia," *Early Education and Development*, vol. 20, no. 6 (2009), pp. 978–91; Magdalena Janus and Daniel Offord, "Development and Psychometric Properties of the Early Development Instrument (EDI): A Measure of Children's School Readiness," *Canadian Journal of Behavioural Science*, vol. 39 (2007), pp. 1–22.

25. Australian Bureau of Statistics, *2006 Census of Population and Housing: Socio-Economic Indexes for Areas*, ABS catalogue 2033.0.55.001(Canberra, ACT: 2008).

26. Centre for Community Child Health and Telethon Institute for Child Health Research, "A Snapshot of Early Childhood Development in Australia: Australian Early Development Index (AEDI) National Report 2009" (Canberra, ACT: Australian Government Department of Education, Employment, and Workplace Relations, 2009).

27. Ibid.

28. Mary Sayers and others, "Starting School: A Pivotal Life Transition for Children and Their Families," invited paper submitted to *Family Matters*, the research journal of the Australian Institute of Family Studies, Melbourne.

29. Ilan Katz, "Community Interventions for Vulnerable Children and Families: Participation and Power," *Communities, Children and Families Australia*, vol. 3, no. 1 (2009), pp. 19–32; John Wiseman, "Local Heroes: Learning from Community Strengthening Policy Developments in Victoria," *Australian Journal of Public Administration*, vol. 65, no. 2 (2006), pp. 95–107.

30. Katz, "Community Interventions for Vulnerable Children and Families"; Tony Vinson, *Markedly Socially Disadvantaged Localities in Australia* (Canberra, ACT: Department of Education, Employment, and Workplace Relations, 2009); Wiseman, "Local Heroes."

31. Betty Hart and Todd R. Risley, *Meaningful Differences in the Everyday Experience of Young American Children* (Baltimore, Md.: Paul H. Brookes, 1995); Betty Hart and Todd R. Risley, *The Social World of Children Learning to Talk* (Baltimore, Md.: Paul H. Brookes, 1999).

32. Feinstein, "Inequality in the Early Cognitive Development of British Children"; Feinstein and Duckworth, *Development in the Early Years*.

33. Neal Halfon, Kandyce Larson, and Shirley Russ, "Why Social Determinants?" *Healthcare Quarterly*, vol. 14 (2010), pp. 8–20; Avram Denburg and Denis Daneman, "The Link

between Social Inequality and Child Health Outcomes," *Healthcare Quarterly*, vol. 14 (2010), pp. 21–31; Clyde Hertzman, "Social Geography of Developmental Health in the Early Years, *Healthcare Quarterly*, vol. 14 (2010), pp. 32–40.

34. Australian Institute of Health and Welfare, *A Picture of Australia's Children 2009*.

35. David James Purslove Barker, *Fetal and Infant Origins of Adult Disease* (London: British Medical Publishing Group, 1992); David James Purslove Barker, *Mothers, Babies, and Health in Later Life* (Edinburgh, Scotland: Churchill Livingstone, 1998).

36. Nicholson and others, "Socioeconomic Inequality Profiles."

37. Sheena Reilly and others "Predicting Language Outcomes at 4 Years of Age: Findings from Early Language in Victoria Study," *Pediatrics*, vol. 120, no. 6 (2010), pp. e1441–e1449.

38. National Assessment Program Literacy and Numeracy, *NAPLAN Summary Report: Achievement in Reading, Writing, Language Conventions, and Numeracy* (Canberra, ACT: 2010).

39. Sue Thomson and others, *Challenges for Australian Education: Results from PISA 2009* (Melbourne, Vic.: ACER, 2011).

40. Stephen Carbone and others, *Breaking Cycles, Building Futures: Promoting Inclusion of Vulnerable Families in Antenatal and Universal Early Childhood Services: A Report on the First Three Stages of the Project* (Melbourne, Vic.: Department of Human Services, Victoria, 2004); Patricia Moran and Deborah Ghate, "The Effectiveness of Parenting Support," *Children and Society*, vol. 19, no. 4 (2005), pp. 329–36; Gail Winkworth and others, *Working in the Grey: Increasing Collaboration between Services in Inner North Canberra: A Communities for Children Project* (Dickson, ACT: Institute of Child Protection Studies, Australian Catholic University, 2009).

41. Julian Tudor Hart, *The Inverse Care Law*, Socialist Health Association (www.sochealth.co.uk/history/inversecare.htm).

42. Martin White, Jean Adams, and Peter Heywood, "How and Why do Interventions That Increase Health Overall Widen Inequalities within Populations?" in *Health, Inequality, and Public Health*, edited by Salvatore J. Babones (Bristol, U.K.: Policy Press, 2009).

43. Jane Barlow and others, "Health-Led Interventions in the Early Years to Enhance Infant and Maternal Mental Health: A Review of Reviews," *Child and Adolescent Mental Health*, vol. 15, no. 4 (2010), pp. 178–85; June Statham and Marjorie Smith*, Issues in Earlier Intervention: Identifying and Supporting Children with Additional Needs*, Research Report DCSF-RR205 (London: Department for Children, Schools, and Families, 2010); Feinstein, Duckworth, and Sabates, *Education and the Family*.

44. Department of Epidemiology and Public Health, *The Marmot Review: Fair Society, Healthy Lives: Strategic Review of Health Inequalities in England Post-2010* (London: University College London, 2010).

45. Centre for Community Child Health, *Services for Young Children and Families: An Integrated Approach*, CCCH Policy Brief 4 (Melbourne, Vic.: Royal Children's Hospital, 2006).

46. Halle and others, *Disparities in Early Learning and Development*.

47. Sharon Goldfeld and others, *Kids in Communities Study Phase 1: Pilot* (Melbourne: VicHealth) (www.vichealth.vic.gov.au/en/Publications/Health-Inequalities/Kids-in-Communities-Study.aspx).

7

Economic Inequality and Children's Educational Attainment

MARY E. CAMPBELL, ROBERT HAVEMAN, AND BARBARA WOLFE

The past three decades have witnessed substantial growth in the United States in economic inequality among families and the neighborhoods in which they live. For example, between 1980 and 2008, a standard measure of inequality in family income—the Gini coefficient—rose from .40 to .47, an increase of nearly 20 percent.[1] The income gains leading to the increase in inequality were largely concentrated in high-income families. In 1975, the income of households at the 90th percentile was 8.5 times that of those at the 10th percentile; by 2009, the rich family had 11.4 times the income of the poor family.[2] Wealth (family assets) inequality is far greater; in 1980, the top 1 percent of households held about 7 percent of the nation's wealth, but by 2008, that had increased to nearly 17 percent.[3] This increase in economic inequality has led to an increase in the concentration of affluent families in high-income neighborhoods, with poor families living in poor neighborhoods with poor schools.[4] It has also led to a decline in the quality of the urban neighborhoods in which many poor and minority children live.[5] This pattern of increasing disparities is also associated with changes in a wide variety of other social, economic, and political dimensions, including the development and educational

We thank the Russell Sage Foundation and its program on the social dimensions of inequality for support for this research and Cecilia Rouse, Peter Saunders, and the editors for their helpful suggestions. Special thanks to Andrea Voyer for her insights and help in thinking through dilemmas as they arose and to Gary Sandefur, who worked with us on the first version of this paper. We are very grateful for everything that they have added to our study and for their generous willingness to share both their time and their effort. We also thank David Chancellor, Deborah Johnson, and Dawn Duren of the Institute for Research on Poverty for their superb help in turning our technical words into understandable prose that is also technically accurate. The authors are listed in alphabetical order; all contributed equally to the chapter.

attainments of children who have experienced the resulting increase in disparities among families, schools, and neighborhoods.[6]

This chapter contributes to the meager literature on how changes in the inequality of family income and geographic/neighborhood resources are linked to the attainments of the children who live in them. We study the relationship between observed increases in family and geographic economic inequality and the schooling attainments of children who have experienced these increases. We concentrate on two measures of children's schooling—the probability of graduating from high school and years of completed schooling. In particular, we provide quantitative estimates of the effects of an assumed change in the inequality of family and geographic economic resources on both the level of schooling of children and the educational disparities among them. Considering the extensive literature on how parents' income is linked to children's attainments, we expect that increased inequality in family income (and geographic environments) will be reflected in the level and inequality of children's schooling attainments.[7] We assume that if family economic resources are positively related to the attainments of children, the growing gaps among families will be reflected in growing gaps in the education of children. Educational attainments of children from higher-income families will increase as the affluence of their family increases, while those of children from lower-income families are likely to decrease. It is not clear whether the increases in schooling for rich children will offset the likely decreases for poor children, making the overall impact of growing inequality on the national level of schooling uncertain.[8]

Prior Literature

Previous empirical research on the intergenerational effects of changes in overall economic inequality is sparse.[9] Susan Mayer's work stands as the primary empirical exploration of the relationship between family and geographical inequality while children are growing up and their later educational attainments.[10] Using data from the Panel Study of Income Dynamics (PSID), she estimated the relationship between state-level income inequality and the later educational attainments of children in high- and low-income families who experienced those inequality levels.[11]

While results from her estimates are not always consistent and frequently are not statistically significant, she tends to find a positive relationship between the level of within-state inequality experienced by children and both the overall level of and inequality in children's educational attainment. When the estimated models allow for increased returns to education and parental income, income inequality tends to increase the educational attainment of higher-income youth by more than it decreases the attainment of youth from lower-income families, leading to overall increases in the level of schooling. However, when state-level investments in education are introduced into the model, this pattern is reversed. In this model, the negative coefficient for lower-income children is large and statistically significant. In addition, the difference between the (positive) effect of increases in inequality on the attainments of higher-income youths and the (negative) effect of inequality on the attainments of youth from lower-income families is statistically significant.[12]

Research Strategy

Here we adopt a new and different approach to studying the effect of economic inequality on children's educational attainment. While Mayer estimated statistical models of the relationship between parental income inequality and youths' level of school completion, we combine such models with simulation methods to provide more detailed estimates of the connection. We also use a broader set of measures of both economic inequality and children's education.

First, we present a new estimate of the relationship between children's family and geographic circumstances and schooling outcomes. We relate a set of family and geographic economic variables for a group of children (recorded between the ages of 2 and 15 years) to their schooling attainment at the age of 25. The variables that we use are consistently identified in the prior literature as significantly related to schooling outcomes.[13] In addition to standard demographic and economic variables, our statistical estimates include variables describing children's exposure to child care, the characteristics of their neighborhoods, and the cost of public postsecondary education in their state.[14]

Second, we directly alter the value of the family variables (for example, income/needs ratio and assets) and geographic indicators of inequality (state-specific changes in the Gini coefficient of family income) to reflect an assumed level of increased inequality in line with state-specific changes between 1970 and 2004.[15]

In a final step, we combine these changed (more unequal) values for individual family and geographic economic variables together with the relevant coefficients from our statistical estimates of the determinants of educational attainment. These allow us to estimate (predict) the schooling attainment outcome for each observation. In this simulation, the actual values of the remaining independent variables are held constant. The resulting simulated changes in individual educational attainments show a distribution of schooling outcomes that reflects the estimated effects of increased inequality on children.

We then compare this simulated distribution of educational attainments with the actual distribution. In appendix 7A, we present the details for both our data and our approach to establishing these links between parental and geographic inequality and children's educational outcomes.

Estimating the Effects of Family and Geographic Economic Circumstances on Educational Attainment

We use a standard framework to establish links between two educational attainment variables and four family and geographic economic variables. Control variables found to have persistent, robust, and statistically significant relationships with educational attainment in prior research studies were included in the estimation.[16] For those characteristics that change over time (such as family income, number of siblings, and county unemployment rates), we average the values of those variables over the individual's life from the ages of 2 to 15 years.

Table 7-1 presents summary statistics for our variables, and table 7-2 presents results from our estimated model. The coefficients on the core socioeconomic explanatory variables consistently identified in the prior literature are significantly related to schooling outcomes, and they have the expected signs. Blacks, women, and those from families in which the head is foreign-born have higher educational attainment than individuals not in these groups, after we control for other relevant characteristics.[17] Parental schooling is positively and significantly related to offspring years of completed schooling and high school graduation. The average number of siblings at home during childhood is negatively associated with years of education but not with high school graduation. The number of residential moves during childhood and the average county unemployment rate are negatively associated with both years of completed schooling and high school graduation.[18] Interestingly, the proportion of years that a child lives with a single parent is not significantly associated with either of the educational outcomes after controls. The percentage of neighborhood residents with less than a high school degree is negatively associated with both of the schooling outcomes. The coefficient on the child care cost variable is negative in both models, but it is not statistically significant. These results suggest that spending considerable time in formal child care between the ages of two and five years is not associated with our schooling outcomes when we included the numerous other control variables.[19]

The primary variables that we use in our simulation analysis also have the expected sign, and they too are statistically significant. Both the log of family income/poverty level when children are 2 to 15 years of age and family wealth

Table 7-1. *Unweighted Descriptive Statistics*[a]

Item	Mean	Standard deviation	Minimum	Maximum
High school graduate	0.749		0	1
Attended college	0.306		0	1
Years of completed education	12.251	1.694	2	17
African American	0.441		0	1
Female	0.469		0	1
Average number of siblings[b]	2.101	1.465	0	8.43
At least one parent graduated from high school	0.633		0	1
At least one parent attended college	0.269		0	1
Education info missing for both parents	0.072		0	1
Log of family income/poverty level[b]	0.663	0.649	−1.52	3.17
Proportion of years with single parent[b]	0.270	0.372	0	1
Number of moves[b]	2.831	2.576	0	12
Head of family foreign born	0.020		0	1
Average county unemployment[b]	6.542	1.91	1.5	30.67
Percent of dropouts in neighborhood[b]	16.708	8.677	0	67.29
Log of positive wealth (1984)	7.621	4.705	0	16.12
Negative wealth (1984)	0.052		0	1
Wealth missing (1984)	0.108		0	1
State Gini index[b]	0.339	0.019	0.299	0.398
Public tuition and fees per full-time student/1,000 (1987)	1.592	0.546	0.705	4.78
Public tuition x youngest age group (born 1970)	0.326	0.693	0	4.78
Child care costs above $1,000[c]	0.158		0	1

Source: Authors' calculations.
a. $N = 1,210$.
b. From 2 to 15 years of age.
c. From 2 to 5 years of age.

are positively and significantly associated with children's educational attainment. That the influence of wealth is generally smaller than that of income suggests a high correlation between wealth and family income. In her preferred model (which included public education support variables), Mayer found that greater income inequality within a state had a small, positive, and statistically insignificant effect on years of schooling for children in higher-income families and a large, negative, and significant effect on years of schooling for lower-income children.[20] In contrast, we find an overall significant negative effect of the state Gini coefficient on years of completed schooling but not on high school graduation.[21] The state public institution tuition variable is negatively and

Table 7-2. *Regression Results*[a]

Item	Years of completed schooling	High school graduate	Attended college
	OLS coefficient	Logit coefficient	Logit coefficient
African American	0.491***	0.563***	0.754***
	(0.110)	(0.198)	(0.205)
Female	0.337***	0.411***	0.571***
	(0.084)	(0.155)	(0.150)
Log of average family income/ poverty level[b]	0.461***	0.453**	0.763***
	(0.110)	(0.201)	(0.205)
Log of positive wealth (1984)	0.059***	0.107***	0.061*
	(0.017)	(0.027)	(0.036)
Negative wealth (1984)	0.298	0.404	0.151
	(0.233)	(0.353)	(0.505)
State Gini index[b]	−6.354**	0.016	−11.436***
	(2.902)	(5.237)	(5.163)
At least one parent graduated from high school	0.395***	0.811***	−0.011
	(0.113)	(0.188)	(0.217)
At least one parent attended college	0.166	0.293	0.183
	(0.114)	(0.240)	(0.185)
Proportion of years with single parent[b]	0.081	−0.017	−0.097
	(0.154)	(0.264)	(0.290)
Average county unemployment[b]	−0.066***	−0.099**	−0.033
	(0.024)	(0.043)	(0.041)
Public tuition and fees per full-time student/1,000 (1987)	-0.169*	0.166	−0.345**
	(0.098)	(0.184)	(0.166)
Public tuition x youngest age group (born 1970)	−0.139**	−0.227**	0.014
	(0.065)	(0.115)	(0.118)
Average number of siblings[b]	−0.082**	−0.045	−0.182***
	(0.035)	(0.060)	(0.068)
Number of moves[b]	−0.063***	−0.088***	−0.043
	(0.018)	(0.030)	(0.035)
Head of family foreign born	1.129***	2.113*	1.036**
	(0.306)	(1.111)	(0.508)
Child care costs above $1,000[c]	−0.160	−0.245	−0.034
	(0.122)	(0.225)	(0.212)
Percent of dropouts in neighborhood[b]	−0.022***	−0.028***	−0.025**
	(0.006)	(0.010)	(0.010)
Constant	14.440***	0.565	3.254
	(1.137)	(2.077)	(2.005)
Observations	1,202	1,202	901

Source: Authors' calculations.

a. Standard errors in parentheses. Models also include indicator variables for missing information on parental schooling and wealth. *Significant at 10 percent; **significant at 5 percent; *** significant at 1 percent.

b. From 2 to 15 years of age.

c. From 2 to 5 years of age.

significantly associated with the years of completed schooling variable but not with high school graduation—a pattern that seems quite sensible.[22]

The Effect of Increased Inequality in Family and Geographic Economic Circumstances on Educational Attainment

In simulating the effects of increased inequality on children's schooling attainments, we first developed new and more unequal values for the family and geographical income and wealth values. For family income/needs, we chose values for each family designed to reflect the actual change in the standard deviation of family income/needs from 1970 to 2004 in the state in which the family lived.[23] We followed a similar procedure in simulating the effects of an increase in the inequality of family assets (wealth).[24] Finally, we used the state-specific change in the Gini index for the state of residence from 1970 to 2004, reflecting the effect of changes in overall state inequality on the individual. We added or subtracted the change over time in the observed state-specific Gini value for the individual observations.

While these symmetrical assumed changes in income/needs and state income inequality values reflect overall changes in the observed inequality in these values over the 1970 to 2004 period, they do not reflect changes in the skewness or asymmetry of the distributions. In contrast, those for wealth do take skewness into account. Indeed, the economic processes that generated the increases in inequality during this period led to larger proportional increases above the mean than below the mean. Extensive literature documents that the ratio of the income of a household at the 90th percentile to the income of a household at the 50th percentile increased substantially more than the ratio of the income of a household at the 50th percentile to the income of a household at the 10th percentile over this period.[25] As described in appendix 7A, several public sources of data were used to estimate these relevant increases in inequality.

We then used the model coefficient estimates in table 7-2 together with these constructed—and more unequal—values of family income/needs, family wealth, and state income inequality to predict for each child the value of schooling attainment that would be expected with these increased levels of family and geographic inequality. This procedure assumes that the coefficients for the family and geographic economic variables remain constant when the variation in their distributions is increased in the simulation and that these relationships are as estimated in the statistical models. In other words, although we are simulating a change in income, we are assuming that the *relationship* between income and educational outcomes remains the same. We also assume that the actual values of the remaining variables are unchanged from those observed in the data. This procedure is described in more detail in appendix 7A.

Effects of Increased Economic Inequality on Educational Attainment

The effects of our assumed changes in family and geographic economic inequality on children's schooling attainments can be seen by comparing the actual distribution of schooling attainments with the distribution reflecting the levels of increased inequality.[26] Figures 7-1 and 7-2 present our estimates of the effect of the assumed increases in economic inequality on the full distributions of years of completed schooling and high school graduation. Each figure shows the relative frequency distributions of both *actual* children's schooling attainment predicted using actual values of the independent variables and the model coefficients and predicted schooling based on the adjusted (more unequal) values of the three family and geographic economic variables (family income/needs, family wealth, and state-specific Gini coefficients of family income).

The effect of the assumed increase in all three indicators of economic inequality on educational attainments is reflected in the difference between the base distribution (the solid line) and the distributions reflecting the effect of increased economic inequality (the various dashed lines). Clearly, the increases in inequality in schooling attainments reflect the increase in economic inequality. Consistent with the small estimated impact of family and geographic economic factors on the probability of graduating from high school (table 7-2), the simulated increase in family and geographic inequality has a smaller effect on the distribution of the probability of graduating from high school (figure 7-2) than on the distribution of years of schooling (figure 7-1).

In table 7-3, we report the *average level* (mean and median) and the *inequality* (standard deviation) of children's schooling attainments, using both the actual values (predicted from the model using the respondent's real characteristics on all of the independent variables) and the adjusted (more unequal) values for the three family and geographic economic variables (family income/needs, assets, and state-specific Gini coefficients).[27] Because the observed changes in inequality in each of the distributions of the economic and geographic economic variables reflect changes in the same underlying social forces and economic arrangements, the estimates reflecting the joint change in these variables indicate the overall effects of increases in economic inequality on

Figure 7-1. *Years of Schooling Distribution*

Density

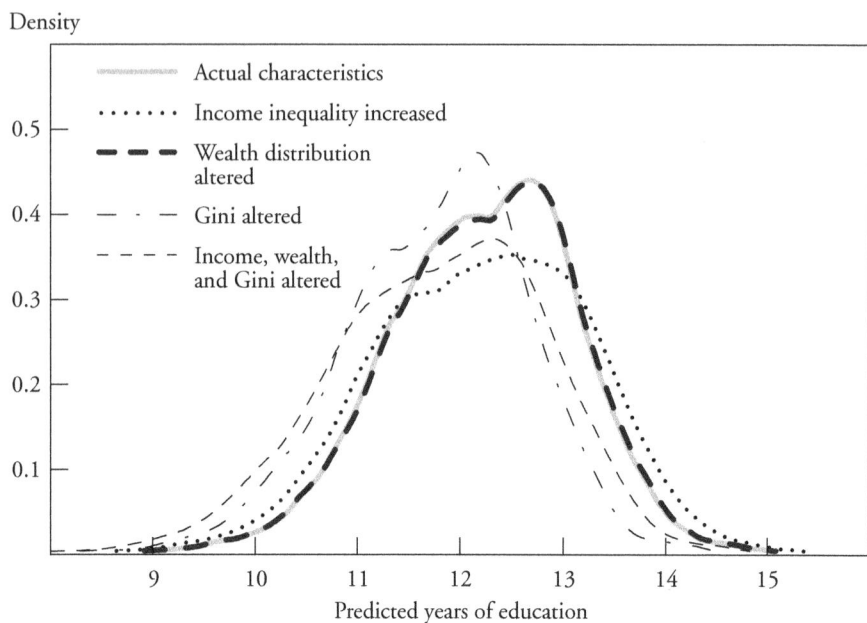

Predicted years of education

Source: Authors' calculations.

the distribution of educational attainment. Our results are weighted to reflect national levels of attainment for this cohort of individuals.

The top bank of table 7-3 indicates that the increase in inequality of family income/needs and wealth is associated with a very small increase in the average level (mean and median) of years of schooling, implying that the schooling gains for those at the top of the distribution exceed the schooling losses for those at the bottom. However, the inequality (standard deviation) of the distribution of years of schooling increases substantially—from .80 to .95, about 19 percent—when the adjusted and more unequal values of income/needs (alone) and more unequal values of both income/needs and wealth are substituted for the actual values. Most of this change is attributable to the increase in inequality of family income/needs. In contrast, the increase in state-specific income inequality (the state Gini index) decreases the mean and median years of schooling from about 12.6 years to about 12.2 years and marginally reduces the level of inequality in the distribution of years of schooling, from .80 to .79. Finally, when the effects of all three inequality changes are combined (a simulation that is inherently more consistent than changing one at a time), the simulations suggest a decline in median and mean years of schooling of about 3 percent. When the effect of

Figure 7-2. *Completion of High School Distribution*

Density

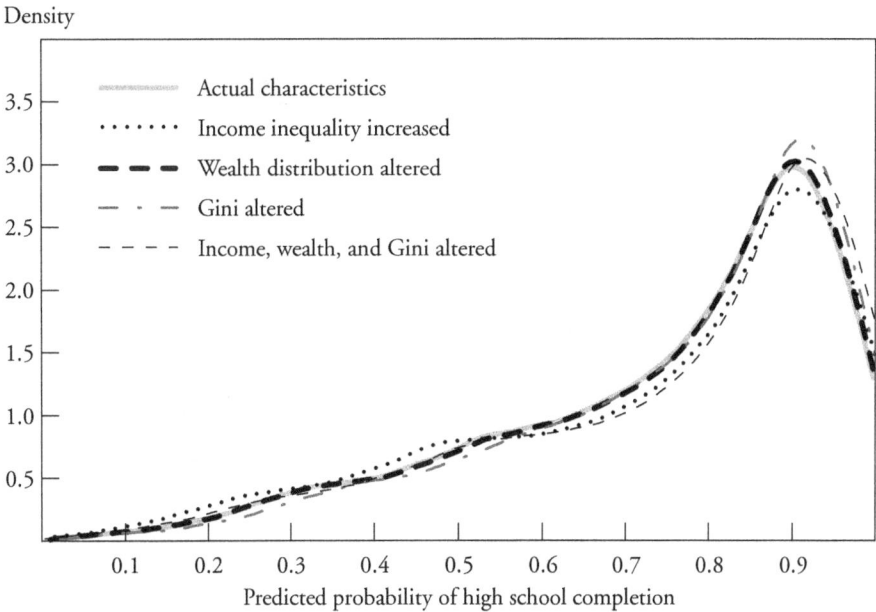

Source: Authors' calculations.

increased inequality in all of the family and geographic indicators is simulated, the standard deviation of the years of schooling variable increases from .80 to .93, or about 16 percent.

Given the small coefficient estimates on family income/needs, wealth, and geographic income inequality in the model estimating the probability of graduating from high school in table 7-2, the small effect of increased family and geographic inequality on the mean and standard deviation of the probability of graduating from high school is not surprising. This pattern is seen when the effects of the increases in economic inequality are estimated either individually or simultaneously (see the middle panel of table 7-3). The mean (median) probability of graduating from high school is about .83 (.88) when the actual values of the family geographic variables are simulated. When the effect of joint increases in the inequality of family income/needs, family wealth, and state income inequality is simulated, the mean and median probabilities increase by a small amount. The inequality (standard deviation) of the distribution of probabilities increases slightly when inequality in the family indicators is increased.[28] Overall, these estimates suggest that the observed state-specific increases in the inequality of family and geographic economic resources lead to a

Table 7-3. *Comparison of Predicted Values of Educational Attainment under Simulated Conditions, Weighted*

	Mean years	Median years	Standard deviation
Years of education			
Actual	12.60	12.65	0.80
Standard deviation of log family income/ needs + state-specific increase	12.67	12.75	0.95
Wealth + percentile changes	12.62	12.66	0.81
Gini + state-specific increase	12.13	12.18	0.79
All economic factors changed	12.22	12.32	0.93
Only income and wealth changed	12.69	12.77	0.95
	Mean predicted probability	*Median predicted probability*	*Standard deviation*
High school graduation			
Actual	0.83	0.88	0.16
Standard deviation of log family income/ needs + state-specific increase	0.83	0.89	0.17
Wealth + percentile changes	0.83	0.89	0.16
Gini + state-specific increase	0.84	0.90	0.15
All economic factors changed	0.84	0.91	0.16
Only income and wealth changed	0.83	0.90	0.17
	Mean predicted probability	*Median predicted probability*	*Standard deviation*
College attendance			
Actual	0.43	0.42	0.20
Standard deviation of log family income/ needs + state-specific increase	0.47	0.48	0.24
Wealth + percentile changes	0.44	0.42	0.20
Gini + state-specific increase	0.27	0.25	0.16
All economic factors changed	0.32	0.29	0.21
Only income and wealth changed	0.47	0.48	0.24

Source: Authors' calculations.

small increase in overall years of schooling and substantial increases in the inequality of schooling attainment. We estimate an increase of about 19 percent in the inequality of years of completed schooling and a negligible change in the inequality of the probability of graduating from high school.

The patterns for college attendance, found in the bottom panel of table 7-3, suggest that an increase in family income inequality or income inequality combined with an increase in wealth inequality leads to an increase in the probability of college attendance as well as an increase in the inequality of college attendance. The mean predicted probability of attending increases to .47 from .43; the median increases to .48 from .42; and the standard deviation increases from .20 to .24. The changes are dominated by the change in family income/needs. In contrast, the increase in state-specific income inequality (the state Gini index) decreases the probability of college attendance substantially from .43 (median .42) to .27 (median .25) and reduces the level of inequality from .20 to .16. Finally, when the effects of all three inequality changes are combined (a simulation that is inherently more consistent than changing one at a time), the simulations suggest a decline in median and mean probability of attending college of 11 to 13 percentage points. When the effect of increased inequality in all of the family and geographic indicators is simulated, the standard deviation of the probability of attending college increases slightly (from .20 to .21).

Race-Specific Effects of Increased Economic Inequality on the Distributions of Educational Attainment

We also estimated our model with a racial variable (black = 1) interacted with parental schooling, income/needs, state public tuition, county unemployment, and child care costs (results are available from the authors). We find that family income/needs appears to have a greater role in determining both high school graduation and years of schooling for blacks than for whites, but the difference is not statistically significant in either estimate. Then, using these estimates, we simulated the effects of increased inequality in family and geographic economic variables on schooling attainment. Table 7-4 summarizes the results of our simulations for these two racial groups. The base levels of both indicators of educational attainment are lower for blacks than for whites. While the standard deviation of years of education is larger for whites than for blacks, there is very little difference in inequality between the two groups in the probability of graduating from high school. Estimates of the effects of increases in family and geographic economic inequality (using the results from the joint change in the family income/needs, family wealth, and state Gini variables) indicate that increases in family and geographic inequality result in increases in the inequality of educational attainment for both racial groups. However, the percentage increases are larger for blacks than for whites for both years of schooling and high school graduation. For example, the standard deviation of years of schooling increases by nearly 10 percent for whites and nearly 32 percent for blacks, while the standard deviation of the probability of graduating from high school increases by about 7 percent for whites but by nearly 18 percent for blacks.

Table 7-4. *Comparison of Predicted Values of Educational Attainment under Simulated Conditions*[a]

Years of education	Mean years	Median years	Standard deviation
Whites			
Actual	12.69	12.76	0.83
Standard deviation of log family income/ needs + state-specific increase	12.78	12.86	0.93
Wealth + percentile changes	12.71	12.77	0.83
Gini + state-specific increase	12.25	12.30	0.80
All economic factors changed	12.36	12.46	0.91
Blacks			
Actual	12.15	12.11	0.63
Standard deviation of log family income/ needs + state-specific increase	12.05	11.91	0.81
Wealth + percentile changes	12.17	12.13	0.63
Gini + state-specific increase	11.72	11.67	0.65
All economic factors changed	11.63	11.50	0.83
High school graduation	Mean predicted probability	Median predicted probability	Standard deviation
Whites			
Actual	0.85	0.90	0.16
Standard deviation of log family income/ needs + state-specific increase	0.85	0.91	0.16
Wealth + percentile changes	0.85	0.91	0.15
Gini + state-specific increase	0.86	0.92	0.15
All economic factors changed	0.87	0.93	0.15
Blacks			
Actual	0.73	0.77	0.17
Standard deviation of log family income/ needs + state-specific increase	0.69	0.73	0.21
Wealth + percentile changes	0.73	0.78	0.17
Gini + state-specific increase	0.76	0.80	0.16
All economic factors changed	0.73	0.78	0.20

Source: Authors' calculations.
a. Weighted model with race interactions.

Sizable increases in the racial schooling gap, irrespective of the measure of educational attainment, also are observed. Using the results for the joint changes in the three economic variables, the white-to-black ratio of mean/median attainment increases from 1.04/1.05 to 1.06/1.08 (for years of schooling) and from 1.16/1.17 to 1.19/1.19 (for probability of graduating from high school).

Increasing Inequality Reflected in Growing Schooling Gaps Among Children

In this study, we attempt to understand the implications of increased economic inequality among American families and neighborhoods for the educational attainment of children affected by the increased disparities. We first estimated a model of determinants of children's educational attainments (identifying the independent role of family and geographic economic characteristics when subjects were children) and then simulated the effects of increasing the inequality in the distribution of these determinants on the distribution of children's educational attainments. Our estimates suggest that the simulated increase in family and geographic inequality (of a magnitude similar to that experienced in the United States over the 1970–2004 period) leads to sizable increases in the gaps among children in years of completed schooling while also modestly increasing overall levels of schooling.

Overall, these results are interesting, though rather modest—particularly given the very large increase in inequality that has occurred in the United States over the period. The decline in mean years of schooling—around five months, from 12.6 to 12.2 years (slightly more for blacks)—is perhaps the most notable result, although the large increase in the variation in schooling outcomes for blacks also is striking.

Perhaps the most troublesome aspect of our findings is the increasing racial gap in school attainment attributed to growing inequality. This increased racial gap implies that increased inequality leads those at the bottom of the educational distribution to fall even further from the mean, suggesting a relative loss of human capital among those who have the least of it. Given the link between schooling attainments and labor market success, the increase in inequality in educational attainments is also likely to be reflected in increased earnings inequality.

Our simulation of the effects of observed changes in inequality on the dispersion of educational outcomes parallels the actual pattern of changes in U.S. educational attainment during past decades. Using data from the Current Population Survey (CPS), we estimate that among adults aged 22 to 25 years, the standard deviation of years of schooling increased by 0.08 years up to the year 2000, a value that is about one-half of our simulated increase of 0.15 years.[29]

Our results have implications for public policy. They suggest that the increase in economic inequality observed in the nation will be reflected in future increases in educational inequality—and hence in inequality in wages, earnings, and income—unless policies are enacted to counter the increase. It seems likely that if actions are not taken, the growth in inequality in income and wealth observed in the last few decades will result in a spiral in which children in higher income/wealth families get more schooling while those in families with few economic resources fall further behind. Our results further indicate that living in a state with more income inequality is tied to an overall reduction in average years of schooling.

Measures are available both to mitigate growing inequality in family income and wealth and to increase educational attainment for those youth with few educational opportunities. Increased resources allocated to preschool opportunities for three- and four-year-olds and needs-based assistance for postsecondary education immediately come to mind.[30] Evidence indicates that if low-income children attend preschool beginning at age three, they will be more likely to succeed in school and have higher attainment. Investing in preschool is a commitment that a state can make, as, for example, the U.S. state of Georgia has done. It is also a commitment that the federal government can make by implementing a more extended Head Start–type program that provides children in lower-income families a high-quality preschool experience. Extending hours to permit parents to work full-time may help accomplish two goals—decreasing the inequality in educational attainment and increasing the incomes of lower-income families (and hence decreasing income inequality).

Further, both state and federal governments could increase their efforts to encourage lower-income students to attend four-year or two-year colleges. For example, states can invest in high-quality two-year colleges and establish a process whereby students can easily transfer from a two-year college to a four-year university. States also set tuition levels at public colleges and universities, and they could establish sliding-scale tuition schedules to encourage young adults from lower-income families to attend college. The federal government could allocate increased support to Pell Grants, the financial aid program for low-income young adults; provide more generous fellowships under new programs; and explore other approaches to encourage children from lower-income families to attend and, especially, to graduate from college.

Appendix 7A
Data and Methods

We used data from the Panel Study of Income Dynamics (PSID) and selected the 2,609 children who were born from 1966 to 1970. We followed them from 1968, the first year of the PSID (or their year of birth, if later), for thirty-one years, or until 1999.[31] Our estimation sample included only individuals who remained in the survey until they reached the age of 21 years. Educational outcomes were measured at age 25 (although to limit missing data, some respondents' outcomes were measured as late as age 29). After omitting observations for which information on core variables was missing, we were left with 1,210 individuals.[32]

These data contain extensive longitudinal information on the status, characteristics, and choices of family members, family income and net worth, living arrangements, neighborhood characteristics, and background characteristics such as race, education, and location for each individual. In order to make comparisons between individuals with different birth years, we tied the variables that change over time to the age of the respondent.[33] All monetary values are expressed in 1993 dollars, using the consumer price index. Census tract (neighborhood) information from the 1970 and 1980 censuses on the percentage of residents who were high school dropouts were matched to the specific location of the children in our sample for each year from 1968 to 1985.[34] Finally, we merged into our data estimates of the state-specific Gini coefficient of family income when subjects were from 17 to 21 years of age.[35]

Table 7-1 provides unweighted descriptive statistics for all variables included in our models, averaged over the 1,210 observations in our sample: three-fourths of our sample of youths graduated from high school; 30 percent attended college; and they had an average of 12.25 years of completed schooling.[36] The corresponding weighted values are 84 percent (high school graduation = 1), nearly 40 percent (attend college = 1), and 12.63 (years of completed schooling). Unweighted average log of family income/needs is 0.663 (ages 2 to 15 years). Unweighted average log of family net worth is 7.621, and average state public tuition and fees is $1,592.[37]

From these data, we measured three educational attainment outcomes (at age 25) for each young person in our sample: completion of high school,[38] college attendance, and years of completed schooling. We then studied the effects of changes in the inequality of the three family and geographic economic variables (family income relative to needs,[39] family net worth,[40] and the state-specific change in the Gini coefficient) over the period from 1990 to 2004 on these schooling outcomes.

Our simulation procedure is designed to reveal the effect on the distribution of children's educational outcomes of increases in inequality in family income/needs, family assets, and state-specific Gini indices. We assume an increase in inequality in these variables that roughly corresponds to that observed in the United States over the period from 1970 to 2004 and translate the increases into changes in individual values of the income, asset, and state inequality measures for the observations in our sample. Then, relying on the estimated model coefficients on these variables, we calculate the simulated (predicted) effect of changes in the variable values on changes in the educational outcomes of each sample observation. Comparing the predicted value of educational values with the actual values of the variables reveals the impact on the full distribution of each of the educational outcomes.

We assume increases in family income inequality that correspond to changes in the standard deviation of state-specific family income between 1970 and 2004. We regard this as the effect of changes in individual-specific inequality over the period. The average person in our sample lived in a state that experienced a 56 percent increase in the standard deviation of income during that time; a small number of respondents lived in a state with a decline in income inequality, but most experienced an increase.

We also analyze the effects of the increase in the standard deviation of family wealth over the period 1989–2004. Using table 4 in Kennickell, we calculate the percentage change in household wealth at various constructed class intervals of the distribution of wealth for our sample over the 1989–2004 period.[41] For example, the increase at the 25th percentile is 64 percent. At the 75th percentile, the increase is 35 percent. This procedure assumes that a family observed at the beginning of the period remains in the same percentile of the wealth distribution until the end of the period. Finally, we use the state-specific change in the Gini index for the state of residence from 1970 to 2004.[42] This state-level inequality measure reflects the effect of changes in overall state inequality on the individual.

We use these state-specific family income and Gini values as well as the global increase in wealth inequality to "spread out" the individual sample values. We add a state-specific value to the respondent's actual value of logged family income/needs for each observed value greater than the mean, and we subtract the same state-specific constant from each value below the state mean. For wealth we simply multiply the original reported value of wealth by the proportionate change in the wealth for families in that part of the wealth distribution, using a national rather than a state-specific value. Finally, we add or subtract the real change over time in the observed Gini value for the individual observations based on the subject's state of residence.

Using logged family income/needs as an example, we increase the standard deviation of logged income/needs in our sample by a state-specific amount by increasing the logged income of each family above the mean by the amount required to attain the correct overall increase in the standard deviation (the specific amount used was the state change in the standard deviation of income between 1970 and 2004 divided by $35,000 and logged) and decreasing the logged income of each family below the mean by the same value. After creating these "spread out" distributions of logged family income/needs, family wealth, and state-specific Gini coefficients, we use the estimated coefficients reported in table 7-2 together with the adjusted (more unequal) values of those independent variables being studied (and the actual values of the remaining independent variables) to predict the value of the relevant schooling attainment outcome for each observation. Again using years of education as an example, we created new predicted values of years of education under the assumption that the overall effect of the variables remained the same (the coefficients from the model remain the same), but we substituted new values of logged family income/needs, family wealth, and state-specific Gini indices for each individual in the sample. The effect of increased economic inequality is obtained by comparing the weighted distributions of predicted years of education with and without the increase in family and geographic economic inequality.

Notes

1. The Gini coefficient is a measure of inequality that consists of a number between zero and one: zero = perfect equality; 1 = perfect inequality. In discussing family income, the higher the Gini coefficient, the greater the level of income inequality.

2. U.S. Census Bureau, "Selected Measures of Household Income Dispersion: 1967 to 2009" (www.census.gov/hhes/www/income/data/historical/inequality/taba2.pdf).

3. Edward N. Wolff, *Top Heavy: The Increasing Inequality of Wealth in America and What Can Be Done About It* (New York: New Press, 2002); Lisa A. Keister and Stephanie Moller, "Wealth Inequality in the United States," *Annual Review of Sociology*, vol. 26 (2000), pp. 63–81.

4. See Douglas Massey, "The Age of Extremes: Concentrated Affluence and Poverty in the Twenty-First Century," *Demography*, vol. 33, no. 4 (1996), pp. 395–412.

5. However, after the late 1990s many neighborhoods improved, in part because of the increase in work by poor mothers in response to the 1996 welfare reform, according to Paul Jargowsky and Isabel Sawhill, "The Decline of the Underclass," CCF Brief 36 (Center on Children and Families, Brookings, January 2006). See also Paul Jargowsky, *Poverty and Place: Ghettos, Barrios, and the American City* (New York: Russell Sage Foundation, 1997).

6. The Russell Sage Foundation, the PEW Charitable Trust, and the Carnegie Corporation have supported extensive research on the links between growing economic inequality and a wide variety of social phenomena, including political participation and civic engagement, education, families and children, health, marriage, media, neighborhoods, public

policy, wealth, and work. See the Russell Sage Foundation (www.russellsage.org/research/social-inequality).

7. See Robert Haveman and Barbara Wolfe, *Succeeding Generations: On the Effects of Investments in Children* (New York: Russell Sage Foundation, 1994); Robert Haveman and Barbara Wolfe, "The Determinants of Children's Attainments: A Review of Methods and Findings," *Journal of Economic Literature*, vol. 33, no. 4 (1995), pp. 1829–78; Sara McLanahan and Gary Sandefur, *Growing Up with A Single Parent: What Hurts? What Helps?* (Harvard University Press, 1994); and Robert Haveman and others, "Inequality of Family and Community Characteristics in Relation to Children's Attainments," prepared for University of Wisconsin Russell Sage Working Group on Inequality (New York: Russell Sage Foundation, 2001) (www.russellsage.org/research/reports/family-and-community).

8. See Christopher Jencks and Susan Mayer, "The Social Consequences of Growing Up in a Poor Neighborhood," in *Inner City Poverty in the United States*, edited by Lawrence Lynn Jr. and Michael McGeary (Washington: National Academy of Sciences Press, 1990), pp. 111–86; Nancy E. Adler and others, "Socioeconomic Status and Health: The Challenge of the Gradient," *American Psychologist*, vol. 49 (1994), pp. 15–24; Michael G. Marmot and others, "Health Inequalities among British Civil Servants: The Whitehall II Study," *Lancet*, vol. 337 (1991), pp. 1387–93; Ana Diez-Roux and others, "Neighborhood Environments and Coronary Heart Disease: A Multilevel Analysis," *American Journal of Epidemiology*, vol. 146, no. 6 (1997), pp. 48–63; Ichiro Kawachi and Bruce P. Kennedy, "The Relationship of Income Inequality to Mortality: Does the Choice of Indicator Matter?" *Social Science and Medicine*, vol. 45 (1997), pp. 1121–27; Susan Mayer, "How Much Does a High School's Racial and Socioeconomic Mix Affect Graduation Rates and Teenage Fertility Rates?" in *The Urban Underclass*, edited by Christopher Jencks and Paul Peterson (Brookings, 1991); and Susan Mayer, "How Economic Segregation Affects Children's Educational Attainment," *Social Forces*, vol. 8, no. 1 (2002), pp. 153–76.

9. For a discussion of the limited research on the link between children's educational attainment and neighborhood and school segregation indicators of economic inequality, see Mayer, "How Much Does a High School's Racial and Socioeconomic Mix Affect Graduation Rates and Teenage Fertility Rates," and Mayer, "How Economic Segregation Affects Children's Educational Attainment."

10. Susan Mayer, "How Did the Increase in Economic Inequality between 1970 and 1990 Affect Children's Educational Attainment?" *American Journal of Sociology*, vol. 107, no. 1 (2001), pp. 1–32.

11. Mayer's sample of children consists of all observations in the dataset at 12 to 15 years of age and at 20 and 23 years of age (when the relevant educational outcome data were available). Measures of within-state economic inequality and control variables were obtained when the children were between the ages of 12 and 15. Mayer considered four educational outcomes: the probability of high school completion by age 20; the probability of beginning college by age 23; the probability of completing four years of postsecondary education by age 23; and the number of years of completed schooling by age 23. High- (low-) income families were defined as families above (below) the median level of family income when children were 12 to 15 years old. Mayer created state-specific Gini coefficients of family income at ages 12 to 15 by using linear interpolations from decennial census data and assigned them to adolescents on the basis of state of residence at age 14. Mayer's control variables included measures of individual-specific returns to education, region, year, percent African American or Hispanic in the state, the log of family income and state-specific mean

household income, the unemployment rate, and measures of investment in education and the level of economic segregation. It should be noted that the link between changes in the state-level economic environment and children's attainment would tend to be more indirect and diffuse than similar changes in neighborhood-level factors.

12. Mayer again addressed this issue in "The Relationship between Income Inequality and Inequality in Schooling," *Theory and Research in Education*, vol. 8 (March 2010), pp. 5–20. While she again emphasizes that changes in government education policies tend to somewhat mitigate the impact of increased income inequality on inequality in schooling, the tie between increases in income inequality and increases in education inequality persists.

13. A large number of studies have addressed the relationship between family resources and choices and children's attainment and have adopted numerous approaches to understanding the patterns of causality in estimated relationships. Haveman and Wolfe, *Succeeding Generations,* and Haveman and Wolfe, "The Determinants of Children's Attainments," assess these approaches for empirical estimation and critique the numerous estimates available in the literature. See also Robert Haveman, Barbara Wolfe, and Kathryn Wilson, "The Role of Expectations in Adolescent Schooling Choices: Do Youths Respond to Economic Incentives?" *Economic Inquiry,* vol. 43, no. 3 (August 2005), pp. 467–92. A summary of results from the numerous available studies is Haveman and others, "Inequality of Family and Community Characteristics," and Haveman and others, "Trends in Children's Attainments and Their Determinants as Family Income Inequality Has Increased," in *Social Inequality,* edited by Kathryn Neckerman (New York: Russell Sage Foundation, 2004), pp. 149–89. While there is little doubt that this relationship is positive, some researchers fail to be convinced that causality plays a major role; see Susan Mayer, *What Money Can't Buy* (Harvard University Press, 1997), where recent studies of this relationship are described. See also Yunju Nam and Jin Huang, "Changing Roles of Parental Economic Resources in Children's Educational Attainment," Working Paper 08-20 (St. Louis: Center for Social Development, 2008), which suggests that the income-education tie may be increasing over time. Arnaud Chevalier and others, "The Impact of Parental Income and Education on the Schooling of Their Children," Working Paper 05/05 (London: Institute for Fiscal Studies, 2005), reports that the strength of the link is positively related to the degree to which the measure of family income is "permanent" and to the use of appropriate statistical methods. Our specification rests on the findings of these studies and balances the goals of both accurately estimating causal relationships and obtaining a model of the determinants of children's educational attainment appropriate for simulation. The inclusion of the extensive set of variables that are plausibly related to schooling outcomes constrains the domain of unmeasured variables and mitigates concerns regarding endogeneity.

14. While Mayer measured family and state characteristics only for ages 12–14, we measure these characteristics at nearly all ages until age 16.

15. These economic variables and procedures are defined more fully below. In particular, we increase the inequality (standard deviation) of the family income/needs variable by altering observed values above and below the mean to reflect observed state-specific changes in inequality in the distribution of this variable between 1970 and 2004. For the wealth variable, we adjust the observed values by the changes in wealth experienced by families in the matched decile of the wealth distribution that took place over the 1989–2004 period. For the geographic variable, we add or subtract the change from 1970 to 2004 in the observed state-specific Gini index for the state of residence for each individual observation.

State of residence is primarily a political or administrative variable and use of the change in state-specific inequality as a determinant of children's schooling attainment requires some discussion. Ideally, we would prefer a measure of inequality change measured at a geographic level that is more proximate to children's experience. We use the state inequality change as a proxy for a neighborhood-based variable. In our view, gaps between rich and poor observed by children are likely to influence their perceptions, aspirations, and choices. For example, if only children from higher-income families are perceived to be committed to hard work and study and hence seen as "college material," children from poor families may well lose hope and fail to advance in school.

16. These variables include race, gender, number of siblings, parental schooling, family structure, foreign-born family head, geographic moves, county unemployment rates, the state-specific tuition and fees variable, and the percentage of neighborhood or census tract individuals who dropped out of high school. In addition, we include a variable indicating whether or not more than $1,000 was spent on out-of-home child care from ages two to five as a proxy for having spent extended periods in nonfamily child care. Unfortunately, we do not have information on Head Start, subsidies from the Child Care and Development Block Grant, Title I child care, and other relevant public programs. Only two variables—having at least one parent who graduated from high school and having at least one parent who graduated from college—are used to capture the effect of parental education on children's educational outcomes. More detailed parental education variables were used in alternative specifications with little effect on the magnitude of the family and geographic resource variables.

17. This background-controlled effect among blacks is a common finding in studies of educational attainment.

18. This includes all residential moves, regardless of the geographic distance.

19. Note that this variable may also be a very crude and noisy estimate of the extent of time spent in early child care.

20. Mayer, "How Did the Increase in Economic Inequality between 1970 and 1990 Affect Children's Educational Attainment?" and Mayer, "The Relationship between Income Inequality and Inequality in Schooling."

21. This difference between our results and those of Mayer may be due in part to our smaller sample. However, Mayer's results are themselves inconsistent across specifications, with state inequality negatively associated with education inequality in two of five models and positively associated with educational inequality for the other three. Mayer, "The Relationship between Income Inequality and Inequality in Schooling," also notes the sensitivity of her results to model specification.

22. The interaction variable where tuition is measured at age 17 (for the youngest children in our study) suggests a stronger negative effect of higher tuition on years of schooling but also a negative influence of higher tuition on the probability of graduating from high school.

23. In particular, we added a state-specific percentage value to income/needs values above the mean income for the family's state and subtracted the same percentage value from those below the mean income for the state. This procedure does not reflect the large increase in incomes at the top of the distribution that has characterized recent increases in U.S. economic inequality. This procedure assumes that children's educational attainment depends on absolute levels of family income and wealth rather than relative values. As an alternative, we tested a similar model that instead used national-level estimates of the increase in inequality to increase the inequality in income and wealth, ignoring the state-level variation that we focus on here. In that set of simulations, we increased the income values above the mean and decreased the income values below the mean by the same percentage, then adjusted the income/needs values so that the original (pre-simulation) mean value of family income/needs

was maintained. (These results are very similar to those reported and are available from the authors on request.)

24. In particular, using Arthur Kennickell, *Ponds and Streams: Wealth and Income in the U.S., 1989 to 2007*, Finance and Economics Discussion Series 2009-13 (Washington: Federal Reserve Board, 2009), table 4, we calculate the percentage change in household wealth at various constructed class intervals of the distribution of wealth for our sample over the 1989–2004 period; see appendix 7A.

25. An alternative but equally arbitrary simulation could have made use of estimated relative changes among quintiles of the relevant distributions.

26. Our simulated schooling outcomes assume that the supply of available education slots is unconstrained at existing relative prices. In analyzing the impact on the earnings distribution of policies that change the distribution of abilities, Robert M. Costrell and Glenn C. Loury, "Distribution of Ability and of Wages in a Hierarchical Job Assignment Model," *Journal of Political Economy*, vol. 112, no. 6 (December 2004), pp. 1322–63, examines the comparative statics of mapping ability onto earnings in a model of endogenous job assignment. Because job assignment and hence output level are endogenous (additional workers of other ability levels affect the assignment of workers of any ability level and therefore aggregate output), the net effect of any exogenous policy will differ from the gross effect. Our assumption avoids the complexity of this labor market analysis and the need for a general equilibrium solution; were the supply of education slots not elastic, our analysis would also need to account for the effect of assignment.

27. The first row in each bank of table 7-3 reports the actual (predicted) values of the relevant educational outcomes. The next three rows report predicted values of these outcomes when adjusted (more unequal) values of the family and geographic economic variables, taken one at a time, are used together with the table 7-2 coefficients. The final rows summarize the predicted outcome values when adjusted values of all of the changes in family and geographic inequality or only of family income/needs and wealth are assumed.

28. We also estimated the effect of changes in family and state inequality on the probability of attending college. This estimate is problematic, as the college attendance variable is conditional on the completion of high school. This simulation indicates that the increase in the state Gini index has a substantial negative effect on the probability of attending college, suggesting that increased disparities in the economic environment may be associated with reductions in state support for public higher education; increased tuition; and increased costs of attendance. Youths from lower-income families are likely to find these barriers important. This pattern suggests the need for additional study of this effect. The effect of increases in the state Gini dominates the effects of changes in income/needs and wealth inequality; when all of the family and state inequality factors are included in the simulation, the average probability of college attendance falls substantially but the inequality in attendance is little affected. Results are available from the authors.

29. These CPS-based values include other changes in the underlying population of U.S. adults 22–25 years of age as well as changes in the K–12 and higher education systems and the aggregate economy. Our procedure holds these characteristics constant and models only the effect of changes in inequality in the distribution of family income/needs, wealth, and state public college tuition. The CPS estimates use the final weight as provided by the CPS. We thank Cecelia Rouse, who first suggested this comparison.

30. See James J. Heckman and Dimitriy Masterov, "The Productivity Argument for Investing in Young Children," Working Paper 5 (University of Chicago, Invest in Kids

Working Group, Committee for Economic Development, 2004), and James J. Heckman and Alan B. Krueger, *Inequality in America: What Role for Human Capital Policies?* (MIT Press, 2003).

31. We use this period in order to isolate the influence of inequality in family income and wealth on children's educational attainment. By using only one broad cohort and then focusing on subsequent changes in income and wealth inequality, we are better able to capture the "pure" influence of changes in income and wealth rather than the influence of other changes in the propensity to complete high school or of changes in years of education more generally.

32. Some persons observed did not respond in an intervening year but reentered the sample the following year. Such persons are included in our analysis, and the missing information was filled in by averaging the data for the two years contiguous to the year of missing data. For the first and last years of the sample, that is clearly not possible, and we assign the contiguous year's value, adjusted if appropriate by using other information reported. Studies of the PSID find little reason for concern that attrition has reduced the representativeness of the sample. See Sean Becketti and others, "The PSID after Fourteen Years: An Evaluation," *Journal of Labor Economics*, vol. 6, no. 4 (September 1988), pp. 472–92; Lee Lillard and Constantijn W. A. Panis, "Attrition from the PSID: Household Income, Marital Status, and Mortality" (Santa Monica, Calif.: RAND, 1994); and Haveman and Wolfe, *Succeeding Generations: On the Effects of Investments in Children*. A more recent study finds that although "dropouts" from the PSID panel do differ systematically from respondents retained, estimates of the determinants of choices such as schooling and teen nonmarital childbearing generated from the data do not appear to be significantly affected. See John Fitzgerald, Peter Gottschalk, and Robert Moffitt, "An Analysis of Sample Attrition in Panel Data: The Michigan Panel Study of Income Dynamics," *Journal of Human Resources*, vol. 33, no. 2 (1998), pp. 251–99.

33. Rather than have the information defined by the year of its occurrence (say, 1968 or 1974), this time-varying information is assigned to the child by the child's age, allowing us to compare the process of attainment across individuals with different birth years.

34. The links between the neighborhood in which each family in the PSID lives and small-area (census tract) information collected in the 1970 and 1980 censuses have been (painfully and painstakingly) constructed by Michigan Survey Research Center (SRC) analysts. For the years 1968 to 1970, the 1970 census data are used; for the years 1980 to 1985, the 1980 census data are used. In most cases, this link is based on a match of the location of our observations to the relevant census tract or block numbering area (67.8 percent for the 1970 census and 71.5 percent for the 1980 census). For the years 1971 to 1979, a weighted combination of the 1970 and 1980 census data is used. The weights linearly reflect the distance from 1970 and 1980. For example, the matched value for 1972 equals [(.8 x 1970 value) + (.2 x 1980 value)].

35. The state-specific Gini coefficient is averaged over the individual's ages 2 to 15. State-specific Gini coefficients were originally downloaded from Inequality.org and are now available through the Census Bureau's Fact Finder (http://factfinder2.census.gov/faces/nav/jsf/pages/index.xhtml).

36. The low rate of high school completion relative to the national average is due to the oversampling of low-income families and racial minorities in the PSID.

37. The state-specific public tuition/fee variable (for a full-time student, divided by 1,000) is measured in 1987, when the respondents were 17 to 21 years of age. The PSID does not

contain information on actual or expected costs of college attendance, so the estimates of state public university tuition and fees were calculated from state-level data available from the National Center for Education Statistics (http://nces.ed.gov/ipeds/). We would have preferred to use estimates of the minimum tuition and fees facing students in various locations at about age 17, when the decision to attend college is becoming especially pressing, but these data are not available.

38. Those observations with twelve or more years of completed schooling are defined as high school graduates; this includes respondents with a General Educational Development (GED) certificate.

39. The family income-to-needs variable is measured as the logarithm of the ratio of family income in each year from age 2 to 15 of the individual to that year's family-size-specific national poverty line, averaged over subperiods of the age 2-to-15 window. Because an implicit equivalence scale is incorporated into the national poverty lines, they can be treated as family-size-specific income needs standards.

40. The family assets variable is the logarithm of positive family net worth in 1984, when respondents were 14 to 18 years old; variables indicating negative or missing wealth information are also included.

41. Kennickell, *Ponds and Streams.*

42. The state-specific Gini coefficient is averaged over each year from 2 to 15 years of age. State-specific Gini coefficients were originally downloaded from Inequality.org and are now available through the Census Bureau's Fact Finder (http://factfinder2.census.gov/faces/nav/jsf/pages/index.xhtml).

8

Pathways of Social Disadvantage from Adolescence into Adulthood

KATHLEEN MULLAN HARRIS AND HEDWIG LEE

A fundamental paradigm in the social mobility literature reveals the persistence of social disadvantage both within and between generations. This literature examines how growing up in a disadvantaged family limits social mobility out of disadvantage as children transition from adolescence and settle into adulthood.[1] Research on intergenerational mobility examines changes in social status that occur across generations, focusing on the reproduction of social disadvantage from the parent to the child generation. Research on intragenerational mobility examines changes in social status across an individual's life course, focusing on the extent to which social disadvantage in childhood remains intractable during the transition to adulthood and during the adult years.

This chapter examines both inter- and intragenerational mobility in a current cohort of young people in the United States. We focus on the environmental and behavioral sources of social disadvantage across the early life course as adolescents make their transition to adulthood at the turn of the twenty-first century. By analyzing unique environmental and longitudinal data, we identify the

We gratefully acknowledge research support to Kathleen Mullan Harris from the National Institute of Child Health and Human Development through grant P01 HD31921 as part of the Add Health program project. This research was also supported by center grant R24 HD050924 and training grant T32 HD007168, awarded to the Carolina Population Center at the University of North Carolina at Chapel Hill by the Eunice Kennedy Shriver National Institute of Child Health and Human Development. This research uses data from Add Health, a program project directed by Kathleen Mullan Harris and designed by J. Richard Udry, Peter S. Bearman, and Kathleen Mullan Harris at the University of North Carolina at Chapel Hill and funded by grant P01-HD31921 from the Eunice Kennedy Shriver National Institute of Child Health and Human Development, with cooperative funding from twenty-three other federal agencies and foundations.

roots of social disadvantage in the social contexts of adolescent life, including the family, peer, school, and neighborhood environments, and trace the roles that early social disadvantages play in social mobility pathways to adulthood.

Background and Theoretical Model

The intergenerational transmission of social and economic inequality is a key mechanism for understanding social stratification processes in all societies around the world and across time. The most basic empirical evidence of transmission is found in the correlations between social, economic, and educational outcomes of parents and children. Early studies of occupational attainment and income documented a fairly weak connection between fathers and sons, indicating substantial opportunity for social and economic mobility and a role for policy intervention.[2] More recent evidence, however, indicates a stronger intergenerational link between the social status and economic success of parents and their children in adulthood,[3] stimulating research on the mechanisms of transmission in order to inform policy designs that facilitate social mobility.[4]

The transmission of social and economic success across generations, however, remains something of a black box because there has been less research on the processes by which social and economic mobility is achieved or thwarted. A large body of social science research emphasizes the role of childhood experiences in the development of social and economic inequalities in adulthood, but the research lacks the longitudinal data needed to track the pathways from childhood social and economic origins to adult attainment outcomes. Recent studies tapping longitudinal data from the National Longitudinal Studies (NLS) and the Panel Study of Income Dynamics (PSID) have contributed to reducing this gap and have begun to untangle some of the mechanisms.[5] This research, however, still tends to draw data from two points in time across the life course (in childhood and adulthood) or focuses only on individual and family contexts. Pathways of disadvantage from childhood into adulthood are molded by multiple social and economic environments during key developmental stages across the life course. The roles of neighborhood and school context have been studied (and that of peers to a lesser degree) but primarily with respect to outcomes in childhood or adolescence.[6] Moreover, more attention has been devoted to the family and individual environment in early childhood[7] and less on adolescence and the transition to adulthood life, when young people have more autonomy and control in decisionmaking regarding their futures. Research indicates that social disadvantage in one context (for example, the family) is highly related to social disadvantage in other contexts (for example, neighborhoods and schools) and that its effects are both additive and interactive.[8]

Our research contributes to this literature by focusing on the developmental stage of adolescence and following young people through their transition to adulthood; we identify sources of social disadvantage in the multiple environments of adolescent life and their role in creating pathways to social disadvantage in adulthood. We document the ways that social disadvantage in the multiple social contexts of adolescent life is linked to social disadvantage in adulthood and analyze behavioral and prosocial mediating mechanisms that represent potential policy levers to facilitate social mobility during the period of transition to adulthood.

The transition to adulthood is a critical developmental stage for understanding pathways of social disadvantage because it represents the link between the launching context of the family and the establishment of independent individual life trajectories into adulthood.[9] This link is highly variable and dynamic both across and within families and social groups and allows for considerable change and potential movement into or out of social disadvantage. During adolescence, families, schools, and neighborhoods prepare young people for becoming independent adults who can manage their own personal and work lives and support themselves and their future families. Young people from disadvantaged families face considerable hurdles in their transition to self-sufficiency in adulthood because of low parental income and education, attendance at low-quality schools, and growing up in depressed and sometimes dangerous neighborhoods. On the other hand, the transition to adulthood may be one of the first opportunities for young people to move out of disadvantage by attending college or finding stable employment that may allow them to reach independence in early adulthood.

While there is considerable evidence on the impact of family disadvantage for outcomes in the transition to adulthood, the roles that other social contexts play in setting pathways of social disadvantage into adulthood have not been well studied. In addition, research on mediating mechanisms tends to focus on family- or neighborhood-level mechanisms in childhood or adolescence.[10] Very little research has explored mechanisms during the transition to adulthood, when young people begin to develop independent lives of their own and when policy interventions might be most salient in helping to improve their later life outcomes.

We use a longitudinal life course framework to understand pathways of social disadvantage, incorporating the theoretical concepts of linked lives, historical time, and life course transitions.[11] The concept of linked lives emphasizes the ways in which children's opportunities and constraints for their future outcomes are linked to their parents' socioeconomic status, representing the intergenerational links in social disadvantage pathways that we examine in this work. Historical time refers to the current time period, which uniquely defines inter- and intragenerational pathways of social disadvantage for this Add Health cohort of young adults, whose critical developmental transition from adolescence into young adulthood at the beginning of the twenty-first century we observe. We furthermore use an ecological conceptual model that argues for additive and interactive effects of the multiple social contexts of young people's lives.[12] The ecological model argues that examining adolescent development in only one context, typically the family, ignores the reality of lived lives, which take place in multiple contexts with multiple influences, particularly in adolescence when young people begin to spend more time with their peers in the school and neighborhood environment. We therefore examine the role of social disadvantage during adolescence among peers, in the family, in the school, and in the neighborhood in relation to social status in adulthood. We use nationally representative, rich, detailed data on the social environments of adolescent life and extensive behavioral and socioeconomic indicators across the life course into early adulthood. Our conceptual model, shown in figure 8-1, illustrates that disadvantage in the social contexts of adolescent life is linked to socioeconomic status (SES) in adulthood and that these links may operate through behavioral and prosocial mechanisms during the transition to adulthood.

Research Objectives

We have three research objectives. First, we examine the extent to which social disadvantage in adolescence, when young people are developing their future expectations for adult roles and status, sets trajectories to social disadvantage in adulthood, defined by socioeconomic status (indicated by the top direct arrow in figure 8-1). That is, does social disadvantage in adolescence predetermine poor social and economic outcomes in adulthood? Second, we identify the adolescent contexts of social disadvantage that are most detrimental in limiting social mobility in pathways to adulthood. Third, we examine potential behavioral and prosocial mediators during the transition from adolescence to adulthood that either reinforce pathways of social disadvantage or facilitate mobility out of social disadvantage (shown by the intervening arrows in figure 8-1).

Data

We use data from the National Longitudinal Study of Adolescent Health (Add Health), a nationally representative study of adolescents in grades 7 through 12 in 1994–95 (wave 1) in the United States who were tracked through three follow-up waves of interviews in 1996 (wave 2), 2001–02 (wave 3), and 2008 (wave 4) when the cohort was 24 to 32 years of age. Add Health was designed to study the effects of the social contexts of adolescent life on the health and behavior of adolescents

Figure 8-1. *Conceptual Model*

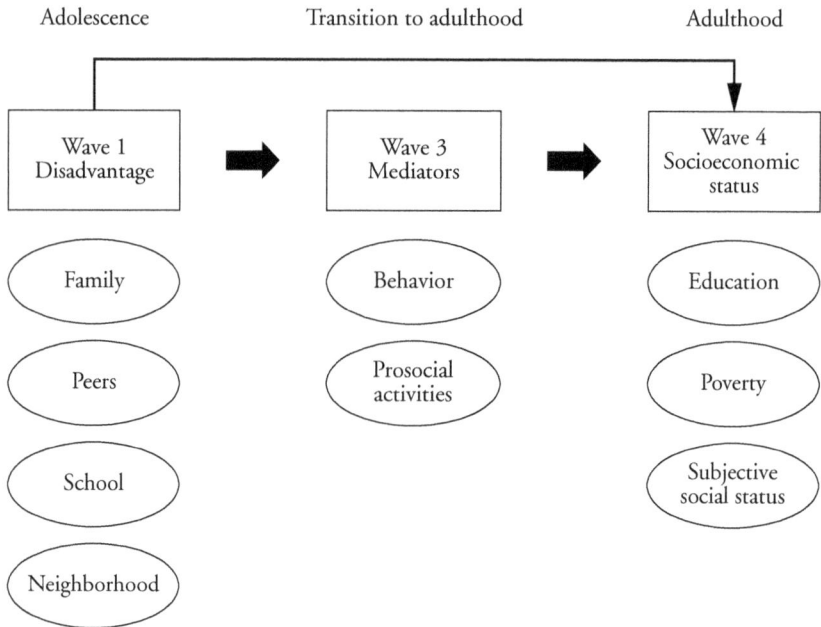

Source: Kathleen Mullan Harris and others, "The National Longitudinal Study of Adolescent Health: Research Design," 2009 (www.cpc.unc.eduprojects/addhealth/design).

and their outcomes in adulthood. The innovative design allows us to directly measure social disadvantage in the family, peer, school, and neighborhood contexts of adolescents and trace the effects of disadvantage in those contexts on adult social status and mobility.

Add Health used a multistage, stratified, school-based, cluster sampling design. A stratified sample of eighty high schools was selected with a probability proportional to the size of the school. For each high school, a feeder school was also selected with a probability proportional to the size of its student contribution to the high school. The school-based sample therefore has a pair of schools in each of eighty communities. An in-school questionnaire was administered to every student who attended each school selected on a particular day during the period from September 1994 to April 1995 and provides school context data. School rosters were used as the sampling frame, and a gender- and grade-stratified random sample was then selected for in-home interviews, producing a total sample size of 20,745 adolescents in wave 1, when respondents were 12 to 20 years of age (79 percent response rate).

A parent, generally the mother, also was interviewed in wave 1. All adolescents in grades 7 through 11 in wave 1 were followed up one year later for the wave 2 in-home interview in 1996 (88 percent response rate). The original wave 1 in-home respondents represent the eligible pool for each follow-up wave of interviews. In 2001–02, a third in-home interview was conducted with the original respondents from wave 1, who were 18 to 26 years old and in the transition to adulthood. Over 15,000 Add Health respondents were reinterviewed at wave 3, for a response rate of 77 percent. In 2008, a fourth in-home interview was conducted with the original wave 1 respondents, who were now 24 to 32 years of age and settling into their adult roles and responsibilities. Almost 16,000 respondents were reinterviewed at wave 4, for a response rate of 80 percent.[13]

We use data from the various survey components available in Add Health, including the in-school data (for peer- and school-level social disadvantage), the parent data (for family-level social disadvantage), and the wave 1, 3, and 4 in-home respondent data. At all waves, respondent addresses were geo-coded and merged with geographical data at multiple levels of spatial units. We use the spatial data measured at the tract level for neighborhood social disadvantage from waves 1 and 3.

Our analysis sample is based on females and males who participated in the in-school and wave 1, 3, and 4 in-home interviews and who had valid sampling weights, resulting in a sample size of 5,892 females and 4,928 males. We conducted all analyses by gender because the fundamental processes that operate in pathways of social disadvantage, in particular the mediating mechanisms, differ by gender. We used sampling weights that adjust for the complex sampling design and differential attrition by wave 4 and corrected all variance estimates for the clustered design in our analyses.

Measures

Three sets of variables were used to measure social disadvantage in adolescence (wave 1); social and economic status in adulthood (wave 4); and mediating mechanisms during the transition to adulthood (wave 3) (see figure 8-1). We included a number of control variables at the individual, family, and neighborhood levels, described below. Descriptive statistics of variables used in analyses are shown in table 8-1.

Wave 1 Disadvantage and Controls

Individual-level variables were measured at wave 1 during adolescence. In all analyses, we controlled for demographic differences in age, race/ethnicity, and immigrant generation. While immigrant generation is associated with family

Table 8-1. *Descriptive Statistics, by Gender*[a]

Wave	Females (N = 5,892)		Males (N = 4,928)	
	Mean	Standard error	Mean	Standard error
Wave 1 disadvantage and controls				
Individual level				
Age (12–21)	15.24	0.13	15.43	0.13
Race/ethnicity				
White (reference)	0.69	0.03	0.70	0.03
Black	0.16	0.02	0.14	0.02
Hispanic	0.11	0.02	0.12	0.02
Asian	0.04	0.01	0.04	0.01
Other	0.003	0.001	0.005	0.002
Family disadvantage index (0–4)	1.54	0.04	1.47	0.04
Neighborhood disadvantage index (0–4)	1.00	0.11	1.05	0.10
School disadvantage index (0–5)	1.41	0.12	1.41	0.12
Peer disadvantage index (0–5)	1.20	0.05	1.16	0.05
Wave 4 outcomes				
College degree	0.35	0.02	0.29	0.02
Poverty/welfare status	0.33	0.02	0.26	0.01
Subjective social status (1–10)	4.98	0.05	5.02	0.05
Wave 3 mediators				
Idle	0.16	0.01	0.13	0.01
High school dropout	0.08	0.01	0.10	0.01
Teen childbirth	0.26	0.01	–	–
Arrest/prison	–	–	0.15	0.01
Civic participation	0.29	0.01	0.28	0.01
Presence of mentor	0.79	0.01	0.75	0.01

Source: Add Health (www.cpc.unc.edu/projects/addhealth).

a. Means are weighted and standard errors are adjusted for design effects. Range of interval-scaled measures are in parentheses.

disadvantage in socioeconomic status, it is also associated with behavioral advantages in education and health among adolescents, so we include it here as a control.[14] In all multivariate analyses we further controlled for mental health, self-esteem, future expectations, cognitive ability, and high school grade-point average (GPA). A full description of the measurement of these variables can be found in appendix 8A.[15] Note also that we present only results for the fundamental controls of age and race/ethnicity here.

To measure social disadvantage in the contexts of adolescents' lives at wave 1, we constructed disadvantage indexes by sex for the family, neighborhood, school, and peer environments using a cumulative risk methodology common in the human development and epidemiological literature.[16] The cumulative risk model assumes that the accumulation of risk factors across a variety of domains, rather than a single risk factor, best captures the lived experience of social disadvantage. The cumulative disadvantage indexes therefore represent a count of multiple dichotomous measures of disadvantage that exist in each social context. We describe the cumulative risk methodology and construction of these indexes in appendix 8A.[17]

Family social disadvantage is measured by parents' education, family structure, welfare or poverty status, and parental incarceration. The wave 1 family disadvantage index represents a count of the following four items: not living in a household with two biological parents; highest educated parent had less than a college degree; a parent was incarcerated before the respondent turned age 18; and receipt of welfare or in poverty before age 18. The wave 1 family disadvantage index therefore ranges from 0 (no family disadvantage) to 4 (all family disadvantage risk factors were present).

Unique contextual measures were constructed to capture social disadvantage in family structure, parent/adult education, and poverty status at the neighborhood, school, and peer levels during adolescence at wave 1. School measures came from the in-school survey administered to all students in the schools that Add Health wave 1 respondents attended, from which aggregate measures were constructed. In the in-school survey, adolescents nominated their five best female and five best male friends from the school roster, and those friends also participated in the in-school survey. From their responses, parallel measures of peers' family structure and levels of parental education were constructed. We also constructed aggregated school- and peer-level measures of behaviors that define social disadvantage, including low school attachment, behavioral problems at school, and risk behavior. Neighborhood measures came from tract-level census data linked to the adolescents' geo-coded home residence.

The wave 1 neighborhood disadvantage index, which ranges from 0 to 4, includes four items indicating that the neighborhood has a high proportion of families with income below the poverty level; female-headed households with children under the age of 18; unemployed males; and adults 25 years or older with less than a college degree. Respondents who were in the top 20th to 30th percentile of disadvantage for these continuous measures of neighborhood composition were categorized as experiencing high neighborhood disadvantage on each of these items. The cut-off percentile varied by measure and by sex.

The wave 1 school disadvantage index includes five items indicating that adolescents in the school had a high proportion of parents with less than a college degree; a high proportion of single-parent families; low school attachment; a high number of school problems; and high levels of risk behavior. The peer disadvantage index, which ranges from 0 to 5, includes the same five items (see table 8-1). The items that go into these indexes were dichotomized into a "high" disadvantage group in a fashion similar to that for the neighborhood-level measures. We included a control for those adolescents with no peer data and substituted the school-specific average peer-level values for their missing data. We also controlled for racial dispersion and urbanicity at the neighborhood level.[18]

Wave 4 SES Outcomes

Adult outcomes were measured at wave 4, when the Add Health cohort was 24 to 32 years of age. Educational achievement is a dichotomous measure of whether the respondent obtained a four-year college degree. Poverty or welfare status is a dichotomous variable that combines a longitudinal measure of any welfare or food stamp receipt over the last five years or 2007 personal earnings below the poverty level for the average person in families or households according to the 2007 poverty guidelines.[19] "Subjective social status" measures a common sense of social status across SES indicators; it is especially salient for young adults who may be in the process of attaining their future social status and have fewer concrete measures for comparison, such as income, but who can make a subjective assessment based on their current trajectory.[20] Respondents were presented with a picture of a ladder with ten steps, on which 1 is the lowest rung and 10 is the highest rung. They were asked to "pick the number for the step that shows where you think you stand at this time in your life, relative to other people in the United States." Responses range from 1 to 10.

Wave 3 Mediating Mechanisms

Mediators during the transition to adulthood that potentially explain the patterns of association between social disadvantage in adolescence and social disadvantage in early adulthood include behavioral and prosocial indicators. Behavioral indicators in the transition to adulthood that reinforce pathways of social disadvantage include idle status, dropping out of high school, teenage childbearing for females, and having been arrested or incarcerated for males.

The term "idle" has been used in social science and policy research to classify young adults who are neither working nor attending school.[21] With rich Add Health data, we were able to create a more refined measure of idle status at wave 3. Respondents were considered idle at wave 3 if they were not engaged in one of the following activities: attending regular school; working ten hours a week or more; in full-time duty in the military; or receiving job training. In addition, married respondents (regardless of sex or parenthood status) were coded as not being idle even if they were not engaging in any of the four activities listed above if their household income was reported as $50,000 dollars or more (at or above median household income in 2008).[22] Being a high school dropout, which was best measured at wave 3, when the sample was 18 to 26 years of age, is a dichotomous variable indicating that a respondent was a high school dropout rather than a high school graduate or GED holder. Teen childbearing is a dichotomous measure based on the complete fertility history in Add Health for whether the female ever had a live birth before the age of 20. Females were coded 0 on teen childbearing if they never gave birth or were 20 years or older at first childbirth. Ever being arrested or incarcerated is a dichotomous variable indicating whether the respondent was ever arrested when 18 years old and/or older or was incarcerated at the time of the wave 3 interview. Because so few females were ever arrested or incarcerated at wave 3, this outcome was analyzed for males only.

Prosocial mediators that may facilitate upward mobility include involvement in community service work and the presence of a mentor. Civic participation is a dichotomous variable based on the answer to the question "During the last 12 months did you perform any unpaid volunteer or community service work?" The presence of a mentor is a dichotomous variable based on the response to the question "Other than your parents or step-parents, has an adult made an important positive difference in your life at any time since you were 14 years old?"

Methods and Analytic Framework

Following the conceptual model in figure 8-1, we began by focusing on the links between social disadvantage in adolescence (wave 1, ages 12 to 20) and adulthood (wave 4, ages 24 to 32). We explored the bivariate associations between social disadvantage in adolescence and social disadvantage in adulthood to establish intergenerational links (family disadvantage and young adult SES disadvantage) and intragenerational links (for example, peer, school, and neighborhood disadvantage and young adult SES disadvantage) in social disadvantage across generations and the life course of individuals. In order for our theoretical mechanisms to potentially mediate pathways of social disadvantage out of adolescence, they must be empirically related. We therefore examined the bivariate associations between social disadvantage in adolescence and the mediating mechanisms (idle status, being a high school dropout, teen childbearing, having ever been arrested or incarcerated, civic participation, and presence of a mentor).

We then used longitudinal multivariate models to trace pathways of social disadvantage and test for important mediating effects. We modeled adult outcomes as a function of adolescent individual factors, demographic controls, and social disadvantage at family, neighborhood, school, and peer levels; the analytic technique used depended on the form of the dependent variable. In a second model we included the behavioral and prosocial mediating mechanisms to observe the degree to which the mechanisms explained the association between adolescent and adult social disadvantage.

A final descriptive analysis focused on social disadvantage pathways and the extent of social mobility out of disadvantage from adolescence into adulthood. Exploiting the longitudinal data, we constructed social disadvantage trajectories to describe young people who experienced social disadvantage in adolescence and in adulthood according to the intensity of social disadvantage at both life stage points by using the disadvantage indexes that we constructed at the family, neighborhood, school, and peer levels in adolescence and a wave 4 disadvantage index in adulthood based on the SES outcomes of no college degree, welfare receipt or poverty, and low subjective social status (see appendix 8A).

The intensity of disadvantage cumulates the various contextual disadvantage indexes in adolescence and the various disadvantage outcomes in adulthood, which we categorized into low (bottom quartile), medium (middle two quartiles) and high (top quartile) intensities of disadvantage in adolescence (wave 1) and adulthood (wave 4). We then cross-classified these three-category intensity indexes of social disadvantage at each life stage so that the diagonal indicates those who experienced no mobility or change in social status across the life course and the off-diagonal identifies those who either moved out of social disadvantage by adulthood (social disadvantage was high in adolescence and low in adulthood) or into social disadvantage in adulthood (social disadvantage was low in adolescence and high in adulthood). We then classified trajectories according to mobility (upward, downward, and no change) and examined differences in trajectories by gender and race/ethnicity to identify risk groups for policy interventions and by prosocial mediating mechanisms to identify potential policy levers in social mobility pathways.

Analysis and Results

We begin with descriptive analysis that explores the bivariate relationships between the adolescent disadvantage indexes and mediating mechanisms during the transition to adulthood and SES outcomes in adulthood. We then conduct multivariate analysis of our SES outcomes in adulthood based on our conceptual model in figure 8-1.

Descriptive Analysis

In table 8-2 we show the bivariate relationship between wave 1 disadvantage indicators and wave 4 SES outcomes for females and males. The analytic technique used to estimate each SES outcome depended on its distributional form. We used logistic regression to estimate the binomial outcomes of college degree and poverty/welfare and used linear regression to estimate the interval-scaled outcome "subjective social status." All models controlled for age, race/ethnicity, and immigrant generation. We show the regression coefficients where bolded coefficients indicate that the bivariate relationship was statistically significant at the .05 level, at least (the vast majority are significant at the .01 level).

Note first that all of the relationships in table 8-2 are statistically significant, indicating pervasive and persistent associations between disadvantage in adolescence and SES outcomes in adulthood. Social and economic disadvantage experienced in the family, neighborhood, school, and peer contexts during adolescence is associated with lower socioeconomic status in young adulthood for both men and women, including a lower likelihood of completing a college degree, lower subjective social status, and a higher likelihood of being in poverty or receiving welfare. Social disadvantage in the family environment during adolescence is most strongly linked to social disadvantage in adulthood for both men and women. Among females, for example, each additional disadvantage experienced in the family environment reduces the odds of completing a college degree by 56 percent ($1-e^{-.83}$), increases the odds of poverty and welfare receipt by 63 percent ($1-e^{.49}$), and reduces subjective social status by .37 of a point on the 10-point scale. Disadvantage in the peer environment during adolescence is the next-strongest link to college degree and subjective social status disadvantage in adulthood, whereas neighborhood, school, and peer disadvantage seem to be similarly associated with poverty and welfare status in adulthood.

Table 8-3 explores the bivariate relationships between social disadvantage in adolescence and the mediating mechanisms (idle status, being a high school dropout, teen childbearing, having ever been arrested or incarcerated, civic participation, and presence of a mentor) during the transition to adulthood for females and males. Here relationships are stronger for females than for males and for social disadvantage links with adverse behavioral mediators than with prosocial mediators. Among females, disadvantage in all social contexts—family, neighborhood, school, and peer—is significantly associated with all mediating mechanisms with the exception of presence of a mentor. Again, family disadvantage during adolescence is more strongly linked with the adverse behavioral mediators of idleness, being a high school dropout, and teen birth than is disadvantage in the neighborhood, school, or peer environment, and it is negatively

Table 8-2. *Bivariate Associations between Disadvantage at Wave 1 and SES Outcomes at Wave 4, by Gender*[a]

	SES outcomes for females (N = 5,892)					
	College degree		Poverty/ welfare		Subjective social status	
Wave I disadvantage indicators	Coefficient	Standard error	Coefficient	Standard error	Coefficient	Standard error
Family disadvantage index	**−0.83**	0.05	**0.49**	0.04	**−0.37**	0.03
Neighborhood disadvantage index	**−0.37**	0.05	**0.32**	0.04	**−0.19**	0.03
School disadvantage index	**−0.37**	0.07	**0.32**	0.05	**−0.17**	0.04
Peer disadvantage index	**−0.47**	0.05	**0.31**	0.03	**−0.23**	0.03

	SES outcomes for males (N = 4,928)					
	College degree		Poverty/ welfare		Subjective social status	
Wave I disadvantage indicators	Coefficient	Standard error	Coefficient	Standard error	Coefficient	Standard error
Family disadvantage index	**−0.81**	0.06	**0.41**	0.05	**−0.31**	0.03
Neighborhood disadvantage index	**−0.37**	0.05	**0.19**	0.04	**−0.13**	0.03
School disadvantage index	**−0.37**	0.06	0.14	0.05	**−0.13**	0.03
Peer disadvantage index	**−0.45**	0.05	0.18	0.05	**−0.19**	0.04

Source: Add Health (www.cpc.unc.edu/projects/addhealth).

a. Bolded coefficients are statistically significant at (at least) the $p < .05$ level. All models control for age, race/ethnicity, and immigrant generation. Models using peer-level measures control for having no friends.

linked with the prosocial mediators of civic participation and having a mentor during the transition to adulthood. For example, with each additional disadvantage factor in the family disadvantage index for females, the chances of being idle increase by 54 percent, of dropping out of high school by 123 percent, and of a teen birth by 75 percent and civic participation is reduced by 32 percent and having a mentor by 15 percent. In contrast, with each additional disadvantage factor in the neighborhood disadvantage index, the chances of being idle increase by 31 percent, of dropping out of high school by 40 percent, and of a teen birth by 23 percent and civic participation is reduced by 10 percent and having a mentor by 8 percent.

The pattern of results is similar among males with the exception that family and peer disadvantage seem to be more significantly and equally associated with

Table 8-3. *Bivariate Associations between Disadvantage at Wave 1 and Mediating Mechanisms at Wave 3, by Gender*[a]

| | Mediating mechanisms for females (N = 5,892) | | | | | | | | | |
| | Idle | | High school dropout | | Teen birth | | Civic participation | | Mentor | |
	Coefficient	Standard error	Coefficient	Standard error	Coefficient	Standard error	Coefficient	Standard error	Coefficient	Standard error
Wave 1 disadvantage indicators										
Family disadvantage index	0.43	0.06	0.80	0.07	0.56	0.04	-0.38	0.04	-0.16	0.04
Neighborhood disadvantage index	0.27	0.05	0.34	0.06	0.21	0.04	-0.11	0.03	-0.08	0.04
School disadvantage index	0.25	0.05	0.47	0.06	0.23	0.05	-0.16	0.05	-0.06	0.05
Peer disadvantage index	0.33	0.06	0.43	0.08	0.31	0.04	-0.29	0.04	-0.11	0.04

| | Mediating mechanisms for males (N = 4,928) | | | | | | | | | |
| | Idle | | High school dropout | | Arrest/prison | | Civic participation | | Mentor | |
	Coefficient	Standard error	Coefficient	Standard error	Coefficient	Standard error	Coefficient	Standard error	Coefficient	Standard error
Wave 1 disadvantage indicators										
Family disadvantage index	0.40	0.07	0.54	0.06	0.23	0.04	-0.28	0.05	-0.19	0.05
Neighborhood disadvantage index	0.21	0.05	0.22	0.05	0.02	0.05	-0.11	0.04	-0.16	0.04
School disadvantage index	0.15	0.05	0.26	0.06	0.01	0.06	-0.10	0.04	-0.13	0.08
Peer disadvantage index	0.48	0.06	0.34	0.08	0.17	0.05	-0.24	0.04	-0.15	0.04

Source: Add Health (www.cpc.unc.edu/projects/addhealth).

a. Bolded coefficients are statistically significant at (at least) the $p < .05$ level.

All models control for age; race/ethnicity; and immigrant generation. Models using peer-level measures control for not having friends.

the mediating mechanisms during the transition to adulthood, suggesting that peers may play a more important role in social stratification pathways from adolescence into adulthood for males. These results suggest that these behavioral and prosocial mechanisms—idle status, being a high school dropout, teen birth, incarceration, civic participation, and presence of a mentor—during the transition to adulthood potentially mediate the links between social disadvantage in adolescence and social disadvantage in adulthood and represent potential policy variables that may facilitate social mobility during the transition from adolescence to adulthood. We move to that analysis next.

Multivariate Analysis

We conducted multivariate analysis on our three SES outcomes in adulthood (wave 4); results for college degree are presented in table 8-4, for poverty and welfare receipt in table 8-5, and for subjective social status in table 8-6 for females and males. We estimated two models. Model 1 includes individual characteristics and controls and the four disadvantage indexes for the family, neighborhood, school, and peer environments. This model allows us to examine the independent effects of disadvantage in each context of adolescent life, adjusted for individual characteristics. Model 2 enters the five behavioral and prosocial mechanisms that occur during the transition to adulthood, enabling us to observe the extent to which social disadvantage in adolescence operates through the mediating mechanisms in pathways to social disadvantage in adulthood.

Turning to the results of the logistic regression for college degree in table 8-4, we discuss only the significant effects (bolded coefficients) of social disadvantage and focus on the degree to which the mechanisms in model 2 mediate the disadvantage associations found in model 1. When disadvantage operates at multiple levels of the social environment in model 1, family disadvantage continues to show the strongest independent link to college education. After we controlled for individual characteristics and neighborhood, school, and peer disadvantage in adolescence, each additional disadvantage factor in the family disadvantage index reduces the odds of achieving a college degree by 42 percent for females and 37 percent for males. To a lesser extent, neighborhood and peer disadvantage are also associated with reduced chances of attaining a college degree. Increasing age is associated with higher odds of completing a college degree. We get a curious positive coefficient for black race, which is due to the inclusion of multiple control variables and especially the disadvantage indexes, which cause the bivariate negative black race coefficient with college degree to change signs in multivariate models. These controls produce results consistent with expectations in all subsequent models of SES outcomes.

Model 2 indicates that all mediators are significantly associated with college degree for females. Whereas being idle, dropping out of high school, and experiencing a teen birth during the transition to adulthood are associated with lower odds of attaining a college degree, prosocial engagement in community service or having a mentor improves the odds. These mechanisms mediate some of the association between family disadvantage and college degree for females, reducing the coefficient by about one-fifth, and completely explain the association between peer disadvantage and college degree, rendering it insignificant in model 2. Neighborhood disadvantage does not operate through these mechanisms in its association with college degree for females. The results are similar among males, except presence of a mentor is not significant and being a high school dropout indicates a stronger association with college degree than do other mechanisms and that association is stronger among males than it is among females. Being idle, being a high school dropout, and ever having been arrested or incarcerated reduce the chances of attaining a college degree, while civic participation improves the chances. However, there is little mediation of the disadvantage links with college degree for males, and what mediation there is likely operates through being a high school dropout.

Table 8-5 shows multivariate results for the association between disadvantage in adolescence and poverty status in adulthood for females and males. Among females, social disadvantage in all adolescent contexts is associated with poverty and welfare receipt in adulthood, as shown in model 1. When behavioral and prosocial mechanisms are added in model 2, there is some mediation of family disadvantage (the coefficient reduces by one-third) and neighborhood disadvantage (the coefficient reduces by one-fourth), but very little of the school and peer disadvantage link is explained. Evidently part of the link between family and neighborhood disadvantage in adolescence and poverty in adulthood among females is due to adverse behavioral choices in the transition to adulthood such as being a high school dropout, idle status, and teen childbearing. Having a mentor during the transition to adulthood reduces some of the risk of poverty in adulthood due to family and neighborhood disadvantage in adolescence.

Among males, family disadvantage and neighborhood disadvantage are independently associated with poverty status in adulthood (shown in model 1). Family disadvantage is not explained by mechanisms added in model 2, but neighborhood disadvantage is completely mediated. This social disadvantage pathway indicates that males living in disadvantaged neighborhoods in adolescence are more likely to drop out of high school and remain idle during the transition to adulthood, which in turn increases their chances of poverty in adulthood.

Table 8-4. *Multivariate Analysis for College Degree Attainment at Wave 4, by Gender*[a]

| | Females (N = 5,892) | | | | Males (N = 4,928) | | | |
| | Model 1 | | Model 2 | | Model 1 | | Model 2 | |
	Coefficient	Standard error	Coefficient	Standard error	Coefficient	Standard error	Coefficient	Standard error
Wave 1 disadvantage indicators								
Individual level								
Age	0.05	0.03	0.07	0.03	0.07	0.03	0.07	0.03
Race/ethnicity								
White (reference)								
Black	0.99	0.21	1.06	0.20	0.79	0.18	0.84	0.18
Hispanic	0.01	0.22	0.18	0.23	0.24	0.22	0.27	0.22
Asian	-0.20	0.32	-0.08	0.36	0.62	0.28	0.60	0.29
Other	0.15	0.66	0.17	0.71	0.57	0.66	0.70	0.71
Family disadvantage index	-0.54	0.04	-0.44	0.05	-0.47	0.05	-0.42	0.05
Neighborhood disadvantage index	-0.17	0.06	-0.15	0.06	-0.17	0.05	-0.16	0.05
School disadvantage index	-0.11	0.07	-0.09	0.07	-0.07	0.07	-0.09	0.07
Peer disadvantage index	-0.14	0.05	-0.08	0.05	-0.20	0.06	-0.18	0.06

	Coef.	SE	Coef.	SE	Coef.	SE	Coef.	SE
Wave 3 mediators								
Idle	−1.14	0.17			−0.50	0.23		
High school dropout	−1.28	0.56			−2.74	0.77		
Teen birth (females)/Arrest or prison (males)	−1.02	0.16			−0.31	0.15		
Civic participation	0.90	0.10			0.76	0.12		
Presence of mentor	0.44	0.14			−0.08	0.15		
Constant	−9.07	0.79	−8.67	0.80	−10.51	1.09	−9.79	1.08

Source: Add Health (www.cpc.unc.edu/projects/addhealth).

a. Bolded coefficients are statistically significant at (at least) the $p < .05$ level.

All models control for immigrant generation; mental health; self-esteem; future expectations; cognitive ability; high school GPA; no friendship information; and wave 1 neighborhood racial dispersion and urbanicity.

Model 2 also controls for wave 3 neighborhood disadvantage index.

Table 8-5. *Multivariate Analysis for Welfare/Poverty at Wave 4, by Gender*[a]

	Females (N = 5,892)				Males (N = 4,928)			
	Model 1		Model 2		Model 1		Model 2	
	Coefficient	Standard error	Coefficient	Standard error	Coefficient	Standard error	Coefficient	Standard error
Wave 1 disadvantage indicators								
Individual level								
Age	-0.10	0.03	-0.09	0.03	-0.02	0.03	0.00	0.03
Race/ethnicity								
White (reference)								
Black	0.58	0.13	0.63	0.13	0.20	0.16	0.03	0.16
Hispanic	-0.20	0.18	-0.27	0.19	-0.42	0.22	-0.48	0.23
Asian	-0.05	0.29	-0.09	0.29	0.05	0.28	0.07	0.28
Other	-0.09	1.14	-0.01	1.07	-1.18	1.04	-1.22	1.13
Family disadvantage index	0.30	0.04	0.21	0.04	0.28	0.05	0.24	0.05
Neighborhood disadvantage index	0.19	0.04	0.15	0.04	0.10	0.04	0.02	0.04
School disadvantage index	0.13	0.05	0.11	0.04	-0.02	0.06	-0.03	0.06
Peer disadvantage index	0.11	0.03	0.08	0.03	0.07	0.05	0.08	0.05

Wave 3 mediators

Idle			0.76	**0.10**			0.76	**0.13**
High school dropout			0.63	**0.18**			0.44	**0.18**
Teen birth (females)/Arrest or prison (males)			0.48	**0.09**			0.15	0.12
Civic participation			−0.18	0.10			−0.03	0.12
Presence of mentor			−0.26	0.12			−0.15	0.11
Constant	**3.11**	**0.71**	**2.08**	**0.72**	0.37	**0.76**	**−0.93**	**0.78**

Source: Add Health (www.cpc.unc.edu/projects/addhealth).

a. Bolded coefficients are statistically significant at (at least) the $p < .05$ level.

All models control for immigrant generation; mental health; self-esteem; future expectations; cognitive ability; high school GPA; no friendship information; and wave 1 neighborhood racial dispersion and urbanicity.

Model 2 also controls for wave 3 neighborhood disadvantage index.

Finally, table 8-6 shows multivariate results for the associations between disadvantage in adolescence and subjective social status in adulthood for females and males. We used linear regression to estimate the subjective scale, and bolded coefficients and standard errors indicate significant results. Among females, family disadvantage and, to a lesser degree, neighborhood disadvantage and peer disadvantage in adolescence are independently associated with reports of lower subjective social status in adulthood. Model 2 results show some mediation indicating that family, neighborhood, and peer disadvantage reduce subjective social status by increasing the likelihood of being idle, dropping out of high school, and teen childbearing during the transition to adulthood, and these mechanisms completely explain the marginally significant peer disadvantage link.

Among males, only family disadvantage and peer disadvantage during adolescence are associated with subjective social status in adulthood, and these associations are mediated slightly in model 2 (but enough to render the peer coefficient insignificant). The results suggest that males who grow up in disadvantaged families and have disadvantaged friends but who avoid being idle or dropping out of high school or engage in civic participation during the transition to adulthood consider their social status higher than do their disadvantaged adolescent counterparts.

Mobility Pathways

The final analysis presents a description of mobility pathways from adolescence to adulthood using the wave 1 and wave 4 indexes of disadvantage intensity described previously. We created a categorical measure of disadvantage intensity based on the cumulated index of disadvantage across all contexts in adolescence and all SES outcomes in adulthood, which we classified into low (bottom quartile = 1), medium (middle two quartiles = 2), and high (top quartile = 3) levels at each life stage and cross-classified these categorical indexes to create a 3x3 table to observe social mobility trajectories from adolescence into adulthood (upward, downward, and no change). We define upward mobility for those in cells below the diagonal who move from level 2 (moderate disadvantage intensity) in adolescence to level 1 (low disadvantage intensity) in adulthood or from level 3 (high disadvantage intensity) in adolescence to levels 1 or 2 by adulthood. Downward mobility is defined for those in cells above the diagonal who move from level 1 in adolescence to levels 2 or 3 in adulthood or from level 2 to level 3. No social mobility is observed for those along the diagonal of the 3x3 table. Because there are large substantive differences between those who experience no mobility but low disadvantage and those who remain at the high end of disadvantage intensity from adolescence into adulthood, we classify the no-mobility trajectories according to where they begin in adolescence (low, medium, and high disadvantage intensity). These pathway measures are admittedly crude, but they provide a useful description of the general patterns of social mobility from adolescence into adulthood. We present these pathways by race and ethnicity in table 8-7 for females and males.

We focus first on gender differences in social mobility pathways in the total columns of table 8-7. More than half of females (53 percent) and males (57 percent) experience some social mobility, with the balance tipped somewhat toward downward mobility for males. Among those who experience no change in their disadvantage status across the early life course, females tend to be more evenly distributed across the three disadvantage levels than males, who tend to be more clustered in the moderate level of disadvantage. Black females and males have much less downward mobility (10 to 15 percent) than whites and Asians (~35 percent). Similarly, blacks are more likely to experience upward mobility (40 to 43 percent) than whites and Asians (~21 percent). Hispanics experience considerable upward mobility as well (31 to 36 percent). Of course, this result is due to the fact that blacks begin their adolescent SES trajectory at a much higher level of disadvantage, as shown in the last row of table 8-7. More than one-third of black females and 24 percent of black males experience the highest level of disadvantage intensity in adolescence and have no social mobility almost fifteen years later in adulthood. Less than 9 percent of whites and 2 percent of Asians experience high disadvantage intensity and no mobility over time. In contrast, about one-fifth of whites and more than a quarter of Asians experience no to very little disadvantage in adolescence and remain at this low disadvantage level into adulthood. Hispanics' patterns are more dynamic and diverse than those of other racial groups. About one-fourth remain at moderate levels of disadvantage intensity and 60 percent experience change from adolescence to adulthood. Hispanic females experience downward and upward mobility equally, but Hispanic males tend to experience more upward mobility from adolescence into adulthood. Hispanics experience the most mobility overall.

In table 8-8 we explore differences in mobility pathways by prosocial mediating mechanisms to identify potential policy implications for social mobility. The distributions show the percent in each mobility pathway who reported having a mentor (column 1) or who engaged in civic participation (column 2) for females and males. We find that the presence of a mentor is especially important for reinforcing levels of high social status across the life course, and those who remain in high disadvantage trajectories over time lack mentors. The presence of a mentor, however, does not seem to be associated with upward mobility, especially among males. Civic participation, on the other hand, is associated with upward mobility, especially among females, and differentiates patterns of no

Table 8-6. *Multivariate Analysis for Subjective Social Status at Wave 4, by Gender*[a]

| | Females (N = 5,892) | | | | Males (N = 4,928) | | | |
| | Model 1 | | Model 2 | | Model 1 | | Model 2 | |
	Coefficient	Standard error	Coefficient	Standard error	Coefficient	Standard error	Coefficient	Standard error
Wave 1 disadvantage indicators								
Individual level								
Age	**0.11**	**0.02**	**0.11**	**0.02**	**0.07**	**0.02**	**0.07**	**0.02**
Race/Ethnicity								
White (reference)								
Black	0.07	0.10	0.06	0.10	0.02	0.12	0.03	0.12
Hispanic	−0.12	0.15	−0.09	0.14	0.11	0.15	0.12	0.15
Asian	0.01	0.13	0.03	0.13	−0.23	0.17	−0.25	0.16
Other	−0.55	0.46	−0.60	0.44	0.13	0.35	0.19	0.34
Family disadvantage index	**−0.22**	**0.03**	**−0.18**	**0.03**	**−0.19**	**0.03**	**−0.16**	**0.03**
Neighborhood disadvantage index	**−0.08**	**0.03**	**−0.06**	**0.03**	−0.04	0.03	−0.04	0.03
School disadvantage index	−0.04	0.04	−0.03	0.04	−0.01	0.03	−0.01	0.03
Peer disadvantage index	**−0.07**	**0.03**	−0.06	0.03	**−0.08**	**0.04**	−0.07	0.04

190

Wave 3 mediators

Idle			−0.34	0.08			−0.31	0.11
High school dropout			−0.32	0.14			−0.52	0.13
Teen birth (females)/Arrest or prison (males)			−0.22	0.07			−0.14	0.09
Civic participation			0.15	0.08			**0.28**	**0.07**
Presence of mentor			0.03	0.05			−0.002	0.09
Constant	0.75	0.45	1.35	0.45	0.45		1.57	0.63	2.31	0.61

Source: Add Health (www.cpc.unc.edu/projects/addhealth).

a. Bolded coefficients are statistically significant at (at least) the $p < .05$ level.

All models control for immigrant generation; mental health; self-esteem; future expectations; cognitive ability; high school GPA; no friendship information; and wave 1 neighborhood racial dispersion and urbanicity.

Model 2 also controls for wave 3 neighborhood disadvantage index.

Table 8-7. Mobility Pathways from Adolescence to Adulthood, by Race/Ethnicity and Gender

Mobility pathway	Race/ethnicity for females						Race/ethnicity for males					
W1 —> W4	White	Black	Asian	Other[a]	Hispanic	Total	White	Black	Asian	Other[a]	Hispanic	Total
Downward Mobility												
Percent	30	10	35	—	29	27	35	15	38	—	23	31
Number	999	181	140	—	192	1,519	968	182	147	—	202	1,506
Upward Mobility												
Percent	22	40	20	—	31	26	21	43	20	—	36	26
Number	728	548	55	—	319	1,655	595	365	62	—	291	1,317
No Change (low disadvantage)												
Percent	19	2	31	—	7	16	14	2	27	—	6	12
Number	661	67	112	—	64	909	448	37	95	—	45	633
No Change (medium disadvantage)												
Percent	19	13	13	—	23	19	22	15	15	—	26	21
Number	629	215	49	—	225	1,121	612	167	75	—	218	1,074
No Change (high disadvantage)												
Percent	9	35	2	100	12	13	7	24	—	—	9	9
Number	260	335	7	21	85	688	180	155	—	—	59	398
Total (percent)	100	100	100	100	100	100	100	100	100	100	100	100
Number	3,277	1,346	363	21	885	5,892	2,803	906	382	22	815	4,928

Source: Add Health (www.cpc.unc.edu/projects/addhealth).

a. Results on "Other" race group are not shown because some cell sizes are less than 5 and therefore, according to Add Health security procedures on deductive disclosure, cannot be displayed. Other cells with low frequency are not shown for the same reason.

Table 8-8. *Means of Prosocial Mechanisms at Wave 3 by Mobility Pathways from Adolescence to Adulthood, by Gender*

| Mobility pathway | Females (N = 5,892) | | | | Males (N = 4,928) | | | |
| | Mentor | | Civic participation | | Mentor | | Civic participation | |
W1 —> W4	Percent	Number	Percent	Number	Percent	Number	Percent	Number
Downward mobility	77	1,519	26	1,519	77	1,506	24	1,506
Upward mobility	78	1,655	31	1,655	74	1,317	27	1,317
No change (low disadvantage)	88	909	52	909	82	633	50	633
No change (medium disadvantage)	78	1,121	22	1,121	74	1,074	26	1,074
No change (high disadvantage)	72	688	13	688	65	398	14	398

Source: Add Health (www.cpc.unc.edu/projects/addhealth).

mobility across the life course at the low- and high-intensity levels of disadvantage for both males and females. Among males who remained at the high level of disadvantage from adolescence into adulthood, only 14 percent engaged in community service during the transition to adulthood; in contrast, 50 percent of those who remained at the low level of disadvantage across time did so. The results for females are similar. Clearly civic participation reinforces advantage pathways from adolescence into adulthood.

Discussion and Conclusion

The policy issue addressed by this research is how to alter adolescent pathways of social disadvantage to enable upward mobility into adulthood. With this objective and rich longitudinal data that follow individuals from adolescence into adulthood, we documented first how the multiple contexts of adolescent social disadvantage are linked to social disadvantage in adulthood and, second, potential mediating mechanisms in the transition to adulthood through which social disadvantage in adolescence operates to either reinforce or redirect pathways of social disadvantage into adulthood.

Sources of disadvantage exist in multiple social environments of adolescent life, not only at the individual and family levels but also within the neighborhood, school, and peer contexts. Multiple sources of disadvantage also vary by social group, with native-born racial and ethnic minorities (blacks and Hispanics) experiencing more disadvantage than other groups (results available on request). Not surprisingly, disadvantage in one context is highly related to disadvantage in other contexts, but our multivariate results indicate that these effects are additive, further disadvantaging vulnerable social groups. Not taking these multiple and interrelated sources of disadvantage into account does not capture the complete picture of social disadvantage that young people face during the critical stages of development in adolescence and the transition to adulthood.

We found strong links between social disadvantage in adolescence and social disadvantage in adulthood, especially among females. Equally strong and consistent links between social disadvantage in all contexts of adolescent life were found with behavioral mechanisms (idle status, being a high school dropout, teen childbearing, and incarceration) and the prosocial mechanism of civic participation during the transition to adulthood. These unique longitudinal data in Add Health reveal that social disadvantage trajectories are set early in life and create a momentum for continuing environmental and behavioral disadvantage as young people transition into adulthood.

Multivariate analysis indicates that college degree was the adult outcome most associated with the multiple contexts of social disadvantage in adolescence for both females and males, particularly disadvantages in the family, neighborhood, and peer context. Poverty status and subjective social status were also highly associated with social disadvantage pathways, but more so for females than for males. Family disadvantage was the strongest and most consistent link to disadvantaged SES outcomes in adulthood for females and males, though neighborhood disadvantage was also important across all outcomes for females. Disadvantage in all contexts—family, neighborhood, school, and peers—was associated with poverty status in adulthood for females. These associations were independent and additive, suggesting that even if females are not disadvantaged in the family context, experiencing disadvantage in the school or neighborhood or among peers increases the chances of experiencing poverty in adulthood. Indeed, previous ethnographic research supports this finding, showing precarious outcomes for black middle-class adolescents living in racially segregated neighborhoods that often were close to disadvantaged neighborhoods.[23]

Although we document strong links in social disadvantage across the early life course, our results also provide some promise that policy intervention can help to redirect these disadvantage pathways during the transition to adulthood. We find that some of the disadvantages in the social contexts of adolescent life are mediated by key behavioral decisions and prosocial activities during the transition to adulthood, when young people strike out on their own and begin to control their futures. For example, among females, the pathway from peer disadvantage in adolescence to low education in adulthood can be redirected by presence of a mentor or civic participation and by avoiding idle status, completing high school, or avoiding teen childbearing during the transition to adulthood. These mechanisms also mediate some of the association between family disadvantage and lack of a college degree. Among males, family disadvantage operates through being idle, dropping out of high school, and becoming incarcerated to reduce the chances of a college degree in adulthood, while civic participation helps to ameliorate some family disadvantage by increasing the chances of a college degree. These findings are especially salient for African American males, who face disproportionately high levels of incarceration, further blocking educational opportunities in social mobility pathways.[24]

These findings have important implications for policy. First, programs targeting disadvantaged youth should base eligibility to participate on experience with disadvantage in the multiple social contexts, including disadvantaged schools, peer networks, and neighborhoods, not only the family context. This may be particularly salient for African Americans, who may come from a middle-class family but live in more disadvantaged neighborhood and school settings due to patterns of neighborhood segregation.[25] Second, targeted programs that facilitate obtaining a high school education and work or training to avoid being idle, prevent teenage childbearing, encourage civic participation, and promote mentoring relationships will help young females, in particular, move out of social disadvantage pathways during the transition to adulthood. Disadvantage in adolescence seems to be more persistently related to low educational achievement in adulthood for males, indicating less policy leverage to improve educational outcomes for males. However, keeping males in high school to obtain their diploma seems to be an important positive link in educational pathways among disadvantaged males. As James Heckman has argued, investments in education even earlier in the developmental stages of early childhood probably lay the groundwork for educational achievement across the life course.[26] Unfortunately, Add Health begins to follow its respondents in early adolescence and cannot capture early childhood educational experiences, but secondary school education is clearly an important piece of this pathway. Again, finding ways to keep males, particularly black males, in (high) school is critical, as the risk of incarceration is greatest among those with low education. Indeed, 62.5 percent of black men born between 1970 and 1974 who dropped out of high school were imprisoned at some point in their lives by the ages of 30 to 34 years.[27]

The behavioral mechanisms appear to be more important in reinforcing social disadvantage trajectories from adolescence into adulthood than the prosocial mechanisms are in promoting social mobility. For all SES outcomes (college degree, poverty status, and subjective social status) for both females and males, the lack of human capital development during the transition to adulthood indicated by idle status and being a high school dropout reinforces social disadvantage trajectories coming out of adolescence. For example, these two mechanisms—idleness and dropping out of high school—completely explain the association between peer disadvantage and low subjective social status and between neighborhood disadvantage and poverty status for males. These results point to the policy implication that providing opportunities for schooling, training, or work among male adolescents in socially and economically disadvantaged neighborhoods may help to facilitate social mobility during the transition to adulthood. For both females and males, programs that provide alternative schooling for youth who are not progressing in mainstream educational systems or that provide training or vocational skills development to avoid idleness during the transition to adulthood will facilitate social mobility for disadvantaged youth.

Especially promising is the finding that involvement in community service during the transition to adulthood may facilitate social mobility among disadvantaged youth. Among females, civic participation during the transition to adulthood was associated with a 145 percent increase in the odds of obtaining a college degree (and a 114 percent increase in the odds among males). Community service, both voluntary and required, was more consistently related to social mobility pathways for males, improving educational and subjective status outcomes as disadvantaged males transitioned into adulthood. Involvement in community service may promote human capital development and a sense of productivity when mainstream work and educational opportunities are thwarted among disadvantaged males. Although civic participation may be endogenous to positive SES outcomes in these observational data, the finding that this kind of activity is important in mobility pathways seems worth exploring in further policy research.

In addition to providing skills and training that facilitate work, civic participation may also provide disadvantaged youth with critical noncognitive skills in interpersonal and social interaction. Engagement in community service may broaden networks of social support and increase social capital for disadvantaged youth, thereby facilitating social mobility. A recent review of evaluations (using both experimental and quasi-experimental designs) of positive youth development programs found that programs that included curriculums involving community service and/or mentoring were effective in promoting positive behavioral outcomes, such as increasing school attachment, academic achievement, and interpersonal skills, and in preventing youth problem behaviors, such as misbehavior in school, truancy, and high-risk sexual behavior.[28] The policy impacts of our findings suggest that achieving some level of productivity in the transition to adulthood, whether through continuing education, work, or even community service, helps to elevate one's self-rating of social status and to pave the way for social mobility from disadvantaged neighborhoods and peer networks in which young people grew up.

The presence of a mentor is more important for disadvantaged females, facilitating some social mobility toward obtaining a college degree and moving out of poverty by adulthood. A mentor may influence females' behavioral choices to avoid teen pregnancy, complete high school, and avoid idleness. In a review of positive youth development programs that promote adolescent sexual and reproductive health, programs that included mentors (in some capacity) were associated with increased use of contraception and decreased likelihood of pregnancy for both males and females.[29] In addition, a meta-analysis found that mentoring programs tend to be most beneficial for at-risk and disadvantaged youth.[30] Although there is a large body of research on gender differences in response to helping behaviors, there has been less research on gender differences in the efficacy of mentoring for youth and young adult outcomes,[31] and the available evidence shows mixed results.[32] Therefore, it is difficult to speculate that mentors are less important for males in our study. One possibility is that our measure captured mentorship characterized by emotional closeness, which tends to be more salient for females than for males, who tend to respond more to instrumental and problem-solving support.[33] Despite these findings, it is still important to consider the protective role of mentoring for all at-risk youth, particularly black youth, who face multiple barriers to making a successful transition into adulthood due to reduced employment opportunities, low education, and increased risk of incarceration.[34]

Our analysis of mobility pathways provides evidence of social stratification processes at work during the transition to adulthood stage of the early life course. We find that those in more advantaged pathways, either experiencing upward social mobility or little disadvantage from adolescence into young adulthood, have a higher level of engagement in prosocial activities. For example, the presence of a mentor is especially important for reinforcing levels of high social status across the life course, and those who remain in high disadvantage trajectories over time lack mentors. Similarly, civic participation is more common among those in stable trajectories of high social status, reflecting some selection bias likely associated with engagement in community service. Our finding, however, that disadvantaged youth who experience upward mobility from adolescence into young adulthood have more involvement in community service than youth with downward mobility, coupled with prior experimental evidence and our multivariate results showing significant mediating effects of civic participation, does suggest that there is a potential policy lever associated with civic participation that can help alter social stratification processes coming out of adolescence.

Further evidence was found in an evaluation of the Quantum Opportunities Program (QOP), a multi-year, year-round, comprehensive service program for disadvantaged youth from families receiving food stamps/public assistance in five communities in the United States in 1989.[35] In each community, twenty-five disadvantaged ninth graders were randomly selected to enter the program, which continued through the end of high school (four years). In addition to education and development activities, QOP stressed community service, and each student was provided with a mentor who stayed with the student through the entire four years of high school. Although efficacy varied by study site, students were more likely than the control group to graduate from high school (63 percent versus 42 percent), go on to postsecondary education (42 percent versus 16 percent), and attend a four-year college (18 percent versus 5 percent) or a two-year institution (19 percent versus 9 percent), and they were less likely to drop out of school (23 percent versus 50 percent) or become teen parents (24 percent versus 38 percent).[36] These findings show the substantial impact that interventions based on mentoring and community service can have. Moreover, services for selected students were provided in multiple contexts of their daily lives, including their school and communities. Reaching young people in the contexts in which they live their lives increases the effectiveness and efficacy of interventions like the QOP program and similar programs that intervened at the family/parent level.[37] Programs that are able to intervene in multiple domains have been found to be the most successful.[38]

In summary, we bring attention to two issues often overlooked in policy research. First, programs and interventions to improve the lives of socially disadvantaged youth and their pathways into adulthood need to focus on the complete environment in which adolescents live, including their neighborhood, school, and peer groups as well as family. Youth who live in families with few disadvantages but attend disadvantaged schools or befriend peers who experience family disadvantage, school problems, or risk behaviors or are not engaged in school face disadvantages similar to those faced by youth who live in disadvantaged families but without these additional risks in their social environments. In addition, intervening in the social environment to provide mentoring or opportunities for civic participation is less structurally difficult than intervening in the family context; furthermore, it helps improve chances for social mobility among youth from disadvantaged families. Previous interventions, like QOP, provide evidence of this contention. The lack of data on child development and the environment during the preschool and elementary years imposes some limitations on the conclusions that we can draw about the impact of events and conditions during adolescence on adult outcomes. This limitation may be more critical for the family environment than for peer, school, and neighborhood environments, which become especially salient with respect to adolescent development when young people begin to spend more time outside the family. Thus, the evidence on interventions that occur during adolescence appears to be especially promising in light of our results.

Second, the transition to adulthood is a key developmental period during which critical behavioral decisions and opportunities for prosocial engagement or mentoring support help young people move out of social disadvantage in adulthood. Programs during adolescence and alternative opportunities during the transition to adulthood that steer young people away from negative behaviors such as teenage pregnancy, dropping out of high school, and illegal activities give disadvantaged youth a chance for social mobility in adulthood. These behaviors reinforce pathways of social disadvantage from adolescence to adulthood and explain some of the disadvantage that youth experienced in their family, neighborhood, and peer contexts. In addition, programs that facilitate work or training to avoid being idle, encourage civic participation, and promote mentorship will help young people move out of social disadvantage pathways during the transition to adulthood.

Appendix 8A

This appendix provides details on the construction of measures and cumulative risk methodology.

Wave I Social Disadvantage and Controls

INDIVIDUAL-LEVEL VARIABLES. Individual-level variables are measured at wave 1 during adolescence. Demographic characteristics include age at wave 1 and race and ethnic background (non-Hispanic white, non-Hispanic black, Hispanic, Non-Hispanic Asian, and Other, primarily Native American). We include a control for mental health at wave 1, which is correlated with social disadvantage at wave 1 and confounded with social mobility pathways into adulthood. Mental health is measured using questions from the Center for Epidemiologic Studies Depression (CES-D) scale. The standard CES-D is a twenty-item self-report scale that measures depressive symptoms.[39] We use an abbreviated five-item version of the CES-D.[40] We include self-esteem as an indicator of noncognitive skills measured by the mean of responses to six statements: I have a lot of good qualities; I have a lot to be proud of ; I like myself just the way I am; I feel like I am doing everything just right; I feel socially accepted; and I feel loved and wanted. Likert scale responses ranged from 1 (*strongly disagree*) to 5 (*strongly agree*).

We include two measures of future expectations at wave 1. The expectation to go to college is measured on a Likert scale that asks "On a scale of 1 to 5, where 1 is low and 5 is high, how much do you want to go to college?" The expectation to live to age 35 is also measured on a five-point scale in response to the question? "What do you think are the chances that you will live to age 35?" where 1 is *no chance* and 5 is *almost certain*. Our cognitive measure represents verbal ability as the age- and sex-standardized Add Health Picture Vocabulary Test (AHPVT) score (mean of 100; standard deviation of 15) on an abbreviated picture vocabulary test. We include a missing dummy for AHPVT because this test result was missing for 211 females and 202 male respondents. Our achievement indicator is measured by the grade point average of grades (ranging from A = 4 to D or lower = 1) in math, English or language arts, social studies or history, and science, self-reported by the adolescent at wave 1.

FAMILY-LEVEL VARIABLES. We control for immigrant generation at the family level. Generation 1 comprises foreign-born adolescents with foreign-born parents; generation 2 comprises native-born adolescents with at least one foreign-born parent; and generation 3 comprises native-born adolescents with native-born parents.[41] Family social disadvantage is measured by parents' education, family structure, welfare or poverty status, and parental incarceration. Parents' education, which is based on the higher level of education if two parents were present at wave 1, is measured as a dummy variable for less than a college degree (reference is college degree or higher). Family structure is a set of dummy variables for two biological or adoptive parents (reference), step family, mother only, father only, and other or surrogate parent family (no biological parent present). Welfare or poverty before the age of 18 years is a dichotomous indicator of any welfare receipt before the age of 18 or family income of less than poverty level. This measure is constructed from data on the family's receipt of public assistance or welfare from wave 1 and wave 2 during adolescence in combination with a retrospective report at wave 3 on receipt of welfare and public assistance prior to the age of 18. Based on data from the wave 1 parent questionnaire on reported annual income from 1994, family income is categorized as below poverty level if income was less than $16,000 (roughly the poverty level for a family of four in 1994). We chose a welfare- and income-based measure of poverty over a measure based on income only due to the large proportion of missing data on parental income at wave 1 ($\approx$ 20 percent). Parental incarceration is a dummy variable indicating that either the biological father or mother was incarcerated while the adolescent was growing up (prior to age 18).

Unique contextual measures are constructed to capture social disadvantage in family structure, parent/adult education, and poverty status at the neighborhood, school, and peer levels during adolescence at wave 1. School measures come from the in-school survey administered to all students in the schools attended by Add Health wave 1 respondents, from which aggregate measures are constructed. In the in-school survey, adolescents nominated their five best female and five best male friends from the school roster, and these friends also participated in the in-school survey. From their responses, parallel measures of peers' family structure and level of parental education are constructed. In addition to these contextual measures, we also construct aggregated school- and peer-level measures of behavioral contexts that define social disadvantage, including low school attachment, behavioral problems at school, and risk behavior. Neighborhood measures come from tract-level census data linked to the adolescents' geo-coded home residence.

NEIGHBORHOOD-LEVEL VARIABLES. Social disadvantage in adult education in the neighborhood is measured by the proportion of adults 25 years of age and older who have less than a college education. Neighborhood family structure is measured by the proportion of female-headed neighborhood families that include children. Two social disadvantage measures available at the neighborhood level (but not at the school or peer level) are male unemployment rate and the percent of poor families (income below the poverty line). We include two controls for neighborhood context. Urbanicity distinguishes census tracts that are in completely urbanized areas from those that have any individuals living outside urbanized areas, in rural farm or rural nonfarm locations. Racial dispersion, an indicator that ranges from 0 to 0.93, represents the level of racial heterogeneity in the census tract; higher proportions indicate greater heterogeneity.

SCHOOL-LEVEL VARIABLES. School-level social disadvantage is measured by the percent of all adolescents in the school whose parents have less than a college degree education and the percent who live in a single-parent family. School attachment is an index representing the average response, ranging from 1 (*strongly disagree*) to 5 (*strongly agree*), to the following three items: "How much do you agree or disagree with the following statements? You feel close to people at your school; You feel like you are part of your school; You are happy to be at your school." High values of school attachment represent greater attachment. School problems is an index based on the average response (0 = *never* to 4 = *every day*) to the following four items: "Since school started this year, how often have you had trouble paying attention in school; getting your homework done; getting along with other students; and getting along with teachers?" High values of school problems indicate more problems. Risk behavior is a behavioral index based on the average response (0 = *never* to 6 = *nearly every day*) to the following seven behavioral items: "During the past twelve months, how often did you smoke cigarettes; drink beer, wine, or liquor; get drunk; race on a bike, on a skateboard or roller blades, or in a boat or car; do something dangerous because you were dared to; lie to your parents or guardians; and skip school without an excuse?" High values on risk behavior indicate more risk behavior. Recall that these indexes use aggregate responses from all students in the schools that wave 1 respondents attended and thus represent school census measures.

PEER-LEVEL VARIABLES. We construct parallel measures of social disadvantage at the peer level: percent of peers whose parents have less than a college degree; percent of peers who live with a single parent; average school attachment among peers; average level of school problems among peers; and average risk behavior among peers. We include a control for those adolescents with no peer data (10 percent among females and 16 percent among males) either because they were not in school on the day of the Add Health in-school survey or they did not nominate any friends. For those with no friend data, we substitute the school-specific, average peer-level values.

Social Disadvantage Indexes

We generated social disadvantage indexes by sex for wave 1 family, neighborhood, school, and peer measures using a cumulative risk methodology common in the human development and epidemiological literature.[42] The cumulative risk model assumes that the accumulation of risk factors across a variety of domains, rather than a single risk factor, best captures the lived experience of social disadvantage. Forms of disadvantage rarely occur in isolation and are more likely related to multiple behavioral and social risk factors within and across multiple social environments. Therefore, cumulative disadvantage indexes represent a count of multiple measures of disadvantage that exist at each level of social context. To create an index, all variables in the risk index are transformed into dichotomous variables to represent the presence or absence of the risk factor, where risk = disadvantage measures described above. For continuous variables, individuals who are in the top or bottom 20th to 30th percentile (depending on the direction indicating risk) are given a code of "1."[43] These fairly conservative cut-offs are used to ensure the presence of risk. The measures are summed in a cumulative risk index (CRI) used to calculate the level of cumulative risk for each respondent,

$$(1) \qquad CRI = \sum_{i=1}^{n} x_i = x_1 + x_2 + x_3 + \dots + x_n,$$

where x represents a statistically significant risk factor (with a value of "0" or "1") and n represents the number of statistically significant risk factors included in the cumulative risk index. A risk factor is equal to "1" if the risk factor is present for the respondent; it is equal to "0" if the risk factor is not present.

The wave 1 family disadvantage index contains four items: not living in a two-biological-parent household; parent has less than a college degree; a parent was incarcerated before the child reached the age of 18; receipt of welfare or living in poverty before the child reached the age of 18. The wave 1 neighborhood disadvantage index includes four items: families with income below poverty level; female-headed households including children under the age of 18; male unemployment rate; and adults 25 years or older with less than a college degree. The wave 1 school disadvantage index includes five items: parents with less than a college degree; single-parent families; low school attachment; high school problems; and high levels of risk behavior. The peer disadvantage index includes the same five items. Wave 3 neighborhood disadvantage, which includes the same items as wave 1 neighborhood disadvantage, is used primarily as a control in multivariate analyses. At wave 3 we also control for the proportion of the tract that is an urbanized area, which differs from our wave 1 urbanicity control.

We use a similar approach to create a social disadvantage index at wave 4 based on our SES outcomes. The wave 4 disadvantage index includes three outcomes: no college degree; welfare receipt or poverty after age 18; and a score of less than 4 on subjective social status. We use the social disadvantage index at wave 4 for our mobility pathway analyses.

Notes

1. Samuel Bowles, Herbert Gintis, and Melissa Osborne Groves, *Unequal Chances: Family Background and Economic Success,* 2nd ed. (New York: Russell Sage Foundation, 2005); Robert Haveman and Barbara Wolfe, *Succeeding Generations* (New York: Russell Sage Foundation, 1994); Greg J. Duncan and Jeanne Brooks-Gunn, *Consequences of Growing Up Poor* (New York: Russell Sage Foundation, 1997); Martha S. Hill and Greg J. Duncan, "Parental Family Income and the Socioeconomic Attainment of Children," *Social Science Research,* vol. 16 (1987), pp. 39–73; Harry J. Holzer and others, "The Economic Costs of Childhood Poverty in the United States," *Journal of Children and Poverty,* vol. 14 (2008), p. 41–61; Sara McLanahan and Gary Sandefur, *Growing Up with a Single Parent: What Hurts, What Helps* (Harvard University Press, 1994); Timothy Smeeding, Robert Erikson, and Markus Jäntti, *Persistence, Privilege, and Parenting: The Comparative Study of Intergenerational Mobility* (New York: Russell Sage Foundation, 2011); William J. Wilson, *The Truly Disadvantaged: The Inner City, the Underclass, and Public Policy* (University of Chicago Press, 1987).

2. Peter M. Blau and Otis D. Duncan, *The American Occupational Structure* (New York: Wiley, 1967); Gary S. Becker and Nigel Tomes, "Human Capital and the Rise and Fall of Families," *Journal of Labor Economics,* vol. 4 (1986), pp. S1–S39; Jerry Behrman and Paul Tubman, "Intergenerational Earnings Mobility in the United States: Some Estimates and a Test of Becker's Intergenerational Endowments Model," *Review of Economics and Statistics,* vol. 67 (1985), pp. 144–51; William H. Sewell, Archibald O. Haller, and Alejandro Portes, "The Educational and Early Occupational Attainment Process," *Sociological Review,* vol. 34 (1969), pp. 82–89.

3. Samuel Bowles and Herbert Gintis, "The Inheritance of Inequality," *Journal of Economic Perspectives,* vol. 16 (2002), pp. 3–30; Robert M. Hauser, Solon J. Simmons, and Devah I. Pager, "High School Dropout, Race-Ethnicity, and Social Background from the 1970s to the 1990s" (University of Wisconsin–Madison, Center for Demography and Ecology, 2000); Casey B. Mulligan, *Parental Priorities and Economic Inequality* (University of Chicago Press, 1997); Elizabeth H. Peters, "Patterns of Intergenerational Mobility in Income and Earnings," *Review of Economics and Statistics,* vol. 74 (1992), pp. 456–66; Gary Solon, "Intergenerational Income Mobility in the United States," *American Economic Review,* vol. 82 (1992), pp. 393–408; Gary Solon, "Intergenerational Mobility in the Labor Market," *Handbook of Labor Economics,* vol. 3 (1999), pp. 1761–800; David J. Zimmerman, "Regression toward Mediocrity in Economic Stature," *American Economic Review,* vol. 82 (1992), pp. 409–29.

4. Bowles, Gintis, and Groves, *Unequal Chances: Family Background and Economic Success.*

5. Greg J. Duncan, Ariel Kalil, and Susan Mayer, "The Apple Does Not Fall Far from the Tree," in *Unequal Chances,* edited by Bowles, Gintis, and Groves, pp. 23–80; Tom Hertz, "Rags, Riches, and Race: The Intergenerational Economic Mobility of Black and White Families in the United States," in *Unequal Chances,* edited by Bowles, Gintis, and Groves,

pp. 165–92; Melissa Osborne Groves, "Personality and the Intergenerational Transmission of Economic Status," in *Unequal Chances*, edited by Bowles, Gintis, and Groves, pp. 208–32; Peters, "Patterns of Intergenerational Mobility in Income and Earnings"; Solon, "Intergenerational Mobility in the Labor Market."

6. Duncan and Brooks-Gunn, *Consequences of Growing Up Poor*; Richard M. Lerner and Laurence Steinberg, *Handbook of Adolescent Psychology*, vol. 2, *Contextual Influences on Adolescent Development*, 3rd ed. (Hoboken, N.J.: John Wiley and Sons, 2009).

7. Greg J. Duncan, Kathleen M. Ziol-Guest, and Ariel Kalil, "Early-Childhood Poverty and Adult Attainment, Behavior, and Health," *Child Development*, vol. 81 (2010), pp. 306–25.

8. Duncan and Brooks-Gunn, *Consequences of Growing Up Poor*; David J. Harding, "Cultural Context, Sexual Behavior, and Romantic Relationships in Disadvantaged Neighborhoods," *American Sociological Review*, vol. 72 (2007), pp. 341–64; Gary W. Evans, "The Environment of Childhood Poverty," *American Psychologist*, vol. 59 (2004), pp. 77–92; Michael Rutter, "Protective Factors in Children's Responses to Stress and Disadvantage," in *Primary Prevention of Psychopathology*, vol. 3, *Social Competence in Children*, edited by M. W. Kent and J. E. Rolf (Hanover, N.H.: University Press of New England, 1979), pp. 49–74.

9. Richard A. Settersten Jr., Frank F. Furstenberg Jr., and Rubén G. Rumbaut, *On the Frontier of Adulthood: Theory, Research, and Public Policy* (University of Chicago Press, 2005).

10. Duncan and Brooks-Gunn, *Consequences of Growing Up Poor*; Guang Guo and Kathleen Mullan Harris, "The Mechanisms Mediating the Effects of Poverty on Children's Intellectual Development," *Demography*, vol. 37 (2000), pp. 431–47.

11. Glen H. Elder Jr., "Historical Times and Lives: A Journey through Time and Space," in *Looking at Lives: American Longitudinal Studies of the 20th Century*, edited by Erin Phelps, Frank F. Furstenberg Jr., and Anne Colby (New York: Russell Sage Foundation, 2002), pp. 194–218.

12. Urie Bronfenbrenner, "Ecological Systems Theory," in *Six Theories of Child Development: Revised Formulations and Current Issues*, edited by Ross Vasta (London: Jessica Kingsley Publishers, 1992), pp. 187–249.

13. For more details on the Add Health design and longitudinal data, see Kathleen Mullan Harris and others, "The National Longitudinal Study of Adolescent Health: Research Design," 2009 (www.cpc.unc.edu/projects/addhealth/design).

14. Kathleen Mullan Harris, "The Health Status and Risk Behavior of Adolescents in Immigrant Families," in *Children of Immigrants: Health, Adjustment, and Public Assistance*, edited by Donald J. Hernandez (National Academy Press, 1999), pp. 286–347.

15. See appendix 8A.

16. Evans, "The Environment of Childhood Poverty"; Rutter, "Protective Factors in Children's Responses to Stress and Disadvantage"; Arnold J. Sameroff, "Dialectical Processes in Developmental Psychopathology," in *Handbook of Developmental Psychopathology*, 2d ed., edited by Arnold J. Sameroff, Michael Lewis, and Suzanne Miller (New York: Kluwer Academic/Plenum Publishers, 2000), pp. 23–40.

17. See appendix 8A.

18. Ibid.

19. See "The 2007 HHS Poverty Guidelines," 2007 (http://aspe.hhs.gov.poverty/07poverty.shtml)

20. See "The MacArthur Scale of Subjective Social Status," 2007 (www.maces.ucsf.edu/research/psychosocial.subjective.php).

21. McLanahan and Sandfur, *Growing Up with a Single Parent*; Nancy S. Landale, Ralph S. Oropresa, and Daniel Llanes, "Schooling, Work, and Idleness among Mexican and Non-Latino White Adolescents," *Social Science Research*, vol. 27 (1998), pp. 457–80.

22. Carmen DeNavas-Walt, Bernadette D. Proctor, and Jessica C. Smith, *Income, Poverty, and Health Insurance Coverage in the United States: 2009*, Current Population Reports, pp. 60–238 (U.S. Census Bureau, 2010), table 1, p. 5.

23. Mary Pattillo, *Black Picket Fences: Privilege and Peril among the Black Middle Class* (University of Chicago Press, 1999).

24. Bruce Western and Christopher Wildeman, "The Black Family and Mass Incarceration," *Annals of the American Academy of Political and Social Science*, vol. 621 (2009), pp. 221–42.

25. Pattillo, *Black Picket Fences*.

26. James Heckman, "The Economics of Inequality: The Value of Early Childhood Education," *American Educator*, vol. 35, no. 1 (Spring 2011), pp. 31–47; James Heckman and Flavio Cunha, "Investing in Our Young People," in *Cost-Effective Programs in Children's First Decade: A Human Capital Integration*, edited by Arthur Reynolds and others (Cambridge University Press, 2010), pp. 381–414; James Heckman and Dimitriy V. Masterov, "The Productivity Argument for Investing in Young Children," *Review of Agricultural Economics*, vol. 29 (2007), pp. 446–93.

27. Western and Wildeman, "The Black Family and Mass Incarceration."

28. Richard F. Catalano and others, "Positive Youth Development in the United States: Research Findings on Evaluations of Positive Youth Development Programs," *Annals of the American Academy of Political and Social Science*, vol. 591 (2004), pp. 98–124.

29. Loretta E. Gavin and others, "A Review of Positive Youth Development Programs That Promote Adolescent Sexual and Reproductive Health," *Journal of Adolescent Health*, vol. 46 (2010), pp. S75–S91.

30. David DuBois and others, "Effectiveness of Mentoring Programs for Youth: A Meta-Analytic Review," *American Journal of Community Psychology*, vol. 30 (2002), pp.157–97.

31. Lillian T. Eby and Tammy D. Allen, "Moving toward Interdisciplinary Dialogue in Mentoring Scholarship: An Introduction to the Special Issue," *Journal of Vocational Behavior*, vol. 72 (2008), pp. 159–67.

32. Nancy Darling and others, "Gender, Ethnicity, Development, and Risk: Mentoring and the Consideration of Individual Differences," *Journal of Community Psychology*, vol. 34 (2006), pp. 765–80.

33. Ibid.

34. Ronald B. Mincy, *Black Males Left Behind* (New York: Urban Institute Press, 2006); David Miller, *Man Up: Recruiting and Retaining African American Male Mentors*, "Executive Summary" (www.urbanyouth.org/docs/AfricanAmericanMalePerspectivesOnMentoring_08.pdf).

35. Catalano and others, "Positive Youth Development in the United States: Research Findings on Evaluations of Positive Youth Development Programs."

36. See "Quantum Opportunities," 1994 (www.aypf.org/publications/compendium/C1S37.pdf).

37. Kathleen Ethier and Janet S. St. Lawrence, "The Role of Early, Multilevel Youth Development Programs in Preventing Health Risk Behavior in Adolescents and Young Adults," *Archives of Pediatric and Adolescent Medicine*, vol. 156 (2002), pp. 429–30.

38. Catalano and others, "Positive Youth Development in the United States: Research Findings on Evaluations of Positive Youth Development Programs."

39. Lenore S. Radloff, "The CES-D Scale: A Self-Report Depression Scale for Research in the General Population," *Applied Psychological Measurement*, vol. 1 (1977), pp. 385–401.

40. Krista Perreira and others, "What Are We Measuring? An Evaluation of the CES-D across Race, Ethnicity, and Immigrant Generation," *Social Forces*, vol. 83 (2005), pp. 1567–601.

41. Harris, "The Health Status and Risk Behavior of Adolescents in Immigrant Families."

42. Evans, "The Environment of Childhood Poverty"; Rutter, "Protective Factors in Children's Responses to Stress and Disadvantage"; Sameroff, "Dialectical Processes in Developmental Psychopathology."

43. Karen Appleyard and others, "When More Is Not Better: The Role of Cumulative Risk in Child Behavior Outcomes," *Journal of Child Psychology and Psychiatry*, vol. 46 (2005), pp. 235–45.

9

Poverty, Intergenerational Mobility, and Young Adult Educational Attainment

PATRICK WIGHTMAN AND SHELDON DANZIGER

Equality of opportunity has long been a distinguishing characteristic of the American experiment. Historian James Truslow Adams characterized the "American dream" as "a social order in which each man and each woman shall be able to attain to the fullest stature of which they are innately capable . . . regardless of the fortuitous circumstances of birth or position."[1] Education has been the key to this conception of economic mobility. As early as 1779, as governor of Virginia, Thomas Jefferson proposed a "Bill for the More General Diffusion of Knowledge" that, had it passed, would have taught "reading, writing, and common arithmetic" to "all the free children, male and female."[2] Of course, as with other civil rights, access to public education expanded across the social spectrum only fitfully—compulsory school attendance laws became commonplace only by the end of the nineteenth century. And after decades of resistance, separate schools for white and black children were outlawed by the Supreme Court only recently, in 1954. Even today, the U.S. tradition of basing funding for public schools on local area property taxes means that children residing in affluent communities with relatively high local tax bases attend schools that have more resources than the schools attended by children living in poor communities with low tax bases.

Nevertheless, as a result of the American commitment to the ideal of equality of educational opportunity, raising the educational attainment of poor children

This research was supported in part by cooperative agreement 1U1 AE000002-01 from the U.S. Department of Health and Human Services, Assistant Secretary for Planning and Evaluation, and by funds provided to the Research Network on Transitions to Adulthood by the John D. and Catherine T. MacArthur Foundation. Ariel Kalil and Luke Shaefer provided helpful comments on a previous version. Any opinions expressed are solely those of the authors.

208

was a key goal of President Lyndon Johnson's War on Poverty. In a 1965 special message to Congress, "Toward Full Educational Opportunity," he proposed "that we declare a national goal of Full Educational Opportunity. Every child must be encouraged to get as much education as he has the ability to take. We want this not only for his sake, but for the nation's sake."[3]

In the decade that followed, the federal government enacted many programs that both provided income and services for poor families and sought to increase the human capital of poor children, thereby enhancing their opportunities to break the intergenerational cycle of poverty. Programs included Head Start, federal spending for primary and secondary education, programs to encourage disadvantaged youth to attend college, and the work-study program and subsidies for college tuition, both of which make college more affordable. These initiatives and many others that were implemented or expanded between the mid-1960s and late 1970s continue to form the core of the country's pursuit of equal educational opportunity.

Indeed, educational interventions focused on poor children and young adults garner more public support than programs that provide benefits to their parents, in part because Americans strongly believe that children's opportunities should not be limited by their circumstances at birth. For example, a March 2011 poll by the Economic Mobility Project of the Pew Charitable Trusts asked a random sample of adults to list which of twelve choices was "one of the most important goals the government should work toward."[4] The highest ranked of the choices was "ensuring all children get a quality education," which was endorsed by 46 percent of respondents. In contrast, only 23 percent endorsed "helping people out of poverty" as one of the most important goals. Respondents were also asked to rate "steps that the government could take to help Americans improve their economic situation." Almost 80 percent reported that making college more affordable and 84 percent reported that improving the quality of elementary and high school education would be one of the most effective policies or a very effective policy.

Despite such attitudes toward promoting equal opportunity, the quality of public elementary and secondary schools remains much lower for the poor and access to college is much more restricted for the poor (especially racial and ethnic minorities) than for the affluent. Indeed, since the mid-1970s there has been little progress against poverty and inequality between high and low socioeconomic status (SES) families has widened along most dimensions, including earnings, family income and wealth, and, ominously, the educational attainment of children.[5] In 2005, for example, 53.5 percent of high school graduates whose parents were in the lowest family income quintile enrolled in secondary education (two- or four-year colleges) in the fall immediately after graduation while

81.2 percent of high school graduates whose parents were in the highest income quintile did so.[6] The rates of immediate college enrollment were 42 percent for whites, 32 percent for African Americans, and 25 percent for Hispanics.

This chapter investigates the relationship between family background and young adult outcomes and the extent to which inequalities in parental SES (as measured either by income or by educational attainment) may have affected young adults' educational attainment differently over the past thirty years. In analyzing data from the Panel Study of Income Dynamics (PSID), we find no evidence that the gap in college completion (earning a four-year degree by age 25) between young adults from low- and high-income families and those from low- and high-education families narrowed among cohorts from the mid-1950s through the early 1980s.

We also examine educational attainment differences by SES over three generations, focusing on the outcomes of young adults around age 19 raised by low-income parents who also were raised in low-income households. We find that educational attainment is lower both for those whose childhood SES was low and for those whose parents' childhood SES was low.

Together, our results suggest that despite several decades of spending on compensatory education programs from preschool through college, the educational attainment and hence the economic status and prospects of young adults remain strongly correlated with the status of their parents and even with the status of their grandparents.

Family Background and Young Adult Outcomes

Family background can influence the life-course trajectories of young adults in many ways. Parental income and other economic resources may provide access to better opportunities for human capital accumulation.[7] Other advantages of having high-income parents may be indirect: for example, their ability to provide a cognitively stimulating home environment.[8] Other experiences within the household that are related to socioeconomic status also can influence children's developmental trajectories. Low income contributes to increased parental stress and inconsistent parenting, which in turn are associated with behavioral problems and other impediments to successful development.[9]

The substantial correlation between parental educational and economic outcomes and those of their offspring has been extensively documented empirically.[10] Although these studies show that the children of rich parents fare better than the children of poor parents, they have not addressed whether the increasing inequality in parental economic status over the last three decades has also been associated with increasing gaps in young adult attainment.

The Changing Role of Family Background

In a 2007 study, Guldi, Page, and Stevens examined the effects of parental SES on young adult outcomes at age 30 for two birth cohorts—individuals born between 1950 and 1953 and those born between 1970 and 1973.[11] They note several factors regarding the different time periods during which these individuals transitioned to adulthood that may have increased the correlation between family SES and young adult outcomes. These include the increasing returns to higher education[12] and the subsequent widening of income and educational inequalities (among both the parental and young adult generations); the disparity between high- and low-income families in parental transfers to young adults;[13] and the rise in the percentage of children growing up in single-parent families.[14] Potentially offsetting the widening inequalities were increased government expenditures on disadvantaged children and young adults, especially those born after the late 1960s, through programs such as Head Start and food stamps, Medicaid, expanded access to school-provided meals, and Pell Grants and work-study grants for higher education. Guldi, Page, and Stevens document a strong positive relationship between family SES and young adult outcomes, especially educational attainment, but find little evidence that the relationship was greater for the cohort born in the 1970s than for the cohort born in the 1950s.[15]

There are several reasons why SES differences may influence more recent cohorts differently than previous cohorts, including the two analyzed by Guldi, Page, and Stevens. First, the trends described by those authors have continued, particularly rising income inequality and the prevalence of single parents, putting low- and high-income families on more divergent paths. Also, the declining number of well-paying manufacturing jobs for workers without any college education means that the economic circumstances of children growing up in the 1950s would have been different from those of children growing up in the late 1970s and afterward, even for children growing up in same region. The negative shift in economic opportunities for less-educated workers has increased the importance of obtaining a college education. With regard to government policies, the 1996 federal welfare reform (the Personal Responsibility and Work Opportunity Reconciliation Act) and related state welfare policy reforms may have reduced the resources available to disadvantaged adolescents living with single parents.

These developments suggest that the experiences of recent cohorts vis-à-vis their family background may be different from those of the cohort born in the 1950s and even those born in the early 1970s. However, the net effect of these economic, demographic, and social policy changes is ambiguous. For example, changing economic conditions may have increased young adults' incentives to go to college but may also have hampered the ability of some parents to pay the rising cost of a college education. That might be a particular problem for middle-income households that earn too much to qualify for Pell Grants and other financial aid typically reserved for low-income families but earn too little to afford the expense themselves. In addition, as discussed below, young adults from low-income families may have incomplete information about their eligibility for Pell Grants and other scholarships because of the complexity of the financial aid application process.[16]

Bailey and Dynarski, using the 1979 and 1997 National Longitudinal Surveys of Youth and an analytical framework (cohort comparison) similar to that of Guldi, Page, and Stevens, find significant changes in the association between family background and educational attainment for young adults born between 1961 and 1964 and the association for those born between 1979 and 1982.[17] The rate of college entry (any college experience by age 19) increased by 80 percent for those from top-income quartile homes but only about 50 percent for those from bottom-income quartile homes. The authors also find growing disparity in the rate of college completion (obtaining a B.A. degree by age 25).

Data, Methodology and Descriptive Statistics

We analyzed data from the Panel Study of Income Dynamics, the longest-running longitudinal study of household income in the United States, which since 1968 has collected detailed economic and demographic information over the life course of its respondents. The original sample consisted of approximately 5,000 households. As younger members attain adulthood and move out of their parental household, they are interviewed and integrated into the study as independent PSID households. The survey was conducted annually from 1968 to 1996 and biennially from 1997 forward. The PSID initially comprised two separate subsamples, a national sample and a low-income oversample. Because of that, we used the study-supplied sampling weights, which correct for unequal selection probabilities as well as differential attrition, in all analyses.

The PSID is ideally suited to studying intergenerational relationships. The most distinctive characteristic is the length of the panel—even with the switch to biennial interviews, there are thirty-five waves of data going back nearly forty years. No other data source covers a time period of this length with a similar depth of available information. Because of its design, the sample is self-perpetuating, and with the application of the probability weights, children born into PSID families themselves constitute representative cohorts (of the nonimmigrant population) as they advance through childhood and into adulthood, despite attrition.[18] Moreover, the ability to link family members across multiple representative cohorts is unique to the PSID.

The PSID data have two prominent limitations, sample size and subject matter. Because the sample increases only when participant household members form their own families (for example, through own births, marriages, and stepfamilies), the sample remains relatively small. This limits (to a varying degree) the ability to investigate specific subgroups (for example, the extremely wealthy) and non-black minority populations (for example, Hispanics). Although the content has expanded in recent years to include topics such as respondent health, child care use, and consumer expenditures, analyses using all survey years are restricted to (detailed measures of) education, family structure, employment, and income. In spite of its limitations, the PSID is a unique and valuable source of information on the socioeconomic history of the United States.

Our sample comprises 6,160 PSID participants for whom we had at least three years of information on parental income when the participants were between the ages of 11 and 15 years and whom we subsequently observed at or around the age of 25.[19] These young adults were born between 1956 and 1982. We evaluate the effects of two measures of family background on young adult outcomes: family per capita income (adjusted for inflation) and parental education. For the former, we divided annual total family income by family size for each year and then computed the average for the years when participants were 11 to 15 years old (requiring a minimum of three observations). We then divided per capita income for each cohort into quintiles (weighted) and used the respondent's position within this distribution as our indicator of childhood income—those who grew up in the lowest quintile; those in the middle three quintiles; and those in the top quintile.

For parental education, we used three categories of the highest level of education obtained by either (or the single) parent: a parent completed a high school degree or less; at least one parent had some postsecondary education but less than a four-year degree; and at least one parent had completed a four-year college degree or higher. We examined four-year college completion at age 25. While graduation from college is not sufficient to guarantee economic success, college graduates are much more likely to achieve stable employment at good wages than are those with less education.

Weighted summary statistics are presented in table 9-1; column 1 includes all 6,160 respondents, of whom 22.3 percent had completed college around the age of 25 years. The modal young adult (36 percent) was raised in a household in which at least one parent had finished high school but did not have a four-year college degree; 15.8 percent were raised in households in which no parent had graduated from high school; and 24.8 percent were raised in households in which at least one parent was a college graduate. Blacks made up 14.7 percent of the sample. Only 20.7 percent were born to parents younger than age 24; 58.9 percent were born to parents who were between the ages of 25 and 35; and 20.3 percent were born to a parent older than 35.

Table 9-1 also shows the mean income (divided by family size, in constant 2005 dollars, and divided by 10,000) when these young adults were between the ages of 11 and 15 years. The bottom 20 percent grew up in households with a per capita income of $4,620, about a third of the average for the middle 60 percent ($13,690) and about 15 percent of the average for the top quintile ($31,580).

Our sample differs from that of Guldi, Page, and Stevens in several aspects.[20] First, it is much larger; whereas they focused exclusively on two four-year cohorts, we include all individuals born between 1956 and 1982 who met the stated criteria. Second, ours is younger; whereas they measured young adult outcomes at age 30, we examine outcomes at age 25 in order to include more recent cohorts. By focusing on 25-year-olds, our sample includes individuals born as late as 1982, who grew up in an era of rising economic inequality. As a result, we do not evaluate stable employment and earnings, the measures that they evaluated for 30-year-olds. However, educational attainment at age 25 is a strong predictor of employment stability and earnings at age 30.[21] An important difference is that our sample also includes young adults who resided with their parents. Guldi, Page, and Stevens focused on heads of household and wives, but given that they examined 30-year-olds, the exclusion of dependent adult children is likely to have had little effect on their findings. However, given both the lengthening of the transition to adulthood in recent years and the fact that we examined 25-year-olds, including co-resident adult children, is an important consideration. In this regard, the results presented below are more comparable to those estimated by Bailey and Dynarski.[22]

Finally, in contrast to both Guldi, Page, and Stevens and Bailey and Dynarski, we analyzed long-term trends in the effects of parental SES on young adult attainment rather than differences between two cohorts. We did so in two ways. First, we combined young adults into seven four-year birth cohorts (with the exception of the reference group, which consists only of three years) that cover the span of the PSID: 1956–58 (the reference cohort); 1959–1962; 1963–66; 1967–1970; 1971–74; 1975–78; and 1979–1982. We then included an interaction between each cohort indicator and our SES indicators. That specification allowed us to test for differences across cohorts. The second specification instead models historical trends using a cubic parameterization of time—that is, it includes controls for birth year, birth year squared, and birth year cubed.[23] That allowed us to test for trend differences across SES categories. Each specification

Table 9-1. *Summary Statistics for PSID Participants Born 1956–1982*

Variable	Sample	Bottom	Middle three	Top	No college	Some college	College
		Income quintiles			Parental education		
College degree by age 25	0.223	0.062	0.212	0.424	0.092	0.217	0.503
Parental education							
Dropout	0.158	0.439	0.108	0.017	0.305	...	...
High school	0.360	0.401	0.401	0.194	0.695	...	...
Some college	0.234	0.126	0.272	0.231	...	...	...
College	0.248	0.034	0.220	0.557	...	...	...
Black	0.147	0.394	0.103	0.025	0.213	0.112	0.042
Female	0.498	0.528	0.490	0.491	0.506	0.478	0.502
Head's age at respondents' birth							
Less than 24	0.146	0.222	0.148	0.061	0.171	0.174	0.067
Between 25 and 35	0.448	0.335	0.457	0.536	0.344	0.506	0.610
Over 35	0.203	0.246	0.184	0.215	0.224	0.173	0.186
Region of residence							
South	0.292	0.400	0.263	0.268	0.317	0.270	0.260
Northeast	0.222	0.195	0.225	0.242	0.220	0.188	0.259
North Central	0.298	0.280	0.317	0.256	0.315	0.291	0.269
West	0.161	0.095	0.169	0.208	0.134	0.212	0.172
Alaska/Hawaii/ Foreign	0.003	0.003	0.002	0.005	0.001	0.005	0.004
Average income[a]							
Bottom quintile	0.462 (0.172)	... ...	... ...	... ...	0.446 (0.169)	0.538 (0.166)	0.576 (0.142)
Middle quintiles	1.369 (0.429)	... ...	... ...	... ...	1.233 (0.380)	1.439 (0.421)	1.595 (0.427)
Top quintile	3.158 (1.492)	... ...	... ...	... ...	2.717 (0.959)	2.939 (0.974)	3.417 (1.759)
Sample size	6,160	2,126	3,266	768	3,843	1,268	1,039

Source: PSID and authors' calculations.

a. Income at respondents' ages 11 to 15, in ten thousands of 2005 dollars. Standard deviations are given in parentheses.

acts as sensitivity check against the other. All regressions are estimated using ordinary least squares (OLS) and with PSID-provided sampling weights. All models also include controls for gender (1 = female), race/ethnicity (1 = black), and the age of the household head at the time of the individual's birth.

Figures 9-1, 9-2A, and 9-2B plot the annual PSID data for our sample for college completion, average income by parental income quintile, and parental

Figure 9-1. *College Completion by Age 25*

Percent of 25-year-olds

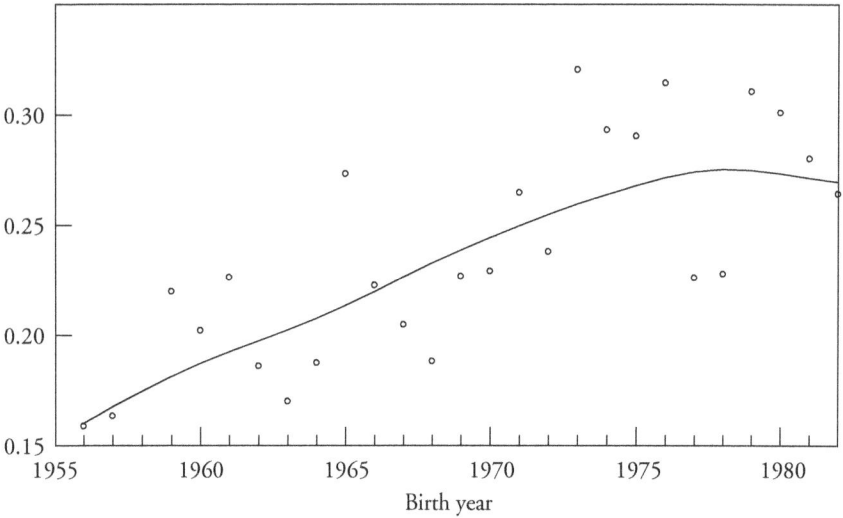

Source: PSID and authors' calculations.

education, respectively. Because of the noisiness of the data, figure 9-1 also presents stylized rates of college completion derived from a locally weighted regression (lowess smoother). The percentage of young adults with college degrees increased on average among those born between the mid-1950s and the late 1970s, at which point the overall trend flattens. Consequently, while only 16 percent of those born in the mid-1950s completed college by 25 years of age, 27 percent of those born in the early 1980s did so.

Figure 9-2A shows average annual household per capita income when the young adults were ages 11–15 for the bottom, middle three, and top quintiles (the y-axis units are ten thousands of 2005 constant dollars). For a respondent born in the mid-1950s, average annual inflation-adjusted income is $3,932 in the bottom quintile and $26,482 in the top quintile. In the early 1980s, those means are $4,898 and $39,002, respectively, representing rates of increase of 24.5 and 47.2 percent. Thus, income inequality increased: the average rate of income growth for families in the top quintile was almost double the rate for families in the bottom quintile.

Figure 9-2B presents the distribution of parental educational attainment. The percentage of young adults who grew up in households in which no parent had any college experience declined dramatically, from 66 percent for those born in mid-1950s to 33.6 percent for those born in the early 1980s. The number of

Figure 9-2A. *Average Income, by Income Quintile*

Tens thousands of 2005 U.S. dollars

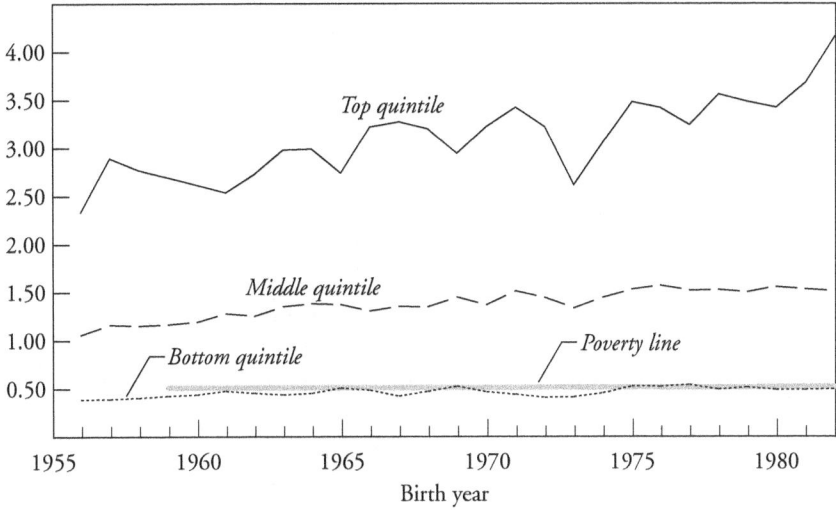

Source: PSID and authors' calculations.

Figure 9-2B. *Parent's Education Level*

Percent at each level

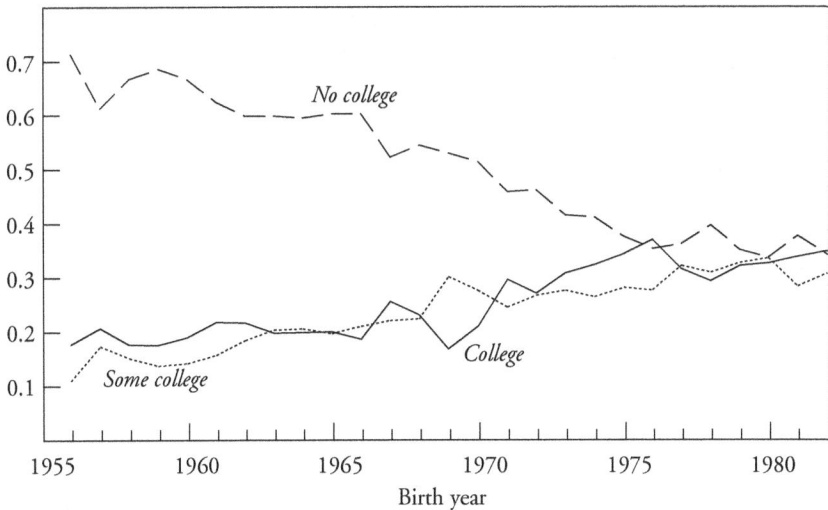

Source: PSID and authors' calculations.

young adults in the same cohorts who grew up with a college-graduate parent nearly doubled, from 19.3 to 34.3 percent.

These data trends illustrate our rationale for using two different measures of family background. Because there are always bottom (and middle and top) quintiles in the per capita income distribution, our first measure captures a relative dimension of parental SES. In contrast, parental education is an absolute measure, in that the number of young adults growing up in households in which no parent had any college experience is not categorically dependent on the number of those who did have such experience. If absolute improvements in the family background of disadvantaged young adults can promote intergenerational mobility, then public policies focused on "raising the bottom" can be effective. In contrast, if relative resources in childhood are what matter, then it will be much more difficult for policies focused on raising the absolute well-being of those at the bottom—which characterize the U.S. social safety net—to promote intergenerational mobility.

The Association between Parental SES and College Completion: Regression Results

Figure 9-3A shows the changing relationship between college completion at age 25 and childhood per capita income, based on the cohort specification (regression results are shown in the first three columns of appendix table 9A-1). Among young adults raised in low-income homes, there is little difference between the predicted completion rate of those born in 1956–58 and those born in 1979–1982 (3 percent and 4 percent, respectively). In contrast, among those growing up in high-income homes, the predicted rate increased from 27 to 54 percent, with most of the increase coming from the cohort born in the 1970s. As a result, the gap between low- and high-income respondents increased from 25 to 50 percentage points.

The results from the cubic time trend specification are similar (see figure 9-3B and the first column of appendix table 9A-2). In this specification the trend among low-income respondents is similarly flat, from 2 to 1 percent. However, the most prominent feature is the increasing gap in the fitted completion rates between young adults from low- and high-income backgrounds (from 24 to 52 percentage points).

Figure 9-4A shows the results for college completion when SES is measured by parental education (regression results are shown in the last three columns of appendix table 9A-1). The predicted completion rate is consistently 6 percent for those whose parents did not have any college experience. Among 25-year-olds with at least one college-graduate parent, college completion increased from

Figure 9-3A. *College Completion, by Family Income*[a]

Regression-adjusted probability

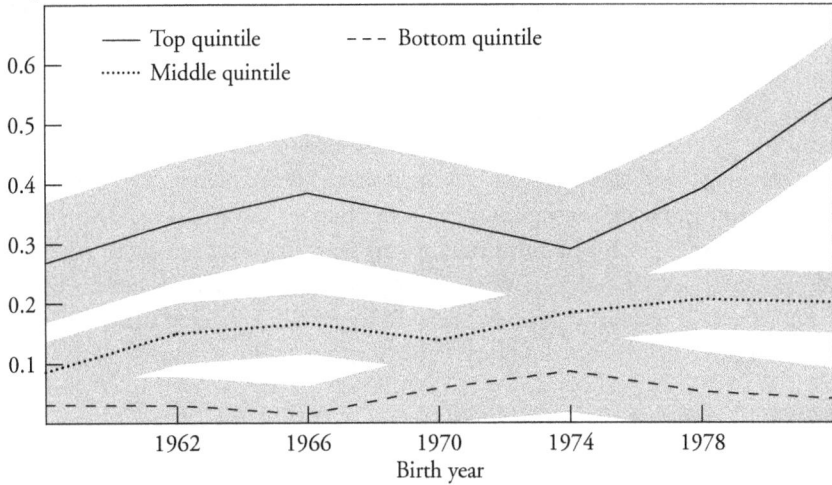

Source: PSID and authors' calculations.
a. With four-year cohort dummies.

Figure 9-3B. *College Completion, by Family Income*[a]

Regression-adjusted probability

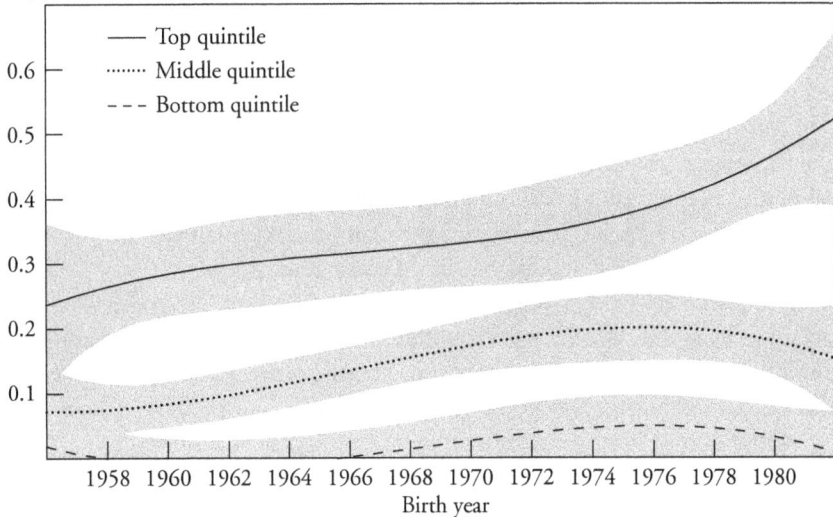

Source: PSID and authors' calculations.
a. With cubic time trend.

35 to 51 percent. As a result, the predicted gap increased from 29 to 45 percentage points.

The results from the cubic time trend specification, presented in figure 9-4B (and the last column of appendix table 9A-2), are very similar. The moderate decline (from 5 to 3 predicted percentage points) in the fitted completion rate among those with parents with no college is statistically not different from zero. However, the increase among those with college-educated parents, from 31 to 46 percentage points, is significant. As a result, the predicted parental-education achievement gap widened significantly, from 26 to 43 percentage points.

In the case of both SES measures, among 25-year-olds born since the mid-1970s, the predicted gap between those with high- and middle-SES backgrounds also is increasing. For example, in figure 9-3A the gap increases from 18 to 34 percentage points; in figure 9-4A, from 22 to 30 points.

Sensitivity Analyses and Limitations

Bailey and Dynarski show that a large part of the increased disparity in educational attainment between high- and low-income families is due to increased college attendance among high-income women.[24] When we estimated the regressions described above separately by gender (results available on request), we found similar results. Women from the highest-income families are completing college at a greater rate (20-percentage-point increase) than similar men (17-point-increase). Among low-income 25-year-olds, the gap between men and women showed a reversal, from 2 percentage points in favor of men to 7 points in favor of women, due primarily to the falling completion rate among men (from 8 to 2 percent). However, given the PSID sample size, those differences are not statistically significant.

While using income quintiles to define "high" and "low" income is arbitrary, the patterns are robust to alternatives—including using income tertiles, income relative to the poverty line, and household income not adjusted for household size to categorize SES. These trends are also robust to childhood income averaged over a longer time frame, from ages 4 to 14 years.

One limitation is that much of the increased income inequality that has occurred over the past forty years is due in large part to gains concentrated among households in the top decile and even the top percentile of the income distribution. Unfortunately, PSID sample size limitations prevent us from analyzing trends only for those at the very top of the income distribution.

Upward mobility is especially limited among low-income blacks.[25] When we control separately for trends among low-income black youth, we find no evidence that they are worse off than low-income whites. However, as can be seen

Figure 9-4A. *College Completion, by Parents' Education*[a]

Regression-adjusted probability

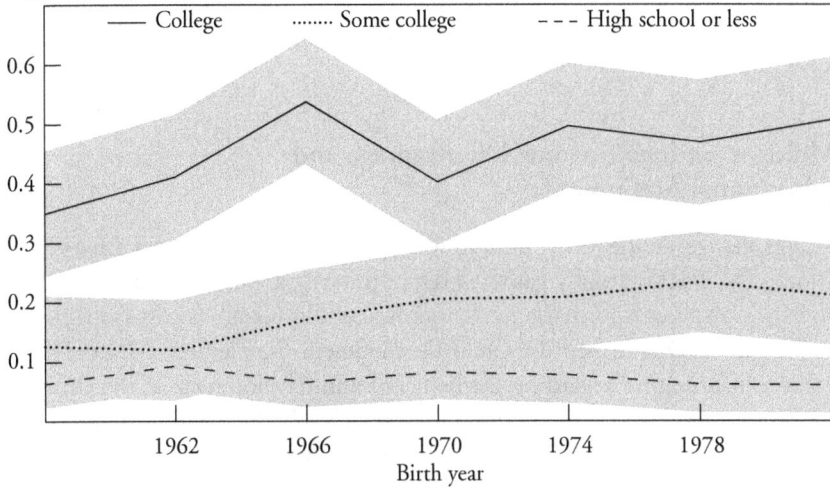

Source: PSID and authors' calculations.
a. With four-year cohort dummies.

Figure 9-4B. *College Completion, by Parents' Education*[a]

Regression-adjusted probability

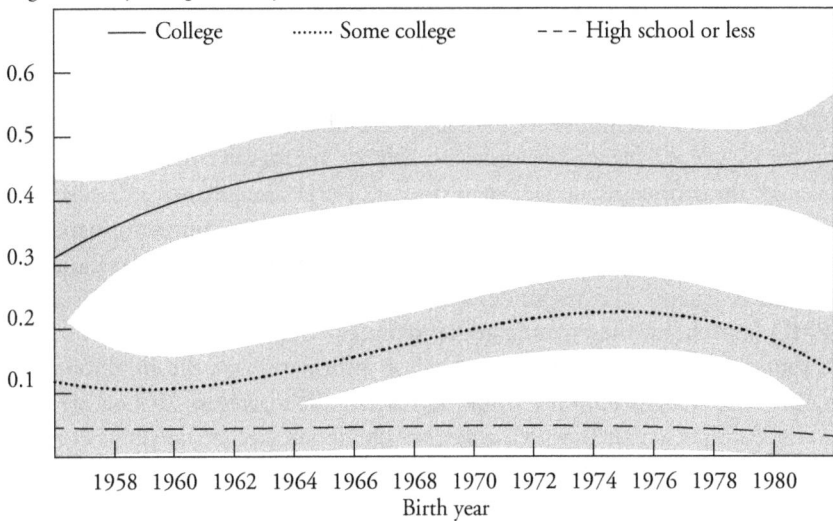

Source: PSID and authors' calculations.
a. With cubic time trend.

in table 9-1, blacks—who make up 14.7 percent of our sample—make up 39.4 percent of the bottom income quintile but only 2.5 percent of the top quintile. Consequently, to the degree that blacks are more likely to be poor (and are much less likely to be wealthy), they show a disproportionate likelihood of not completing college.

Multigenerational Income Disadvantage and Educational Attainment

Recent changes in the PSID allow us to analyze SES patterns across three generations. The PSID initially gathered data primarily about the household head and wife, and less information on other household members was available. In 1997, the PSID launched the Child Development Supplement (CDS), which gathers information regarding the behavior and development of the children (those aged zero to 12 years in 1997) residing in each PSID household as well as measures of the household environment and family relationships. An additional wave of interviews was conducted in 2002 to gather data on these children.

In 2005, CDS-participant children who had finished their high school education (by dropping out or graduating) were recruited into the Transition to Adulthood Supplement (TA). The TA sample consists largely of young adults who reside in their childhood homes (at least for a significant portion of every year) and as a result would not have been interviewed as part of the core PSID. The TA instrument itself is a hybrid of the CDS and core questionnaires, collecting detailed information on respondents' continued development and expectations, together with detailed education and economic data. As of early 2012, the results from TA interviews conducted in both 2005 and 2007 were available.

The TA supplement allows us to expand our analysis in two ways. First, even though the sample is younger than the core PSID sample analyzed above, the TA includes PSID respondents born as late as 1990, including information on their high school completion and participation in postsecondary education. Second, because most TA respondents were born to a parent who was raised in a PSID household, these young adults represent the third generation of PSID respondents. As a result, we have detailed information on the childhood economic resources of both the young adults and their parents. That allows us to investigate the extent to which a parent's childhood circumstances (that is, the SES of the TA respondents' grandparents) influence those of his or her children. To our knowledge this is the first such use of these three-generation PSID data.

Our sample consists of 745 young adults for whom we have a measure of late-childhood (ages 11 to 15 years) average inflation-adjusted per capita family income and the same income measure for their parents when they were at the same age. Because of the smaller sample size, we divide both income measures into two groups instead of three—the bottom and the other four quintiles—and categorize young adults based on their childhood income status in combination with their parents' childhood income status. The average age among first-time TA respondents is 18.7, which means that they are too young to have been included in the analyses discussed above or to have completed college.

Table 9-2 shows weighted sample means for all young adults (column 1), which are then classified into four mutually exclusive categories (two own-childhood income groups x two parental-childhood income groups). We label categories according to the respondent's own childhood income status relative to his or her parents' childhood income status. The low-income category (column 2, 12.3 percent of the weighted sample) comprises young adults who, along with their parents, had low income during childhood. The downwardly mobile category (column 3, 7.3 percent of the weighted sample) consists of those raised in low-income homes by parents who were not raised in the lowest-quintile families. The upwardly mobile category (column 4, 21.2 percent) consists of those raised in quintiles 2 through 5 by parents raised in low-income homes. Finally, the upper-income group (column 5, 59.1 percent) consists of young adults who, like their parents, were raised in quintiles 2 through 5.

Not surprisingly, low-income young adults have the highest dropout rate, 32.9 percent. This figure decreases as we move up the multiple-generation income distribution. The dropout rate is only 6.3 percent for those who were in quintiles 2–5 in both generations. Enrollment in college has the reverse pattern. Among two-generation bottom-quintile young adults, 25.0 percent had some college experience while 78.2 percent of those in the upper-income category did. For the most part, the remaining rows show similar patterns, with two-generation bottom-quintile young adults doing the poorest, followed by the downwardly mobile, the upwardly mobile, and the upper-income respondents, who did the best.

To evaluate the associative effects of low income in two generations, we included a dummy variable for each category associated with at least one generation of low-income status (columns 2-4 in table 9-2) in multivariate regressions for two young adult outcomes: high school dropout and any post-secondary education. In each case, those with incomes in quintiles 2 through 5 in both generations make up the reference group. Each model includes controls for the respondent's age (17–21 years), gender (female = 1), race (nonwhite = 1), the year of his or her first TA interview, and the identity of the PSID parent (whether the respondent's father or mother was raised in a PSID household).

The estimated effects of being raised in these conditions—that is, in parental and multigenerational low-income families—on the probability of dropping out

Table 9-2. *Summary Statistics for Transition to Adulthood Respondents with Parents Raised in PSID Respondent Households*

Variable	Sample	Own childhood income and parents' childhood income			
		Low income (1 / 1)	Downward (1 / ≥ 1)	Upward (≥ 1/ 1)	Upper income (≥ 1/ ≥ 1)
High school dropout	0.096	0.329	0.181	0.115	0.063
Any college, enrolled or completed	0.688	0.250	0.383	0.530	0.782
Average annual childhood income[a]	1.996 (2.094)	0.408 (0.192)	0.468 (0.151)	1.369 (0.511)	2.380 (2.283)
Parent's average childhood income	1.281 (0.811)	0.369 (0.111)	1.262 (0.617)	0.396 (0.125)	1.524 (0.760)
Parents' education					
Neither parent is high school graduate	0.066	0.329	0.236	0.112	0.019
High school graduate is highest parent education	0.241	0.465	0.478	0.393	0.175
Some college is highest parent education	0.378	0.101	0.246	0.318	0.426
At least college	0.315	0.104	0.041	0.177	0.381
Grandparents' education					
Neither grandparent is high school graduate	0.253	0.805	0.501	0.614	0.118
At least one grandparent is high school graduate	0.392	0.111	0.231	0.330	0.443
At least one grandparent had some college	0.166	0.083	0.159	0.050	0.195
At least one grandparent is college graduate	0.188	0.000	0.108	0.006	0.244
Age	18.707 (1.136)	18.997 (1.309)	19.008 (1.122)	18.668 (1.137)	18.661 (1.112)
Female	0.512	0.355	0.479	0.480	0.535
Nonwhite	0.244	0.892	0.448	0.498	0.120
Unweighted sample size	745	91	55	158	441
Weighted sample (percent)	100.0	12.3	7.3	21.2	59.1

Source: Authors' computations.

a. Income at respondents' ages 11 to 15 in ten thousands of 2005 dollars. Standard errors for continuous variables are reported in parentheses.

of high school (relative to being raised in upper-income families) are presented in figure 9-5A (regressions are shown in appendix table 9A-3). Only the two-generation low-income effect is statistically significant at the 10 percent level, but the size of the coefficient, 16.2 percentage points, is large relative to the sample mean, 9.6 percent.

In contrast, the negative effects of any history of low-income status are significant in the postsecondary educational attainment model, presented in figure 9-5B. That is not surprising: while high school attendance is paid for by public funds, postsecondary education requires tuition payments. Two-generation lowest-quintile young adults and the downwardly mobile respondents are much less likely to have enrolled in higher education—37.7 and 32.5 percentage points, respectively—than are two-generation young adults from families in quintiles 2 through 5. Those whose grandparents were in the lowest quintile but whose parents had moved up at least one quintile were also significantly less likely (17.4 percentage points) to have enrolled. Thus, any experience of being in the lowest quintile, even if the experience is a generation removed, is associated with reduced postsecondary enrollment.

Sensitivity Analyses and Limitations

We estimated these three-generation models using parents' education in place of income—specifically whether the respondent's parents and grandparents had less than a high school education (results available from authors on request). These specifications generated similar results: only the respondent's own background had any relationship with high school completion, but in the case of postsecondary education, there was a negative association with either the parents or the grandparents or both generations not having a high school degree. In terms of magnitude, the estimates generated by the education indicators are much larger than those generated by the income indicators.

Given the very large percentage of nonwhites in the low-income and two-generation low-income and low-education families, we also estimated models that included interactions of race with each of the SES indicators. These interactions were not significant, suggesting that even though African Americans are disproportionately represented in these categories, race itself does not have a multiplicative effect on these outcomes. However, sample sizes are rather small.

Discussion and Policy Implications

These new results from the PSID panel data suggest that educational attainment gaps between children growing up in disadvantaged families and other children remain very large despite substantial growth over the last fifty years in government

Figure 9-5A. *Family Socioeconomic Status and High School Dropout*[a]

Percentage points

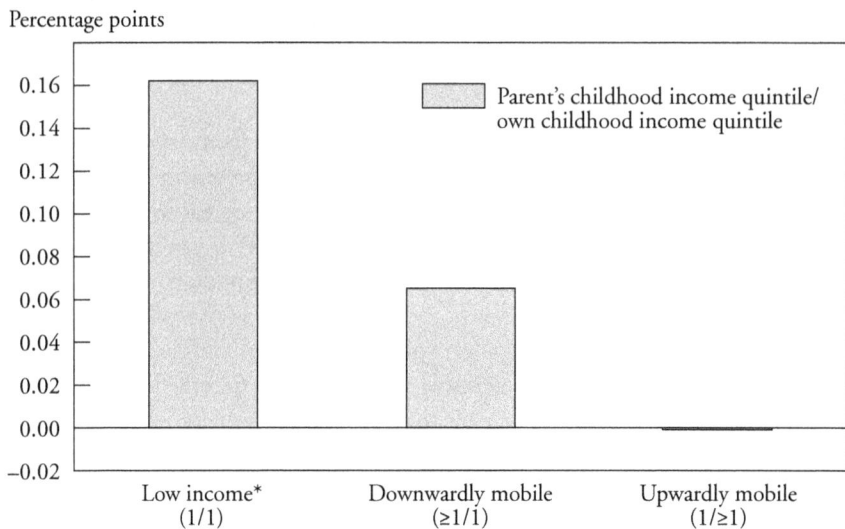

Source: PSID and authors' calculations.
a. OLS coefficient estimates; reference group is upper income (≥1/≥1). *p < .10, **p < .05.

Figure 9-5B. *Family Socioeconomic Status and College Attendance*[a]

Percentage points

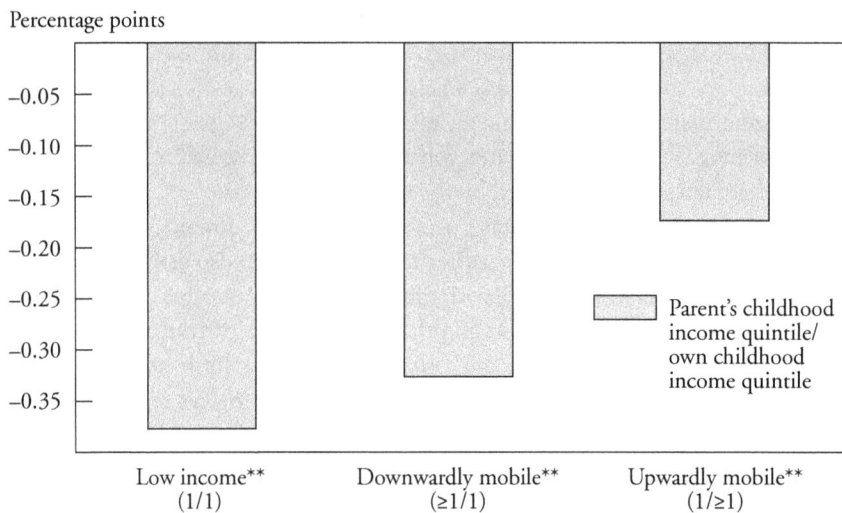

Source: PSID and authors' calculations.
a. OLS coefficient estimates; reference group is upper income (≥1/≥1). *p < .10, **p < .05.

spending on early childhood education and other investments in poor children, including college tuition subsidies. On average, the educational attainment gaps are increasing in many of our specifications.

Several factors may be contributing to the persistence of these attainment gaps. Since the early 1970s, the inflation-adjusted annual earnings of less-educated parents, especially male blue-collar workers, have fallen, whereas the earnings of highly educated parents have increased. Given the rising costs (real and perceived) of college over recent decades, that means that the ratio of college costs to parental income has increased much more for young adults from low-SES than from high-SES families. Many poor young adults may perceive (rightly or wrongly) that college is not a financially feasible option. In addition, government spending on college subsidies for children from low-SES families has not risen as fast as college costs have.

Another potential factor is the increasing gap in academic achievement between children raised in high- and low-SES families. Among school-age children born in the early 1980s, the disparity between the cognitive test scores of those raised in high-income households and the scores of those raised in low-income households was approximately 30 percent larger than it was among those born in the mid-1950s.[26] Thus, in addition to accessibility, college readiness is an important obstacle for low-income youth. While it is beyond the scope of this paper to attribute educational attainment gaps to specific factors, three areas of intervention that might narrow the attainment gap for future cohorts deserve consideration—college readiness, accessibility, and retention.

College Readiness

Perhaps the most effective way to raise the economic prospects of the next generation of young adults is to start early by improving the primary and secondary school experiences and raising high school graduation rates. The current education system falls well short of providing low-income students the skills that they need to prepare for the twenty-first-century labor market. Jacob and Ludwig[27] and Magnuson and Votruba-Drzal[28] document the importance of expanding the scope of early childhood education for low-income children; see also Carneiro and Heckman.[29] The American Recovery and Reinvestment Act of 2009 (ARRA) expanded funding for Early Head Start and Head Start, which serve poor children, yet almost fifty years after Head Start was launched many poor children do not participate because of lack of program capacity.[30] In contrast, Prime Minister Tony Blair proposed Sure Start, an early childhood education program, in the United Kingdom in the late 1990s, and within a decade most low-income children were participating.[31]

The results of these inadequacies manifest themselves early. Reardon, assembling data from a variety of sources, finds that the achievement gap—the disparity between school-age test scores of children from low-income households and scores of children from high-income households—is approximately 50 percent larger among children born in 2001 than among those born in the mid-1970s.[32] While government programs for low-income children have grown relatively slowly, middle- and high-income families have invested more in early childhood skill formation. Reardon finds the relatively greater parental investment in children in middle- and high-income families than in children in low-income families to be a likely explanation for the widening academic achievement gap.

If effective public policies that target early childhood and K-12 education were expanded, the next generation would contain fewer high school dropouts and more college graduates. However, even though educational reforms are more popular than other antipoverty policies with policymakers and the public, most state governments have recently reduced educational spending in response to massive budget deficits caused by the Great Recession. The ARRA included substantial federal government funds to keep school districts from laying off teachers and to induce educational innovations by states and local school districts. However, most of the act's provisions expired by the end of 2011, and the prospects for increased federal spending on education in the near term are dismal.

College Accessibility

Although the United States had the highest percentage of young adults who were college graduates for most of the twentieth century, in recent decades it has fallen behind a number of other countries.[33] President Obama's proposals in the ARRA for making college more affordable included a new tax credit for college students and an increase in the maximum Pell Grant, the program that subsidizes college costs for youth from low-income families. The administration also proposed indexing the maximum value of Pell Grants to inflation and making them an entitlement, but that proposal conflicts with congressional demands for deficit reduction.

Reducing the complexity of the college aid application process could increase the enrollment of low-income youth. To apply for assistance, students must file a Free Application for Federal Student Aid (FAFSA). With about 140 questions, the FAFSA is longer and more complex than the tax forms filed by the typical family.[34] In addition, the timing of the application process makes it difficult for applicants to anticipate the costs that they are expected to pay, making long-term planning challenging and stressful. Bettinger and others conducted an experiment in which a random sample of families were offered the opportunity to have their tax preparer help them complete the FAFSA.[35] High school seniors whose families were selected to participate were 40 percent more likely than those who were not offered assistance to submit an aid application, 29 percent more likely to enroll in college the following fall, and 33 percent more likely to receive financial aid. More fundamentally, Dynarski and Scott-Clayton estimate that streamlining and simplifying the application process itself would create little additional administrative cost and result in considerable gains in terms of college enrollment—7 to 9 percentage points among students from families with income of less than $50,000.[36]

College Retention

Even after enrolling in college, students from low-income backgrounds face additional obstacles to completing their degree. They are more likely to be enrolled in less selective or nonselective institutions such as community colleges, which provide fewer resources to students. As a result, student attachment to these institutions is more tenuous and educational trajectories are more uncertain than they are for students enrolling at more selective (and expensive) four-year colleges. In 2008, the graduation rate for associate (two-year) degree students at community colleges was 27.5 percent (within three years); among bachelor (four-year) degree students, the rate was 55.9 (within six years).[37]

Several recent randomized experiments at two-year community colleges suggest that a combination of increased financial incentives and "enhanced" student support can promote persistence in completing a degree. The Opening Doors project includes programs referred to as "learning communities" that group incoming students together into blocks of classes and offer extra tutoring, programs that provide counseling and monitoring, and programs that offer additional financial incentives for successfully completing courses. These programs, implemented in different combinations by MDRC (formerly Manpower Demonstration Research Project) at six nonselective community colleges, have been successful, to different degrees. The combination of financial aid and learning communities increased both the number of credits attempted and earned, improved the pass rate in the first semester of enrollment, and increased the likelihood of continued enrollment. To date, these programs as well as the similar Student Achievement and Retention Project (STAR) in Canada, remain relatively small in scale.[38]

Summary

Despite the historical commitment in the United States to providing equality of opportunity to children from low-income families, the experience in recent decades has been rather disappointing. It is possible that the large SES gaps in educational attainment that we document reflect the offsetting effects of increased inequalities in parental SES (gap expansion) and increased government spending (gap reduction). Our analysis does not attempt to sort out these separate effects. Yet it is clear that these SES gaps are likely to remain large for the foreseeable future, as there is little likelihood that the large income gap between the top and the bottom of the distribution will narrow or that the large gap between parental education among children of the disadvantaged and parental education among other children will disappear, or that the government will launch major new programs or expand existing ones focused on raising the attainment of children born into low-income families.

In his 1965 special message to Congress, President Johnson concluded: "We are now embarked on another venture to put the American dream to work in meeting the new demands of a new day. Once again we must start where men who would improve their society have always known they must begin—with an educational system restudied, reinforced, and revitalized."[39] Unfortunately, more than forty-five years later, the American dream of equal educational opportunity remains unfulfilled.

Notes

1. James Truslow Adams, *The Epic of America* (New York: Blue Ribbon Books, 1931).

2. Merrill D. Peterson, *Thomas Jefferson: Writings* (Library of America, 1984).

3. Lyndon B. Johnson, "Toward Full Educational Opportunity," Special Address to Congress, January 12, 1965.

4. See "National Survey of Adults," March 24–29, 2011 (www.economicmobility.org/assets/pdfs/EMP_2011_Poll_Toplines.pdf).

5. Finis Welch, *The Causes and Consequences of Increasing Inequality* (University of Chicago Press, 2001); Maria Cancian and Sheldon Danziger, *Changing Poverty, Changing Policies* (New York: Russell Sage Foundation, 2009).

6. National Center for Education Statistics, "The Condition of Education 2007" (U.S. Government Printing Office, 2007), table 25-1.

7. David T. Ellwood and Thomas Kane, "Who Is Getting a College Education? Family Background and the Growing Gaps in Enrollment," in *Securing the Future,* edited by Sheldon Danziger and Jane Waldfogel (New York: Russell Sage Foundation, 2000); Susan M. Dynarksi, "Does Aid Matter? Measuring the Effects of Student Aid on College Attendance and Completion," *American Economic Review*, vol. 93 (March 2003), pp. 278–88.

8. Pedro Carneiro and James Heckman, "The Evidence on Credit Constraints in Post-Secondary Schooling," *Economic Journal,* vol. 112 (October 2002), pp. 705–34.

9. Rand D. Conger and others, "A Family Process Model of Economic Hardship and Adjustment of Early Adolescent Boys," *Child Development,* vol. 63 (June 1992), pp. 526–41; Jean Yeung, M. Linver, and Jeanne Brooks-Gunn, "How Money Matters for Young Children's Development: Parental Investment and Family Processes," *Child Development,* vol. 73 (November 2002), pp. 1861–79.

10. Gary Solon, "Intergenerational Mobility in the United States," *American Economic Review*, vol. 82 (June 1992), pp. 393–408; Greg Duncan and Jeanne Brooks-Gunn, *Consequences of Growing Up Poor* (New York: Russell Sage Foundation, 1997); Richard Settersten Jr., Frank Furstenberg Jr., and Rubén G. Rumbaut, *On the Frontier of Adulthood: Theory, Research, and Public Policy* (University of Chicago Press, 2005); Susan Mayer, "Revisiting an Old Question: How Much Does Parental Income Affect Child Outcomes?" *Focus*, vol. 27 (Winter 2010), pp. 21–26.

11. Melanie Guldi, Marianne Page, and Ann Huff-Stevens, "Family Background and Children's Transitions to Adulthood over Time," in *The Price of Independence: The Economics of Early Adulthood*, edited by Sheldon Danziger and Cecilia Rouse (New York: Russell Sage Foundation, 2007).

12. Peter Gottschalk, "Inequality, Income Growth, and Mobility: The Basic Facts," *Journal of Economic Perspectives*, vol. 11 (Spring 1997), pp. 21–40.

13. Robert Schoeni and Karen Ross, "Material Assistance from Families During the Transition to Adulthood," in *On the Frontier of Adulthood: Theory, Research, and Public Policy*, edited by Richard Settersten Jr., Frank Furstenberg Jr., and Rubén G. Rumbaut (University of Chicago Press, 2004).

14. Lawrence Wu and Jui-Chung Allen Li, "Historical Roots of Family Diversity: Marital and Childbearing Trajectories of American Women," in *On the Frontier of Adulthood*, edited by Settersten, Furstenberg, and Rumbaut.

15. Guldi, Page, and Stevens, "Family Background and Children's Transitions to Adulthood over Time," in *The Price of Independence: The Economics of Early Adulthood*, edited by Danziger and Rouse.

16. Susan M. Dynarski and Judith Scott-Clayton, "College Grants on a Postcard: A Proposal for Simple and Predictable Federal Student Aid" (Brookings, 2007).

17. Martha Bailey and Susan M. Dynarski, "Inequality in Postsecondary Education," in *Whither Opportunity: Rising Inequality, Schools, and Children's Life Chances*, edited by Greg Duncan and Richard Murnane (New York: Russell Sage Foundation, 2011).

18. Greg Duncan and Daniel H. Hill, "An Investigation of the Extent and Consequences of Measurement Error in Labor-Economics Survey Data," *Journal of Labor Economics*, vol. 3 (October 1985), pp. 508–32; John Fitzgerald, Peter Gottschalk, and Robert Moffitt, "An Analysis of Sample Attrition in Panel Data: The Michigan Panel of Income Dynamics," *Journal of Human Resources*, vol. 33 (Spring 1998), pp. 251–99.

19. Our target age is 25, but because interviews were conducted every other year after 1997, we include respondents as young as 24 and as old as 26; this includes respondents who turned 25 in the years that PSID interviews were not conducted. Focusing on outcomes at younger ages maximizes sample size but prevents us from measuring outcomes that are not achieved until later ages—for example, measures of stable employment and earnings.

20. Guldi, Page, and Stevens, "Family Background and Children's Transitions to Adulthood over Time."

21. For example, among those observed in our sample at age 29, only 12 percent of those who had not completed college by age 25 reported obtaining a degree by age 29.

22. Bailey and Dynarski, "Inequality in Postsecondary Education."

23. We arrived at this functional form first by modeling the relationship between family background and college completion as the interaction between our SES measures and the set of single birth-year indicators (twenty-seven total, including the reference group). We then applied a lowess smoother (locally weighted regression) to each group of interaction

coefficients, the results of which suggested that the cubic parameterization provided the best fit for the data.

24. Bailey and Dynarski, "Inequality in Postsecondary Education."

25. Bhashkar Mazumder, *Upward Intergenerational Economic Mobility in the United States* (Washington: Pew Charitable Trusts, 2008).

26. Sean Reardon, "The Widening Academic-Achievement Gap between the Rich and the Poor: New Evidence and Possible Explanations," in *Whither Opportunity: Rising Inequality, Schools, and Children's Life Chances*, edited by Duncan and Murnane.

27. Brian Jacob and Jens Ludwig, "Improving Educational Outcomes for Poor Children," in *Changing Poverty, Changing Policies*, edited by Maria Cancian and Sheldon Danziger (New York: Russell Sage Foundation, 2009).

28. Katherine Magnuson and Elizabeth Votruba-Drzal, "Enduring Influences of Child-hood Poverty," in *Changing Poverty, Changing Policies,* edited by Cancian and Danziger.

29. Carneiro and Heckman, "The Evidence on Credit Constraints in Post-Secondary Schooling."

30. See "Head Start, Early Head Start Programs Received over $2 Billion in Recovery Act Funding" (www.hhs.gov/recovery/programs/acf/hs-ehs.html).

31. Jane Waldfogel, *Britain's War on Poverty* (New York: Russell Sage Foundation, 2010).

32. Reardon, "The Widening Academic-Achievement Gap," in *Whither Opportunity*, edited by Duncan and Murnane.

33. Robert H. Haveman and Timothy M. Smeeding, "The Role of Higher Education in Social Mobility," *Future of Children*, vol. 16 (Fall 2006), p. 125.

34. Susan M. Dynarksi and Judith Scott-Clayton, "Complexity and Targeting in Federal Student Aid: A Quantitative Analysis," in *Tax Policy and the Economy*, vol. 22, edited by James M. Poterba (University of Chicago Press, 2008).

35. Eric P. Bettinger and others, "The Role of Simplification and Information in College Decisions: Results from the H&R Block FAFSA Experiment," Working Paper 15361 (Cambridge, Mass.: National Bureau of Economic Research, September 2009).

36. Dynarksi and Scott-Clayton, "Complexity and Targeting in Federal Student Aid: A Quantitative Analysis." The authors base this prediction on the effects of state-level programs with minimal application requirements.

37. See "Progress and Completion: Graduation Rates" (www.higheredinfo.org/dbrowser/index.php?measure=19).

38. David Demming and Susan M. Dynarski, "Into College, Out of Poverty? Policies to Increase the Postsecondary Attainment of the Poor," Working Paper 15387 (Cambridge, Mass.: National Bureau of Economic Research, September 2009); Susan Scrivener and Erin Coghlan, "Opening Doors to Student Success" (New York: MDRC, 2011).

39. Johnson, "Toward Full Educational Opportunity."

Appendix 9A
Regression Results for Figures

Table 9A-1. *College Completion/Birth-Year Cohort Regression Results*[a]

	Average childhood income			Parents' education		
		Interaction effects			Interaction effects	
	Main effect	Middle quintiles	Top quintile	Main effect	Some college	College degree
Constant/main effect	0.055** (0.022)	0.065** (0.026)	0.247** (0.051)	0.083** (0.019)	0.065* (0.043)	0.291** (0.054)
Born 1959–1962	−0.012 (0.024)	0.062** (0.036)	0.067 (0.070)	0.024 (0.021)	−0.003 (0.057)	0.056 (0.070)
Born 1963–66	−0.035 (0.024)	0.071** (0.037)	0.101* (0.071)	−0.012 (0.021)	0.044 (0.057)	0.182** (0.073)
Born 1967–70	−0.004 (0.030)	0.042 (0.042)	0.060 (0.076)	−0.002 (0.023)	0.074 (0.060)	0.048 (0.074)
Born 1971–74	0.023 (0.035)	0.087** (0.048)	0.010 (0.082)	−0.009 (0.025)	0.082* (0.062)	0.145** (0.073)
Born 1975–78	−0.011 (0.034)	0.111** (0.046)	0.114* (0.079)	−0.022 (0.025)	0.104** (0.060)	0.114* (0.071)
Born 1979–1982	−0.026 (0.026)	0.110** (0.039)	0.268** (0.070)	−0.025 (0.025)	0.085* (0.056)	0.152** (0.067)
Black	−0.050** (0.016)	... ...	... ...	−0.057** (0.014)	... ...	... ...
Female	0.037** (0.013)	... ...	... ...	0.032** (0.012)	... ...	... ...
Between ages 25 and 35	0.069** (0.015)	... ...	... ...	0.040** (0.014)	... ...	... ...
Northeast	0.046** (0.019)	... ...	... ...	0.037** (0.019)	... ...	... ...
North Central	−0.010 (0.017)	... ...	... ...	−0.003 (0.016)	... ...	... ...
West	−0.105** (0.019)	... ...	... ...	−0.094** (0.019)	... ...	... ...
Alaska/Hawaii/Foreign	−0.143* (0.079)	... ...	... ...	−0.137 (0.088)	... ...	... ...
Sample size	6160	.	.	6160	.	.
R squared	0.115	.	.	0.186	.	.

Source: PSID and authors' calculations.
a. Standard errors are in parentheses. ** $p < .05$, * $p < .10$.

Table 9A-2. *College Completion/Cubic Time Trend Regression Results*[a]

	Family income	Parents' education
Nonwhite	−0.051**	−0.057**
	(0.016)	(0.014)
Female	0.038**	0.034**
	(0.013)	(0.012)
Head between ages 25 and 35 at respondent's birth	0.078**	0.049**
	(0.016)	(0.015)
Head over 35 at respondent's birth	0.026	0.021
	(0.017)	(0.016)
Northeast	0.047**	0.036*
	(0.019)	(0.019)
North Central	−0.009	−0.004
	(0.017)	(0.016)
West	−0.104**	−0.095**
	(0.019)	(0.019)
Alaska/Hawaii/Foreign	−0.127	−0.122
	(0.085)	(0.088)
Birth year	−0.022**	−0.005
	(0.010)	(0.008)
Birth year squared	0.002**	0.000
	(0.001)	(0.001)
Birth year cubed	−0.000*	−0.000
	(0.000)	(0.000)
Childhood SES middle	0.056	0.095
	(0.046)	(0.072)
Childhood SES middle* Birth year	0.012	−0.015
	(0.015)	(0.022)
Childhood SES middle* Birth year squared	−0.000	0.002
	(0.001)	(0.002)
Childhood SES middle* Birth year cubed	0.000	−0.000
	(0.000)	(0.000)
Childhood SES high	0.217**	0.254**
	(0.085)	(0.083)
Childhood SES high* Birth year	0.029	0.027
	(0.027)	(0.025)
Childhood SES high* Birth year squared	−0.003	−0.001
	(0.002)	(0.002)
Childhood SES high* Birth year cubed	0.000	0.000
	(0.000)	(0.000)
R squared	0.113	0.185

Source: PSID and authors' calculations.

a. Standard errors reported in parentheses. ** $p < .05$, * $p < .10$.

Table 9A-3. *Multigenerational Low SES and Educational Attainment*[a]

	High school dropout	College attendance
Own childhood income quintile/parent's childhood income quintile		
Low income (1/1)	0.162*	−0.377**
	(0.090)*	(0.086)
Downwardly mobile (≥ 1/1)	0.065	−0.326**
	(0.080)	(0.093)
Upwardly mobile (1/≥ 1)	−0.001	−0.174**
	(0.046)	(0.077)
Age	−0.017	0.026
	(0.011)	(0.018)
Female	−0.011	0.042
	(0.027)	(0.040)
Nonwhite	0.112**	−0.176**
	(0.050)	(0.066)
Year = 2005	0.023	−0.044
	(0.026)	(0.041)
Head PSID parent	0.065**	−0.063
	(0.027)	(0.042)
Constant	0.323	0.351
	(0.210)	(0.343)
R squared	0.098	0.169
Mean of dependent variable	0.096	0.688
Joint significance of SES indicators	0.229	0.000

Source: PSID and authors' calculations.
a. Standard errors reported in parentheses. ** $p<.05$, * $p<.10$.

Contributors

Jennifer Baxter
*Australian Institute of
    Family Studies*

Peter Butterworth
Australian National University

Mary E. Campbell
University of Iowa

Jenny Chesters
University of Canberra

Rebekah Levine Coley
Boston College

Sheldon Danziger
University of Michigan

Sharon Goldfeld
*Centre for Community Child Health,
    Royal Children's Hospital
    Melbourne, and Murdoch Children's
    Research Institute, University of
    Melbourne*

Matthew Gray
Australian National University

Kathleen Mullan Harris
*University of North Carolina at
    Chapel Hill*

Ron Haskins
Brookings Institution

Robert Haveman
University of Wisconsin–Madison

Anna Johnson
Georgetown University

Ariel Kalil
University of Chicago

Liana Leach
Australian National University

Hedwig Lee
University of Washington

Caitlin McPherran Lombardi
Boston College

Tim Moore
*Royal Centre for Community Child
    Health, Royal Children's Hospital
    Melbourne*

Frank Oberklaid
*Centre for Community Child Health,
    Royal Children's Hospital Melbourne*

Rebecca Ryan
Georgetown University

Megan Shipley
Australian National University

Lyndall Strazdins
Australian National University

Patrick Wightman
University of Michigan

Barbara Wolfe
University of Wisconsin–Madison

Index

workforce in, 82; work support system
in, 3–4, 6
Universalism (progressive or proportionate), 137, 138
U.S. *See* United States

Votruba-Drzal, Elizabeth, 227

War on Poverty, 209
Weinraub, Marsha, 103
Welfare, 211
*Welfare, Children, and Families: A Three-
City Study* (Three-City Study), 18, 28

Welfare reform legislation. *See* Personal
Responsibility and Work Opportunity
Reconciliation Act of *1996*
WIC. *See* Women, Infants, and Children
program
Wightman, Patrick, 17–18, 19–20, 208–35
WJ-R. *See* Woodcock-Johnson Psycho-
Educational Battery Revised
Wolfe, Barbara, 16, 144–67
Women, Infants, and Children (WIC)
program, 34, 40
Woodcock-Johnson Psycho-Educational
Battery Revised (WJ-R), 30

www.ingramcontent.com/pod-product-compliance
Lightning Source LLC
Chambersburg PA
CBHW030646270326
41929CB00007B/231